THE MIDDLE GROUP OF AMERICAN HISTORIANS

THE MIDDLE GROUP OF AMERICAN HISTORIANS

BY

JOHN SPENCER BASSETT, Ph.D., LL.D.

Essay Index Reprint Series

BOOKS FOR LIBRARIES PRESS, INC.

FREEPORT, NEW YORK

First published 1917
Reprinted 1966

TO

JESSIE LEWELLIN BASSETT

PREFACE

HISTORY is now being written in the United States by a larger number of persons than ever before. It is also being taught and studied more extensively than ever in our schools, colleges, and universities and with excellent results. Every part of the educational machine has done its share to make this a fat age for the historian. Yet in proportion to the population history is less read to-day by voluntary readers than it was read a hundred years ago. None of our historians command the same degree of respect from the public that men like Bancroft, Prescott, Irving, Motley, and Sparks commanded in their day.

It would be difficult to name a historian who now makes a living out of his profession of historian. Most of those who are writing are able to live from personal incomes or from their salaries as professors of history. We have been used to this state of affairs so long that many intelligent people do not realize that there was once a day in which American writers could trust themselves wholly to history and not be disappointed. If in describing the careers of the men who succeeded in this field in the past century this book can at the same time give historians and the well wishers of history some more confidence in the historian's profession, it will accomplish two very desirable things.

My plan has been to throw up in large outline the most eminent of the men of the group concerned. Jeremy Belknap, George Bancroft, Jared Sparks, William Hickling Prescott, John Lothrop Motley, and Peter Force have been given special prominence, while the work of other men has been treated in an introductory chapter on the development of our history before the civil war. Such an introduction, it is hoped, will serve for a background against which the careers of the most eminent characters may be outlined in bold relief with advantageous results. Probably the American of to-day will derive more pleasure from such a treatment of the subject than from a book in which all the historians within the "middle period" should be treated in space allotments proportionate to their services. The present volume, also, may serve me for an outline of a larger work of the more comprehensive kind just mentioned, if health and years allow me to write it.

In one sense the "middle period" begins with the end of the revolution : in another it begins soon after the war of 1812, let us say about 1826, when Sparks began to give himself to history. The reader may choose the beginning for himself. It is certain that history writing took on a new character with the achievement of independence, and it is also certain that Sparks's widely heralded researches infused a new spirit into the historians of the day.

The end of the period, as I understand it, lies where the scientific spirit secures domination over the patriotic school that had ruled for several decades. Possibly the organization of the American Historical Association in 1884 would be a convenient date to mark the beginning of a new period. On the other hand the Association was in some respects the result rather than the herald of a new school. From 1865 to 1884, however, history in the United States was written in the afterglow of the civil war, and it was not scientific. Keeping in mind both sides of this dilemma, we may say that the new spirit existed fundamentally in the minds of scholars about the middle of the century and that it was not revealed to public view until the cloud of sectional feeling lifted. In this view the year 1884 may well be taken as the dividing point between two periods of historical endeavor in our country.

For my purposes I have chosen to assign Parkman to the new school. While he wrote with that fine appreciation of style which was characteristic of Bancroft and the literary historians, his industry, his research among documents, and especially his detachment seem to place him among the men of to-day. On the whole, the assignment of Parkman to the new school is satisfactory to me, although other persons may not hold the same opinion of it.

Each of the sketches of individuals here submitted
is necessarily a unit in itself. But each man had something to do with another of the group. To give an
account of each career, therefore, has made some repetition necessary. I hope a charitable reader will
believe that I have sought to reduce it to the lowest
terms in keeping with lucid and informing narrative.

The substance of the second, third, and fourth chapters was given in three lectures before the Institute of
Arts and Sciences of Columbia University, in October,
1916; and a large part of the fifth chapter was read in
the same month before the Massachusetts Historical
Society. None of this matter, however, is published
elsewhere than in these pages.

JOHN SPENCER BASSETT.

NORTHAMPTON, MASSACHUSETTS,
    November 1, 1916.

CONTENTS

MIDDLE GROUP OF AMERICAN HISTORIANS

CHAPTER I

EARLY PROGRESS OF HISTORY IN THE UNITED STATES

1. *The Colonial Historians*

THE first historians in the region which is now the United States were European-born Americans, who wrote with the belief that future generations would demand the story of the beginnings of a great state. To them it was a pious duty to record the events they had witnessed. In Virginia and in Massachusetts they were especially notable. For the history of the establishment of the former colony we have Captain John Smith, William Strachey, Edward Maria Wingfield, John Pory, George Percy, Rev. Alexander Whitaker, and George Sandys, all of whom wrote of the first years of the colony. After them came a pause of nearly a hundred years before historians long resident in the colony began to write. For Massachusetts we have the beginnings described by

1

Edward Winslow, Governor William Bradford, and John Winthrop, English-trained men who were deeply loyal to the purposes for which the New England colonies were founded and who wrote in order that posterity might not forget how the early perils had been met and overcome.

Each group was grimly in earnest and very religious, but in different ways. The Virginians were members of the Church of England at a time when it was deeply inspired by the reforms of the Elizabethan age. Puritanism still dwelt within its body, but the genial influence of the Book of Common Prayer was also felt. Early Virginia zeal, therefore, was a thing fit for romantic adventurers staking their all on the favor of God and their own ability. When it expressed itself in historical literature it was freely human. Something of the same cast of thought that gave Shakspere and Ben Jonson their peculiar charm was revealed in it. The Puritan historians were rigidly devout. They belong to the period which saw the triumph of the men who taught rigid simplicity. For the resonant phrases of the Prayer Book they substituted the severe conventions of Calvin. Romance was chased out of the heart and the fear of hell was suspended like a sword over every threshold. Strict morals and godly living were instilled in the minds of young and old. Spontaneity gave place to self-restraint and human feelings were clipped and shorn of all that did not lead to pious thinking.

The Puritan was intellectual. His disputes over dogma sharpened his wits, he delighted in arguments, and his democratic form of society promoted popular education. The early Puritans, therefore, showed more interest than the Virginians in preserving their history, after the first burst of zeal was over. In Virginia idealism quickly gave place to materialism, as tobacco and land became the subjects of thinking and planning. In New England Puritan idealism lost something, no doubt, with the passage of the immediate era of migration, but it remained the strongest fact in these colonies. Thus the impulse to write history was kept alive, a vital thing, and historical works appeared — at great intervals, it is true — but without the long period of silence that left Virginia nearly a century with no voice raised in telling the story of her past.

Let us pursue the contrast a little further. The literary impulse in Virginia was destined to be ephemeral. It could hardly have been otherwise, since it was born of the mere zeal for planting a new dominion of the English stock. Tobacco growing and land speculation soon became the absorbing themes of conversation and striving. Prosperity came apace and a leisure class appeared; but it was not a thoughtful class. Outside nature was most genial, inviting the planters to the soft pleasures of the senses. Courtesy and pleasant manners, hospitality and the love of personal honor went into the standards of the best living;

but severe mental discipline was not a characteristic of either planter, clergyman, or lawyer. Here was no fertile ground for the development of history writing. The first native Virginian to break through the crust of indifference was Robert Beverley, a prominent planter, who published a "History of Virginia" in 1705. He was led to write the book by accident, and not by a desire to assume the rôle of historian. While in London he was shown that part of Oldmixon's "British Empire in America" which related to Virginia. He was disgusted with its defects and undertook to write a better book. He had been secretary of Virginia and was acquainted with the documentary sources of its history. He did not, however, make a large use of them; and the chief value of his work was in his wise and comprehensive views of colonial society.

The other historian of this colony was William Stith. He was a man of true scholarship; and his "History of the First Discovery and Settlement of Virginia," published as part one of a larger work, appeared in 1747. It was accurate, so far as available materials went. He had access to the records of the London Company and drew largely from them and from the works of Captain John Smith. Part one ended with the fall of the company in 1624. Stith had no sense of proportion, and his book did not please the Virginia planters, being too heavy for their taste. They gave it such poor encouragement that he did not carry his researches further. While he is entitled to credit for writing a thoroughly modern book, we can commend neither his lack of adjustment to his public nor his want of devotion to the cause of history. Had he been very earnest in his vocation he would not have been discouraged by the indifference of his compatriots. His failure left Virginia history an unworked field for many a year.

Turning to New England we find a more steady development. Bradford and Winthrop were men of great insight. The first wrote "The History of Plymouth Plantation" from the beginning to 1646, leaving his manuscript unpublished. The book has been preserved in this state, a part of it being published by Bradford's nephew, Nathaniel Morton, in his "New England's Memorial," 1669. The manuscript was in the tower of the Old South Church, in Boston, when the revolution began. It was carried off by British soldiers and was long considered lost; but it came at last to the library of the Bishop of London, where it lay unnoticed in his grace's library at Fulham Palace. Bishop Wilberforce, of Oxford, discovered it and mentioned it in 1844 in a book on the Protestant church in America. Anderson also spoke of it in his "History of the Colonial Church," in 1848. Seven years later two gentlemen in Boston came across the reference in Anderson and took steps to establish the identity of the manuscript. The discovery caused great rejoicing in Boston literary circles. The Bishop of London refused to surrender the precious manuscript, but allowed a copy to be taken, from which the Massachusetts Historical Society published a complete edition in 1856, enriched with notes by Charles Deane. In 1896 the Bishop of London gave up the manuscript, which was deposited in the State Library, in Boston; and in 1912 it was published by the Massachusetts Historical Society in a final authoritative form with valuable additional notes by Worthington C. Ford. Bradford's "History" is a Puritan book in the best sense. It is an earnest and sincere record in a loosely annalistic form, deriving its chief value from its accurate statement of facts and its transparent honesty. It will ever remain one of the most valuable books in the field of American history.

John Winthrop's journal, published first [1] in 1790, is generally known as "A History of New England." It deals with the period from 1630 to 1649. Winthrop, more than anyone else, was the founder of the colony of Massachusetts Bay, and he was long its governor. His book is a careful account of such transactions as he thought worth preserving. It is very full of events relating to Massachusetts, and, like Bradford's book, it abounds in incidents that the author considered manifestations of God's special care for his people. But one who reads it must gain a vivid impression of the life and problems in church and state of the founders

[1] Winthrop's manuscript is in three volumes. The third was lost for a while and did not appear in the edition of 1790. It was, however, discovered in 1816, and a complete edition was published in two volumes in 1825–26 with notes by James Savage. A new edition appeared in 1853.

of New England. Though it has less unity and less charm of narration than the "History of Plymouth Plantation," it is one of the great books of our historical literature.

While some less important books belong to the early period of New England existence, we do not come to another notable group of historical works until we come to the long struggle of the settlers with the Indians. Here was a series of dramatic events which made a deep impression on the people. Other parts of the continent had their Indian wars, but nowhere else was there the same disposition to write about them. The desire to preserve heroic deeds and to attest the goodness of providence in giving victory to his servants was alleged as the object for which the writers wrote; but it may be assumed that one object of the authors was to make money, always the most sustaining motive of popular historical efforts. These narratives were full of a spirit of severity. To the settlers of colonial times, as to the frontiersmen of the nineteenth century, the savages were the embodiment of cruelty. It was rare that one of the narrators showed tolerance for the natives, who in reality were only defending their homes from the aggression of the whites. Acts of cruelty on the part of the Indians were not wanting, but they were probably offset by the retaliation of the white men; and the narratives that have come down to us are full of a spirit of satisfaction for the fell vengeance of the colonial armies.

The Pequot war, King Philip's war, and the long series of struggles that occurred in connection with the conflict between the British and the French in America furnished the themes.   Particularly appealing were the narratives of the suffering captives taken by the Indians and carried off to Canada.   Some of these narratives, notably Rev. John Williams's "Redeemed Captive returning to Zion" and Mrs. Mary Rowlandson's "Narrative of Captivity and Restoration," are extremely vivid and pathetic stories of adventure. This cycle of minor historical narratives stimulated the interest of the people in history and opened the road to more serious things.

Of the writers who wrote about the growth of political and religious life in New England two were most notable, Thomas Prince and Thomas Hutchinson. The first was a minister in Boston.   In his profession he was not eminent, being a thoughtful man whose ministrations were not characterized by eloquent preaching or original theological views.   But he loved the records of the past and possessed the true antiquarian spirit.   He was zealous in collecting documents and works published on New England history. His valuable library was preserved in the tower of the Old South Church until the irreverent British soldiers, who held Boston against the revolting colonists until Washington drove them out in 1776, took the edifice for a riding school and left the books to the mercy of careless intruders.   Some of these treasures survived the

perils of the time and are now in the keeping of the
Boston Public Library. But the most enduring result
of Prince's devotion to history was his "Chronological
History of New England in the form of Annals," the
first volume of which was published in 1736. It was
dull and formless, but it was written in the most careful manner. Accuracy and love of detail make it a
delight to the genealogist and antiquarian. "I cite
my vouchers to every passage," he said, "and I have
done my utmost, first to find out the truth, and then
to relate it in the clearest order." Posterity is willing
to grant that he achieved his object, and it gives him
a place among the most worthy of our historical
scholars. The small sale of his first volume, which
carried the story of New England history to September
7, 1630, caused the publisher to refuse to bring out a
second volume. The author was not able to proceed
at that time, but in 1755 he began a continuation in
serial parts at sixpence each. This venture proved as
unpopular as the first volume, and only three of the
parts were published. Like Stith, in Virginia, he had
not the art of pleasing the public.

Thomas Hutchinson was probably the best historian
who wrote in the colonial period. He was a descendant
of Mrs. Anne Hutchinson, the Antinomian, and something of her free spirit and mental acumen was in him.
He graduated from Harvard when sixteen years old,
became a prosperous Boston merchant, and finally was
called into the service of the colony. He became

lieutenant-governor in 1758, chief justice in 1760, acting governor in 1769, and governor in 1771. For a time he was very popular, but his stand in favor of loyalty in the controversy with the crown brought the whigs down upon him. The stamp act mob destroyed his house and scattered his books and papers through the streets. He tried to reconcile the king and his subjects, hoping to save the integrity of the British empire. In 1774 he went to England, never to return. The king allowed him a pension and Oxford gave him the honorary degree of *doctor civilis juris*, but neither money nor honor could salve a heart that bled for the sufferings of his native land. He died in 1780.

Among the articles of property recovered after his house was wrecked by the stamp act rioters was the soiled manuscript of the second volume of his "History of the Colony of Massachusetts Bay." The first had appeared in 1764, bringing the history of the colony down to 1691. The second volume, so fortunately rescued, was published in 1767. It carried the narrative forward to 1750. After his arrival in London Hutchinson completed a third volume which was left unpublished until 1828. His book is not faultless. The object of abuse by the whigs, he could hardly be expected to give full credit to their motives; but it may be said that he had a fairer sense of the two-sidedness of the controversy than any other person who wrote about it for a hundred years after the revolution was over. In the earlier part of the work the treatment is broad and well balanced, details are subordinated to larger movements, and there is more detachment than in any other New England historian. As a liberal and able man of culture, Hutchinson set out to create a picture of the colony's progress; and he performed his task in the manner of a master.

Not all the colonial historians lived in Virginia and Massachusetts. Outside of these colonies are a few men who would demand notice in a longer sketch than this. Among them are Dr. Cadwallader Colden and William Smith, of New York, Samuel Smith, of New Jersey, and John Lawson, of North Carolina, all men of fair ability. The first, second, and fourth were colony officials of high rank, men who stood out above the mass of colonists in which they lived. The third, Samuel Smith, was a plain Quaker, industrious and conscientious. His book described the history of New Jersey with the pen of an average man, at a time when the difference between average men and their superiors was wider than it is to-day. It has not been entirely superseded. Of all the group only one, John Lawson, had a good literary style.

2. *The Influence of the Revolution*

The immediate effect of the Revolution was unfavorable to the writing of history. It produced a period of confusion, in which the attention of men was demanded by the more serious problems of life. A large portion of the leisure class, those who would either write or read history, were tories, some of whom were driven from the country, while the others were at variance with the spirit of the new government and were not interested in its history. The whigs, however, were zealous for their history, but their zeal oozed out at their finger tips. Ebenezer Hazard, who had in mind great historical projects, gives us the following illuminating statement:

"The war and the numerous avocations consequent upon it, have thrown every man's mind into such an unsettled and confused state that but few can think steadily upon any subject. They hear of useful designs, they give you all the encouragement which can be derived from the warmest approbation of your plan, they will even promise you assistance. Politics intrude — kick you and your designs out of their heads; and when you appear again, why they really forgot that the matter had been mentioned to them. I have been repeatedly served so with reference to my collection." [1]

This complaint was written in 1779, while war was still the chief object of interest. Soon after peace was made, historians of the glorious struggle began to appear; but their chief source of information was British. Out of the records of the thirteen colonies, badly kept and preserved in places widely remote from one another, it was a difficult task to prepare a narrative of what had been done. But in England were all the reports of operations in one collection, sent home by British officers. And out of these reports had been prepared year by year the accounts of military events in the "Annual Register" then conducted under whig

[1] Belknap Papers, I, 12 ("Colls." Mass. Histl. Soc., Ser. V, Vol. II).

influence. At that time the British whigs opposed the American war and believed that the American whigs would have remained loyal Britons had they not been mistreated. Among them was Edmund Burke, who was employed to write the statements in the "Register" referring to the American controversy. He wrote well, giving the facts that made the conduct of the Americans appear in a favorable light.

It was, therefore, to Burke, in the "Annual Register" that the first American historians turned for their information in writing about the revolution. They trusted him implicitly : in fact, they copied large portions of his narrative without quotation marks and with little or no change. Two men were particularly notable in this respect, Rev. William Gordon, D.D., and Dr. David Ramsay. The former was a clergyman living near Boston during the war. He returned to England in 1786 and in 1788 published in London his "History of the Rise, Progress, and Establishment of the Independence of the United States of America," a substantial book in four volumes. It was generally accepted as an original work and was widely read. The present generation, having discovered that most of it was taken from the "Register," holds it in slight honor. Dr. Ramsay's work, "History of the American Revolution," in two volumes, was published in 1789. The author did not hold the view of the British whigs that the revolt was due solely to the mistakes of the tory government. He declared that it was a natural result of general tendencies, the growing disposition of Great Britain to unify the empire and the growing desire of the colonists to rule themselves. But for a large portion of the information in his book he drew directly from the "Annual Register." Dr. Ramsay was a resident of Charleston, South Carolina, and was more noted as an author and political leader than as a physician. He wrote several books besides his work on the revolution: in fact, he was, perhaps, the most active historian of his day in the United States; but none of his other productions had the same vogue as the "History of the Revolution."

The desire to preserve the record of the struggle for independence that resulted in histories of the war led to the writing of biographies of its prominent leaders. Of this class the most famous was Chief Justice Marshall's "Life of George Washington" (5 vols., 1804–1807). Although federalist in spirit, it was a well-constructed work, worthy of the subject and of the author's high position. It was accepted by the friends of Washington as a sufficient tribute, and was issued in several editions. Another biography that had a wide circulation, written also by an eminent statesman and dealing with one of the heroes of the revolution, was William Wirt's "Sketches of the Life and Character of Patrick Henry" (1817). In sentiment and manner it was the opposite of Marshall's book; for it was republican in feeling and light and trivial in treatment. But the author's easy style made it an attractive book of its kind, and it was widely read. At the time these two books were written the market for literature in the United States was dominated by strong personal sentiment. A man bought a biography because it set forth his own political sentiments or his ideas of noble character. Marshall wrote for people holding one kind of political views and Wirt for those holding another kind. Both paid tribute to exalted personal character, and neither wrote impartially. Hume's notable example of critical scholarship had not yet been adopted into the literary thought of the readers of history. We were all partisans of our own cause in the contest with Great Britain and, whether we wished to know its simple history or to read the biographies of its leaders, we demanded narratives that stimulated self-satisfaction.

Another field in which historians wrote in this period was state histories. Colonies had developed into states and hopes for their future ran high. Should not the stories of the states in their early stages of growth be written down? Local pride asserted itself, and the result was several works, as Belknap's "History of New Hampshire" (3 vols., 1784, 1792), Proud's "History of Pennsylvania from 1681 till after the Year 1742" (2 vols., 1797, 1798), Minot's continuation of Hutchinson's history of Massachusetts (2 vols., 1798, 1803) and his "History of the Insurrection in Massachusetts" (1788), and Trumbull's "History of Connecticut" (2 vols., 1818). All these books were well written and have maintained places in our historical literature to this day. Of Proud and Belknap more will be said later on. There were, also, three histories of Southern states originating in this impulse; but they were, unfortunately, less respectable than those already mentioned. They were: Dr. Ramsay's "History of South Carolina" (2 vols., 1809), Burk's "History of Virginia" (3 vols., 1804, 1805), and Dr. Williamson's "History of North Carolina" (2 vols., 1812). These writers had more zeal than industry and were guilty of gross neglect of the sources of information.

Robert Proud has for me a pathetic interest. He was one of the first Americans to combine the functions of historian and schoolmaster.[1] He was very poor and struggled hard against straitened circumstances, producing at the end a book which satisfies many of the qualifications of the modern school of history. He was born in Yorkshire, England, May 10, 1728, and by hard study secured a good preliminary education in the local schools. He fell under the influence of the Yorkshire Quakers and when he came of age settled in London as tutor of the two sons of a prominent Quaker. Being a thoughtful man he took up the study of medicine, but gave it up when he observed that most of the diseases a physician had to treat were the results of vice. Essentially moral, he shrank from a life in which he must deal with those who violated moral laws.

[1] William Stith was also a schoolmaster.

In 1759 he arrived in Philadelphia, where his employment was uncertain for a time. He was a protégé of Anthony Benezet.[1] But in 1761 he became a teacher of Greek and Latin in an academy then just founded by the Friends. When the revolution was about to begin he became a merchant; but as he was a tory, it was an unlucky venture, for the whigs would not trade with him. After the war he again became a pedagogue, and remained one until 1791, when he gave up teaching to complete his history.

Robert Proud was a reticent man and has left few memorials of his life. It is impossible to say when and how he began to write history, but it is certain that he was collecting materials for such a task soon after his arrival in the colony. Considerable progress had been made when the war began, but the work was laid aside because the author saw that it was no time for the people to think about their history. Six years after work was resumed, the first volume was published in 1797, the second followed in 1798.

In colonial days Philadelphia was noted for its progress in science; but in "polite and elegant" literature, its position was below that of Boston. From his surroundings Proud could have got little stimulus.

[1] Hazard wrote in 1784: "Yes, honest Anthony Benezet is dead, and in my opinion this State lost one of her most valuable citizens when he died. I believe no man ever died here who was more universally or more justly beloved: he was truly a *Friend* who embraced all mankind in the arms of his benevolence." "Belknap Papers," II, 356 ("Coll." Mass. Histl. Soc., Ser. V, Vol. II).

Indeed, the state of Pennsylvania cannot be said to have shown great interest in the writing of its own history. Populous and wealthy as it is, it can be asserted that the book written by Robert Proud, a poor schoolmaster who struggled hard against an indifferent public attitude, is the best in scholarship and appreciation of the task before the writer that has yet been produced. This does not mean that the book has no serious faults : the style is heavy and lacking in proportion, and many things are ignored which a modern historian would treat; but there is an abundance of accurate statement, with some valuable documents and every mark of sincerity and industry. It was a drab book, too colorless even for the Quakers themselves. The author's returns for his labor were so small that he repudiated in disgust the career of historian, leaving incomplete the narrative, which the end of the second volume interrupted at the year 1742.

3. *Popular Historical Writers*

From books like Proud's let us now turn to a class of writings that posterity treats with too much contempt,— if posterity would understand how history writing has developed in this democratic country. I refer to some popular books, slight things in themselves, but satisfactory to the people who lived when they were published.

It has been remarked that our revolution was unlike that of the French in its effect on literature : the com-

parison is unjust to us.   In France we have to do with
an old and highly civilized nation whose natural forces,
long kept down by outward social forms, burst forth
into great activity when the old order was changed.
In the United States society was new.   The majority
of the people who in 1776 took hold of the reins of government were those whose ancestors came to the
country two generations earlier in humble stations.
They had been left to wrestle with the ruder problems
of nature, such as clearing the land, building roads,
amassing fortunes, and creating the elementary pro-
cesses of self-government.   They were in no condition
to take up the literary and artistic life.   They liked
their own history, but their taste was not discriminat-
ing; and while a few scholarly men wrote some serious
books for the small class of men who could appreciate
them, the mass of the people demanded something far
less respectable.   To satisfy them was created a class
of books, widely read at the time, which to-day we
throw aside as rubbish.

Of them the most notable were books written by
Mason Locke Weems, who began life as rector of a
parish in Maryland.   It was not the profession for
which nature had fitted him.   In a later phase of our
society he might have become a successful writer of
short stories, but there was no career for a man in that
field when he came upon the stage.   Parson he was by
mere force of convention.   It took little time to show
that he was not suited for his calling, and he became a

writer of religious tracts and popular biography. His
first tract, "Onania," seems to have created trouble for
him. It was not thought becoming in a clergyman to
write such a thing. In 1799 he wrote another, "The
Philanthropist," circulating them both in his own
parish and in nearby regions. Without a regular station he now began a series of journeys that took him
from Maryland to Georgia, selling his own and other
books, and preaching where he got an opportunity.
He was a curious combination of preacher and buffoon,
a fiddler for a country dance or a minister preaching in
any church, chapel, country-house, tavern, or bar-room
that he came across. His facile wit, vigorous figures,
and rather coarse illustrations made him popular with
a class of people who nearly a century later were to
find attractive the sermons of some of our unconventional evangelists. Discovering the extent of his
power in this field, he seems to have resolved to
make the most of it. Some of his tracts had very large
sales. Among them we find such suggestive titles as
"The Bad Wife's Looking-Glass," "God's Revenge
against Murder," "God's Revenge against Adultery,"
"The Drunkard's Looking-Glass," and "Hymen's Re-
cruiting Sergeant, or the Matrimonial Tat-too for old
Bachelors." These titles were evidently employed to
secure the attention of a rough and ready people, the
middle and lower class of society in the South. Reading the tracts themselves we find that they do not contain such extreme matter as we might expect. No

one knew better than Weems how to get the hearing of the people whom he wished to reach, an art which many historians of greater ability may well study in his pages.

Weems's purpose was to make money and to teach morality. Probably he realized that the people to whom he appealed liked nothing more than to be preached to. This purpose found free expression in his biographies, the first of which was a "Life of Washington," published in 1800, within a year after the death of the first president. The work was poor at best, but the first edition was very trivial. In 1804 he brought it out in a larger form, and incorporated in it the well known stories of the cherry tree and the cabbage-bed. The book was well suited to reach the class to which he catered, and its sale was enormous. Along every road in the country it was owned and read in the farm-houses. No one knows how many were sold, but the number of editions is estimated at from forty to seventy. It was followed by biographies of Francis Marion, Benjamin Franklin, and William Penn. All were full of inaccuracies. In fact, no writer of biography in America ever drew more freely on his imagination in composing his books. What he did not know he invented, if it seemed good to him. His works are utterly worthless as books of fact; but he drew vivid pictures of what he thought Washington, Franklin, and Marion ought to be. He sought in his biographies to make virtue attractive, to create real respect for the heroes of the revolution and to make men value the liberties of Americans. Probably he succeeded.

Weems was adjusted to a stage of our literary development now happily in the past. To praise him for his good qualities can no longer incite the younger historians to imitate his defects. The present age is too well convinced of the need of good judgment and accurate statement in writing historical narratives to make it probable that any writer would assume to offer it such a compound of truth and fiction as Weems offered his readers a hundred years ago. We run no risk, therefore, in admitting that he had a remarkable faculty of reaching the popular mind and forming the ideals of a class who otherwise would have remained ignorant of certain historical characters.

In the class of popular works designed to teach history we must rank Washington Irving's "History of New York from the beginning of the World to the End of the Dutch Dynasty, by Diedrich Knickerbocker," the first edition of which appeared in 1809. It was confessedly a burlesque, but it was written with such a clear insight into the character of the Dutch settlers that it gave its readers a fairly acceptable impression of their lives and mental attitude. It was widely read and stimulated interest in real history. It was a forecast of Irving's powers in a better sort of history, a prophecy which he redeemed in such works as "The History of the Life and Voyages of Columbus" (3 vols.,

1828), the "Conquest of Granada" (1829), "The Alhambra" (1832), the "Voyages of the Companions of Columbus" (1831), "Astoria" (2 vols., 1836), the "Adventures of Captain Bonneville" (1837), "Mahomet and his Successors" (1849), and the "Life of Washington" (5 vols., 1855–1859). His clear and well-proportioned narrative, coupled with enough accuracy to satisfy the age in which he wrote, made him a force for good historical interest in the first half of the nineteenth century.

Of course, he far surpassed Weems in literary ability. Irving appealed to men of culture, Weems to men of untutored minds. Between the two stands a New England woman, Mrs. Mercy Otis Warren, sister of James Otis, and author of the most popular book in the field of American history in her own section. Her "History of the American Revolution" (3 vols., 1805) was loosely written, but it appealed to the taste of a people who were fairly well schooled in sober thinking by the village ministers and the public schools of the day. It was enlivened by biographical sketches, but was wholly uncritical.

We should not ignore the popular historians, if we wish to understand the growth of history. They show us in what manner popular taste has limited the performance of the historian. In Weems we have it working in its worst form. Books like his in the present day could not have vogue in any part of the country. Washington Irving, on the contrary, represents popular history at its highest stage. Some of his books will be read years hence for their clear and well-proportioned statement. History as a literary art must ever have a vital relation with the book-buying public, and the wise historian will give a portion of his energy to discovering how he may reach the reader.

4. *Jeremy Belknap and Ebenezer Hazard*

Within the period just after the revolution we find two men with so much of the modern spirit in them that they deserve separate and large notice. One was an industrious and impartial gatherer of information who presented it to his readers with a fine sense of proportion and ease of expression. The other was a collector of historical documents at the time when there was nothing to encourage him in the task but his own devotion to history. Though one was born in Boston and the other in Philadelphia, and one graduated at Harvard and the other at Princeton, and though they lived remote from one another, they were drawn together by similarity of taste, supported one another in their individual efforts, and left a correspondence which throws much light on the conditions under which historians worked in their day.

In the beginning I will confess that I make no claim that Hazard is of first rank among the historians. But he had the modern spirit, and the collection of documents he published was made on the best principles. It came to an untimely suspension, like Stith's

"History of Virginia," because the public would not buy it. But it remained an excellent example for future scholars, and by virtue of its priority it gives the editor the first place in a long line of scholarly editors and compilers. Although he repudiated literature and became a successful business man in Philadelphia, he deserves to have his work in his preferred field commemorated in a sketch like this.

Jeremy Belknap was born in Boston, June 4, 1744. His father dressed leather and sold furs : his mother was a niece of the celebrated Boston minister, Matthew Byles. They were highly esteemed in the town, and though poor were able to send their son to Harvard, where he graduated at the age of eighteen, an age at which our own young men are still in the Freshman Class. His parents desired him to preach, but he held off for some time because he did not feel a call for the ministry. At last he felt "a hope in Christ," as he put it, and in 1766 became assistant pastor of the church in Dover, New Hampshire. He had one hundred pounds a year for salary and one hundred and fifty pounds additional in lieu of a house and garden. In 1767 he married Ruth Eliot, daughter of a prosperous Boston bookseller.

Belknap remained at Dover as assistant pastor and pastor until 1786. He was not a famous preacher and he was disposed to make more of conversion than some of his parishioners liked. Eventually he found the congregation divided and his salary in arrears. Moreover, the colonial currency was depreciated, and altogether his financial situation was distressing. He fought valiantly for his rights, and at last a compromise was made by which he received a note for the arrears, signed on behalf of the congregation by one of his own supporters. He was in debt for a house he had built and assigned this note in payment of the obligation. When it was due the creditor could not collect and had the guarantor arrested for debt. To save his friend Belknap assumed responsibility for the note but proceeded to bring matters to an issue with his congregation. He preached them a sermon in which his whole experience was recounted and closed with the statement that he released the church from all it owed him, claiming on his own part that he considered himself released from his obligation to serve them. The agreement between a minister and congregation in early New England was a two-sided bargain and each was understood to have a sort of property right against the other. When a minister wished to leave it was not a mere matter of resigning: he must have a voluntary discharge of his obligation to serve.

Belknap did not venture to leave outright. He remained for the time, but announced that it was on a voluntary basis. Had he left outright, he would have been charged with breach of contract. Now followed some cross playing, the pastor fencing well. The congregation finally asked if he would renew his contract if paid up in full and given a release. He replied

that he would tell them what he would do after the
contract was released; and they were thus finally
brought to hand him his discharge. It was a moment of triumph for him, and he sent them a letter in
which was a plain piece of his mind. It closed with
the announcement that he would leave the parish.
Belknap's position was now serious. He had six
children and no other dependence for their support
than his own efforts. Temporary engagements at various churches afforded a slender income for a few
months while friends formed plans for his future. One
of them was that he should establish a classical school
in Boston, a scheme which he rejected on the ground
that he was not suited to the life of a pedagogue.
Another was to move to Philadelphia and assume the
editorship of the *Columbian Magazine*, the position to
pay him a salary of one hundred pounds a year with
twenty pounds additional to prepare the historical section of an "Annual Register" which Matthew Carey
proposed to establish. He might have accepted this
offer, made through the kind offices of his friend
Hazard; but before it reached him he had accepted a
call to become the pastor of the Federal Street church
in Boston. It was early in 1787 that he settled in his
new field of labor, where he was to spend the rest of
his life. It was a quiet church, supporting its pastor
in comfort and allowing him time for the literary duties
for which he was well fitted. But it demanded most
of his time, and it is interesting to speculate on the in-

fluence he might have exerted on letters if he had been free to give all his time to their pursuit.

Belknap's fondness for history was manifested in his early youth. While at college he wrote in his commonplace book this sentence showing his early bent: "There are required so many qualifications and accomplishments in an *Historian*, and so much care and niceness in writing an *history* that some have reckoned it *one of the most difficult labors human nature is capable of*." At Dover he came into contact with Governor Wentworth, of New Hampshire, who allowed him access to valuable historical papers. The governor seems to have felt that he had put the young minister under obligations and asked him to assume the education of a favorite nephew at liberal compensation, saying that the pressure of public business made it impossible for him to conduct the task himself. To him Belknap sent a polite but spirited refusal, saying: "If, to use your Excellency's words, you 'find the utter impossibility of your having sufficient time to undertake so important and interesting a charge' by reason of the public business with which our gracious sovereign hath entrusted your Excellency, I may justly hope to stand excused in your view from engaging in that which would in any measure hinder me from faithfully discharging the trust committed to me by the Supreme Ruler." This was said in 1770, but it was worthy of the spirit of 1776, which Belknap shared as fully as any other New Englander.

His sense of loyalty to his profession was soon attacked from another quarter. To Captain Waldron, a friend on whose judgment he relied, he wrote in 1772 : "You cannot help having observed in me an inquisitive disposition in historical matters. I find it so strong and powerful, and withal so increasing with my opportunities for gratifying it, that it has become a question with me, whether I might not freely indulge it, with a view to the benefit of my fellow men, as well as for my own improvement. As it is natural for us to inquire into the ancient state and circumstances of the place of our abode, and to entertain a peculiar fondness for such inquiries in preference to more foreign matters, so I have applied myself in some leisure hours (making it of late my principal amusement) to learn what I can from printed books and manuscripts, and the information of aged and intelligent persons, of the former state and affairs of this town and province." Captain Waldron's reply is not preserved, but we know his correspondent did not relinquish his interest in local history.

He took great interest in the measures of the colonists against the policy of Great Britain restricting action of the colonies. He wrote an appeal to the inhabitants of New Hampshire in behalf of the town of Boston, when it began to feel the effects of the operation of the Boston Port Bill. In the same year, 1774, he wrote a stinging address to British soldiers then in Boston. "Gentlemen, I pity you," he exclaimed. "What have you done to deserve such disgrace? You are sent over into America for the meanest and basest purposes; to terrify the wretched inhabitants of this oppressed town with the apprehension of being murdered in the streets in some insignificant night brawl, and to check that noble spirit which once animated their predecessors to brave every danger, to secure liberty and peace to their posterity, and which still breathes in our present exertions to the same worthy and virtuous purposes." When news of the battle of Lexington reached him he was at the ferry midway between Dover and Portsmouth. Without a moment's delay he set out for Boston to get his aged parents out of the town before the lines were established around it. He accomplished his object with some difficulty, and his parents spent the rest of their days in his home at Dover.

Before the war was over he had ample time to carry forward his studies in local history; and in 1784 he published in Philadelphia, at his own expense, the first volume of his "History of New Hampshire." In the preface he tells how the author came to undertake his task. "Having met with some valuable manuscripts which were but little known, he began to extract and methodize the principal things in them; and this employment was (to speak in the style of a celebrated modern author) his 'hobby-horse.' The work, crude as it was, being communicated to some gentlemen, to whose judgment he paid much deference, he was persuaded and encouraged to go on with his collection, until the thing became generally known, and a publication could not decently be refused." The sales of the book were so poor that Belknap felt little encouragement to go on with it; but after he moved to Boston he took it up again, and published a second volume in 1791 and a third in 1792.

Of this book de Tocqueville said: "The reader of Belknap will find more general ideas and more strength of thought, than are to be met with in any other American historians, even to the present day." The book, in fact, remains to-day one of the best state histories we have. It has both form and matter, and it is written in thorough dependence on original authorities. Washington, when he met the author, said: "I am indebted to you, sir, for the 'History of New Hampshire,' and it has given me great pleasure."

The publication of the history was carefully supervised by Hazard, who had influence in Philadelphia. By the same means Belknap was invited to become a contributor to the *Columbian Magazine*, then the best of such publications in the United States, and in this periodical appeared some of his best pieces. Among them was a series of satirical letters, afterwards published with the title, "The Foresters, an American Tale, being a sequel to the History of John Bull the Clothier." That he could so well hit off the foibles of each side of an ancient controversy, shows his impartiality and his fitness for higher things than the

existing state of literature warranted in our new country. To illustrate the character of the satire a cita-
tion is made here from the third letter, which under-
takes to show how "John Codline quarrels with Roger
Carrier, and turns him out of doors." "Codline" was
made to stand for the orthodox Puritan, and the name
suggests the figure of the Rev. John Cotton, while
"Roger Carrier" represents the founder of Providence
Plantation. Says the satirist:

"It happened that Roger had taken a fancy to dip his head
into water, as the most effectual way of washing his face, and
thought it could not be made so clean in any other way. John,
who used the common way of taking water in his hand to wash
his face, was displeased with Roger's innovation, and remonstrated
against it. The remonstrance had no other effect than to fix
Roger's opinion more firmly; and as a further improvement on
his plan, he pretended that no person ought to have his face washed
till he was capable of doing it himself, without any assistance
from his parents. John was out of patience with this addition,
and plumply told him that, if he did not reform his principles and
practice, he would fine him, or flog him, or kick him out of doors.
These threats put Roger on inventing other odd and whimsical
opinions. He took offence at the letter X, and would have it
expunged from the alphabet, because it was the shape of a cross,
and had a tendency to produce Popery. He would not do his
duty at a military muster, because there was X in the colors.
After a while he began to scruple the lawfulness of bearing arms
and killing wild beasts. But poor fellow! — the worst of all was,
that being seized with a shaking-palsy, which affected every limb
and joint of him, his speech was so altered that he was unable to
pronounce certain letters and syllables as he had been used to do.
These oddities and defects rendered him more and more disagreeable to his old friend, who, however, kept his temper as well as he
could, till one day, as John was saying a long grace over his meat

Roger kept his hat on the whole time. As soon as the ceremony was over John took up a case-knife from the table, and gave Roger a blow on the ear with the broad side of it; then with a quick, rising stroke turned off his hat. Roger said nothing, but, taking up his hat, put it on again; at which John broke out into such a passionate speech as this : 'You impudent scoundrel! is it come to this? Have I not borne with your whims and fidgets these many years, and yet they grow upon you? Have I not talked with you time after time, and proved to you as plain as the nose in your face, that your notions are wrong? Have I not ordered you to leave them off, and warned you of the consequences; and yet you have gone on from bad to worse? You began with dipping your head into water, and would have all the family do the same, pretending there was no other way of washing the face. You would have had the children go dirty all their days, under pretense that they were not able to wash their own faces, and so they must have been as filthy as the pigs till they were grown up. Then you would talk your own balderdash lingo, *thee and thou, and nan forsooth;* and now you must keep your hat on when I am at my devotions; and I suppose would be glad to have the whole family do the same! There is no bearing with you any longer; so now, hear me, I give you fair warning : if you don't mend your manners, and retract your errors, and promise reformation, I'll kick you out of the house. I'll have no such refractory fellows here. I came into this forest for *reformation*, and reformation I *will* have.'

"'Friend John', said Roger, 'dost not thou remember, when thou and I lived together in friend Bull's family, how hard thou didst think it to be compelled to look on thy book all the time that the hooded chaplain was reading the prayers, and how many knocks and thumps thou and I had for offering to use our liberty, which we thought we had a right to do? Didst thou not come hitherunto for the sake of enjoying thy liberty? and did not I come to enjoy mine? Wherefore, then, dost thou assume to deprive me of the right which thou claimest for thyself?'

"'Don't tell me', answered John, 'of right and of liberty; you have as much liberty as any man ought to have. You have liberty to do right, and no man ought to have liberty **to do wrong.**'

"'Who is to be judge', replied Roger, 'of what is right or what is wrong? Ought not I to judge for myself? Or thinkest thou it is thy place to judge for me?'

"'Who is judge?' said John, 'why, *the book* is to judge; and I have proved by the book over and over again, that you are wrong; and therefore you are wrong, and you have no liberty to do anything but what is right.'

"'But, friend John', said Roger, 'who is to judge whether thou hast proved my opinions or conduct to be wrong — thou or I?'

"'Come, come', said John, 'not so close, neither; none of your idle distinctions. I *say* you are in the wrong; I have *proved* it, and *you know* it. You have sinned against your own conscience, and therefore you deserve to be cut off as an incorrigible heretic.'

"'How dost thou know', said Roger, 'that I have sinned against my own conscience? Canst thou search the heart?'

"At this John was so enraged that he gave him a smart kick and bade him begone out of his house, and off his lands, and called after him to tell him, that, if ever he should catch him there again he would knock his brains out."

When we read John's speeches we are apt to feel that he is talking sense; and when we read those of Roger, we agree that he is right. Probably it is a little better to say that Roger was generally right but tiresome and that John was generally wrong but sensible. In these days the average reader knows so little about the ancient disputes of the churches that the majority of intelligent people would probably fail to see the clever points in "The Foresters"; but such was not the case in New England a hundred years ago. Belknap, although a minister, was also a literary man; and in this satire we seem to see the latter side of his nature making faces at his black coat, uttering the jibes he cannot repress for the life of him.   Had he followed his bent for satire in a calling less theological, he would be down in the text-books of to-day as one of our prominent early literary men.

But Belknap himself would have disclaimed the title of satirist, preferring that of historian.   In his researches among documents it early occurred to him that a collection should be made of the lives of distinguished Americans, a thing then unattempted.   He began to collect materials for such a work, but became discouraged and urged Hazard to carry out the plans he had outlined.   He was, he said, "confined, as Pope says, 'to lead the life of a cabbage,' unable to stir from the spot where I am planted," and he thought his friend had better facilities and more leisure for doing the work.   Hazard, however, refused to take it up, since he had a larger task on his hands.   After he went to Boston to live Belknap recurred to the scheme, writing the sketches which appeared in two volumes in 1794, with the title, "American Biography."   The persons treated were mostly early colonial worthies and explorers of the American continent.   In view of the materials available and the standards of the times, the sketches were done with remarkable success.   It was on Belknap's foundation that Jared Sparks, a generation later, laid the plans for his popular "Library of American Biography."

It was through the many-sided activity of Jeremy Belknap that our oldest existing historical society came into existence. While collecting materials for his "History" from collections in private hands, he was impressed with the danger that these collections might be swept away by fire or lost through carelessness. The loss of most of Prince's library in the Old South Church was an appealing example of what might happen to other small collections. His first idea to meet the danger was to have duplicate copies of valuable papers and keep them in different places, and this plan seems to have been in his mind when he moved to Boston in 1787. He soon saw fit to change it for a society with a great collection safely kept. He secured the co-operation of four others, William Tudor, Rev. John Eliot, Rev. Peter Thacher, all of Boston, and James Winthrop, of Cambridge. In 1790 these men and five others held preliminary meetings to form a general plan of the Massachusetts Historical Society. January 24, 1791, they met at the residence of William Tudor in the first regular meeting. After adopting a constitution the society adjourned. At its second meeting each member handed in a list of books, pamphlets, and manuscripts he was willing to give to establish the nucleus of the collection it was proposed to build up. From that time to this it has been a principle well accepted by all the members of the society that they are to build up the collections in its possession. At first the membership was limited to thirty, but in 1794, when the legislature granted a charter, the number was enlarged to sixty; and it has since been in-

creased. In the first years of the society's existence,
when its vitality was slight, most of the work of keeping it going fell on Belknap. It was through his effort
that the first volume of its "Collections" appeared in
1792, a series in which have been published more
original and valuable materials than in any other in
the United States. Of all Belknap did for history it is
probable that the impetus he gave to found the Massachusetts Historical Society is his best service.

Ebenezer Hazard was born in Philadelphia in 1744,
and died in the same city in 1817. His father was well
known among the business men of the place and was
able to send the boy to Princeton, where he graduated
in 1762, the same year that Belknap graduated from
Harvard. He settled in New York, where he became
connected with a firm of booksellers, remaining in that
business until 1775. He was an ardent supporter of
the revolution, and in 1775 became post-master in
New York, under the authority of the committee of
safety. The arrival of the British army on Long
Island brought him an order immediately to "remove
his office to some convenient place near Dobb's Ferry,
till further orders." The command was obeyed with
alacrity. In 1777 he was appointed surveyor of the
post throughout the eastern part of the United States.
In 1782 he was made postmaster-general, succeeding
Richard Bache, who had followed Benjamin Franklin
in that office. In this position he remained until the
government under the federal constitution went into

operation. He would have been pleased to continue under that régime, but he was put aside to give place to a man who had more political friends than he. He then sought other government employment and disappointed in this respect retired to private life.

It was while he was surveyor of the post that he began to collect historical materials. July 11, 1778, he petitioned congress for their patronage in making a collection of American State Papers. He proposed to visit each state and wished aid in the form of recommendations to the various states, so that he might be allowed access to their public documents. The petition was referred to a committee consisting of Richard Henry Lee, William Duer, and Samuel Adams, which recommended that Hazard be allowed to have copies of papers in federal offices at the expense of the public and that he be allowed one thousand dollars for making copies. The report was adopted by congress; but in what respect the sum mentioned was used does not appear.[1] While surveyor he traveled much, and it is certain that he used his leisure while on these journeys to make copies of records. After he retired from the post office he gave himself to the preparation of these documents for publication. In

[1] See Journals of the Continental Congress (Library of Congress edition), XI, 682, 705. Also "Belknap Papers," I, 13 ("Colls." Mass. Histl. Soc., Ser. V, Vol. II). Belknap complained that the states did not furnish him copies of manuscript material, as suggested by congress, and that he had to pay for all he got.

1792 he brought out the first volume of his "Historical Collections," and a second in 1794. In the first of these two large volumes were many miscellaneous documents on the periods of discovery and early colonization, and in the second were the records of the New England Confederation. Although superseded by later and more complete collections, Hazard's documents were for the time excellently selected and reproduced. He began with the purpose of carrying his work into several volumes; but the sale of the two which were published was so disappointing that he gave up the enterprise. He then embarked in the insurance business, in Philadelphia, in which he attained solid prosperity until his death in 1817. His son, Samuel Hazard, published the "Register of Pennsylvania" (16 vols.) and other valuable collections.

It was in 1779 that the correspondence between Hazard and Jeremy Belknap began. The latter, anchored in a provincial town, looked upon the much-traveled Hazard as a happy exponent of the life of the historical scholar; and Hazard recognized in the superior mind of the minister an attractive kindred spirit. They wrote frequent letters, each pouring out his soul, seeking advice, or offering aid as opportunity or necessity offered. Both men were interested in what at that time was called science. Unusual stones were exchanged and deposited in museums, or "cabinets," as the term of the day ran. For example, asbestos excited their curiosity much. A story of a

musical prodigy in England who could play the organ
at three years of age was written down and sent by
Belknap to his friend as a thing worth noting. Sibe-
rian wheat and barley aroused much interest at a time
when most intelligent Americans were concerned with
the introduction into their own country of all kinds of
superior plants and vegetables. Hazard was able to
collect newspapers in connection with the post office
and sent many of them to Dover, where a periodical
from a distant place was very welcome.

He took upon himself to secure the apprenticeship of
Belknap's oldest son to Robert Aitken, whom he called
the best printer in the country. About the same time
Hazard made arrangements with Aitken to do the
printing and binding of the first volume of the "History
of New Hampshire," and circulated subscription lists
in its behalf. He could not have shown more interest
in the project if he had been the author himself. The
appearance of the first volume gave him much pleasure
and he wrote in his eagerness urging that the second
be prepared for the printer at once. His suggestion
elicited the following reply :

"I fully intend it, and have already begun to collect and com-
pile; but considering the situation I am in, and the many duties
that are required of me as a son, a husband, a father, a pastor
and a friend, and making allowance for foreseen and unforeseen
impediments arising out of the nature of the work, it is not a
supposable case that a second volume *can* be got ready for the
press in less than two, or perhaps three, years from this time.
The other cost me, off and on, nine or ten years. I know that it

might be run through in a much shorter time by a Grub Street Gazetteer, who would take everything on trust and had materials ready prepared."

Referring to the statement of Dr. Johnson that "no writer has a more easy task than the historian," Belknap went on to say:

"If he had to write the History of a country, and to search for his materials wheresoever they were likely or *not likely* to be found; if he was to find that the 'treasures' contained in 'records' are to be explained by private papers, and that these are to be sought in the garrets and rat-holes of old houses, when not one in a hundred that he was obliged to handle and decipher would repay him for the trouble; that 'tradition', whatever it might 'pour down', is always to be suspected and examined; and that the means of examination are not always to be obtained,— in short, if he had to go through the drudgery which you and I are pretty tolerably acquainted with, and to humour the passions of those we are obliged to, all the while, he would be fully sensible that to write an History as it should be is not so easy a work." [1]

When we remember that this was written at the time when Gordon and Ramsay were drawing liberally on Dodsley's "Annual Register" for their histories of the revolution, we shall be able to understand how much ahead of their time were Belknap and Hazard in their conception of the historian's art.

In the early part of his literary career Belknap appears as the novice leaning on the superior knowledge of Hazard, the man of the city and friend of editors and publishers. But after he settled in Boston and began to be in demand the relation was reversed.

[1] "Belknap Papers," I, 294 ("Coll." Mass. Histl. Soc., Ser. V, Vol. II).

Hazard, out of his position as postmaster and embarking in the field of history himself, now looked to the more experienced, and really more able, Belknap for advice and encouragement. He was not disappointed. Belknap tried to sell his friend's "Historical Collections" in Boston and gave comfort as he could when the task proved difficult. The two men remained friends until death took away the Boston minister in 1798. At that time Hazard had already relinquished his designs in authorship, and was making money in business.

Judged by what they wrote these two men did not produce a considerable number of important books. Nor did they begin an influence of great magnitude that passed continuously into their successors. After they were gone it was nearly a quarter of a century before we had historians in this country to be compared with them. They are to be considered sporadic manifestations of genius, who worked according to their richly endowed natures, following the gifts they had received at birth, seeking truth earnestly and industriously, and feeling that they were compelled by duty to record it as they could. Of the two, Belknap was the best historian. His sparkling wit,[1] so abun-

[1] The following poem, often republished a century ago, was probably written by Jeremy Belknap, although attributed to his wife. It illustrates his facility in writing humorous satire.

The Pleasures of a Country Life
"Up in the morning I must rise
Before I've time to rub my eyes.

dantly exemplified in his correspondence, and his
facility in expression, relieve his tendency to dwell on
facts merely, and we cannot but think that in a more
favorable age or environment he would have developed
into a leading light of literature. He was a rare spirit
set in a new and unformed world, doing his task well
and overriding limitations that many a man in more
conventionalized surroundings would not have sur-
mounted.

5. *Early Histories of the United States*

The first writers to attempt to treat all the colonies
as a whole were two Englishmen. The first was John
Oldmixon, who as early as 1707 made a sorry attempt
to write a history of the British colonies in America.

> With half-pinned gown, unbuckled shoe,
> I haste to milk my lowing cow.
> But, Oh! it makes my heart to ake,
> I have no bread till I can bake.
> And then, alas! it makes me sputter,
> For I must churn or have no butter.
> The hogs with swill too I must serve;
> For hogs must eat or men will starve.
> Besides, my spouse can get no cloaths,
> Unless I much offend my nose.
> For all that try it know it's true
> There is no smell like colouring blue.
> Then round the parish I must ride
> And make enquiry far and wide
> To find some girl that is a spinner,
> Then hurry home to get my dinner.

> "If with romantic steps I stray
> Around the fields and meadows gay,

The other was George Chalmers, an able writer, who published his "Political Annals of the Present United Colonies" in 1780 and followed it with an "Introduction to the History of the Revolt of the American Colonies" four years later. He had access to British documents not accessible in the colonies. In feeling he was very British, and the Americans rejected him

> The grass, besprinkled with the dews,
> Will wet my feet and rot my shoes.
> If on a mossy bank I sleep,
> Pismires and crickets o'er me creep,
> Or near the purling rill am seen
> The dire mosquitos pierce my skin.
> Yet such delights I seldom see
> Confind to house and family.
>
> "All summer long I toil and sweat,
> Blister my hands, and scold and fret.
> And when the summer work is o'er,
> New toils arise from Autumn's store.
> Corn must be husk'd, and pork be kill'd,
> The house with all confusion fill'd.
> O could you see the grand display
> Upon our annual butchering day,—
> See me look like ten thousand sluts,
> My kitchen spread with grease and guts,—
> You'd lift your hand surpris'd and swear
> That Mother Trisket's self were there.
>
> "Yet starch'd up folks that live in town,
> That lounge upon your beds till noon,
> That never tire yourselves with work,
> Unless with handling knife and fork,
> Come, see the sweets of country life,
> Display'd by Parson B——'s wife."

See "Belknap Papers," III, 228, note ("Coll." Mass. Histl. Soc., Ser. VI, Vol. IV).

as unfair and inadequate; but he stimulated them to attempt a more satisfactory treatment.

The first American historian to write an important general history was Rev. Abiel Holmes, who published the first edition of his "American Annals," in two volumes, in 1805. He wrote with great accuracy, but the style was dull and strictly annalistic. The work did not satisfy those who looked for a treatment worthy of their devotion to the newly established united government. Benjamin Trumbull, whose history of Connecticut has been mentioned, next attempted the same task. The first volume of his "General History of the United States of America, 1492–1792," carrying the story to 1765, was published in 1810. It was a solid piece of work without notable literary merit, and its success was not great enough to warrant its continuation.

Next came the "Political and Civil History of the United States" (2 volumes, 1828), by Timothy Pitkin, a Connecticut lawyer. The author gave much attention to the statistical development of the country, treating his subject in a colorless manner. He was federalist in sympathy and did not subordinate political feelings to truth. For a long time he was considered the best authority on the subject. But he gave chief stress to the affairs of New England, and even the people of that section could but admit that he had failed in his object of writing an adequate history of the whole country. In 1817 he published a

"Statistical View of the Commerce of the United States" which is still held in high esteem.

It was with an idea of making up the deficiencies of such works as Pitkin's, Trumbull's, and Holmes's that George Bancroft was led to begin his history. His sympathy for the democratic party made it certain that his work would not be unduly federalistic; but he did not get beyond the colonial period.

While Bancroft was slowly bringing out his volumes in the intervals of his political activity there appeared in Boston a writer who was about to produce a better, but less popular, book in the same field. This was Richard Hildreth, who was one of the founders of the *Atlas*, an influential newspaper of Boston. He remained with this paper from 1832 to 1840, but his health failing he sought a milder climate in Florida and in Demerara, British Guinea. Returning to the United States, he became a ready writer on many subjects. At last he entered the field of history, and in 1849 published in three volumes the first series of his "History of the United States," followed three years later, 1852, by the second series, also containing three volumes. The whole carried the story of national life down to 1820.

Although Hildreth wrote from the New England standpoint, he sought to avoid sectional bias. It was the time of violent controversy, and he was an earnest opponent of slavery: but his book was nearly free from that kind of bias. He was, also, intent on securing the facts of history, and to this day the student derives much assistance from his accurate and all-embracing statements. His book is one that a man seeking information may well have at hand as a constant reference for details. He wished, moreover, to strip our history of the Fourth-of-July cant with which an earnestly patriotic age had clothed it. A British reviewer said of it : "We encounter the muse of American history descended from her stump, and recounting her narrative in a key adapted to our own ears." Weakness in style and the lack of the faculty of interpreting broad movements are, perhaps, its chief defects.

One other New England historian remains to be mentioned here. Although he falls chronologically outside of the limits assigned to this volume, he belongs in spirit to the early New Englanders. Rev. John Gorham Palfrey was pastor of a church in Boston, professor in Harvard, editor of the *North American Review*, and a prolific writer of religious and historical tracts. He has been called "filo-pietistic" because he was so much devoted to the defense of New England ideals. His "History of New England during the Stuart Dynasty" (3 vols., 1858–1864) was well received by New Englanders. It was, in fact, the result of much labor and was a learned and useful work. But it was a defense of Puritanism written at a time when men like Charles Francis Adams were beginning to criticize with singular sharpness the deeds and ideals of the former ruling class in the land of Winthrop and Bradford. The author wrote a continuation of his work with the title, "History of New England from the Revolution of the 17th Century to the Revolution of the 18th" (2 vols., 1875–1890), the last volume being published with additions after his death. Realizing that his work was too extensive for general use, he published a shorter work in four volumes in 1865–1873, with the title "Compendious History of New England to the first general Congress of the Anglo-American Colonies." In this industrious and capacious writer, Puritanism found a worthy interpreter and defender.

Most of the activities here described were in the region directly adjacent to Boston : the reader must find the reason for himself. Why Philadelphia and New York should have lagged behind is another interesting subject of speculation. Why the South should have been left so pathetically void of literature is a question that has called forth anxious debate. It was evident to the men of the period that the South was having her history written by persons who, however worthy, were at heart not in sympathy with Southern ideals. Newspaper editors scolded at the situation, orators cast reproaches, and conventions passed resolutions, but to little avail. It is true that some creditable state histories appeared, like those of Dr. Hawks, on North Carolina ; Pickett, on early Alabama ; McCall, on Georgia ; Stevens, on Georgia ; Haywood, on Tennessee ; Charles Campbell, on Virginia ; Bozman, on Maryland ; and Broadhead, on New York. But these writers did not attempt large things.

The demand in the South was for a book which would treat the history of the nation in such a way that the presidents who represented the ideals of Southern voters should not be held up as bunglers, and that the part taken by the South in the revolution and later should be presented with as much fullness as the South thought fair. It was in keeping with this demand that a leading Virginian, George Tucker, published his "History of the United States, to the end of the 26th Congress in 1841" (4 vols., 1856–1858). It is not a great book, but a good one, a worthy fulfillment of the purpose which inspired its creation. Its misfortune was that it was offered to a people not accustomed to read large and serious books, and it failed of its object because it was not read as widely as the author had a right to expect. It is known in our own generation chiefly through the impression it made upon those whose defects it was intended to offset, while the South has gone on reading the histories written in the North. Tucker was a man of learning and wrote many fugitive political pieces for local readers. He is also remembered for a valuable "Life of Thomas Jefferson" which appeared in two volumes in 1837.

6. *Gayarré*

In the list of state historians just given the name of Charles Étienne Arthur Gayarré was omitted because it seems to deserve separate treatment. He was born in New Orleans of distinguished creole lineage in 1805.

Educated as a lawyer, he early turned his attention to the history of his native state. In 1830 he published in French his "Essai Historique sur la Louisiane." It was based upon the dry collection of documents which François Xavier Martin had published in 1827 with the title "History of Louisiana," but the style was greatly different. Assuming the manner of an old man addressing young people and making use of the traditions in which creole communities were rich, he wrote a book whose charms appealed to old and young alike. It was not sober history, but historical romance.

In 1835 Gayarré was elected to the United States senate, but at the same time he developed symptoms of a serious disease, which sent him off to Paris for a course of treatment in which seven years were consumed. While in the city he took up the study of Louisiana history as a means of employing his otherwise idle hours. He secured access to the records of the colony in the offices of the ministry of the marine and colonies, and returned to New Orleans with a large mass of notes on his favorite subject. On this basis he published in 1846 and 1847 two volumes in French on the history of Louisiana, from the earliest days to the end of the French domination, 1769.

These volumes had much of the charm that was in all Gayarré's writings, but being in the French language they were not available to the people of the state generally. They belonged to the people of the past, and they must remain in the existing form a sealed book to the future, since no one could doubt that English was to be the language of coming Louisianians. Reflections like these caused the author to begin his work over again in another tongue.

Invited to give a popular lecture in New Orleans, he took for his subject "The Poetry or Romance of the History of Louisiana," confining himself to the deeds of De Soto, Father Marquette, and La Salle. The lecture was so successful that he followed the vein and in 1848 published in the form of a series of lectures a volume called "Romance of the History of Louisiana," carrying the story of the colony, in English, as far as 1717. In closing the volume the author said: "I hope I shall be forgiven for having deviated from historical truth in the preceding pages with regard to particulars which I deemed of no importance. For instance, I changed the name of Crozat's daughter. Why? Perhaps it was owing to some capricious whim — perhaps there is to me some spell in the name of Andrea." In real life she was Marie Anne Crozat. The account of her death at the close of the volume is as dramatic a story as Sir Walter Scott himself could have written. There were numerous other places in the narrative in which his imagination was allowed to have play.

Encouraged by the success of this volume, Gayarré published in 1851 a second installment of "lectures" carrying the story to 1743. In the preface he made this statement: "I was informed that many had taken for the invention of the brain what was but historical truth set in a gilded frame, when, to use the expression of Sir Joshua Reynolds, I had taken but insignificant liberties with facts, to interest my readers, and make my narrative more delightful, in imitation of the painter who, though his work is called *history painting*, gives in reality a poetical representation of facts." He added, however, that, profiting by experience, he had been "more sparing of embellishments" in the second installment. In truth, the second series was less imaginative than the first, but it was still far too much under the sway of an errant fancy and could not command the confidence of readers seeking historical truth. The title of this series is "Louisiana: its Colonial History and Romance." [1]

Immediately after the appearance of the second series came a third, carrying the story in English to the end of the French régime. Here again we see the progress of a sobering judgment. "I looked upon the first four lectures," he said in the preface, "as *nugae seriae*, to which I attached no more importance than a child does to the soap bubbles which he puffs through the tube of the tiny reed, picked up by him for the amusement of the passing hour. But struck with the interest which I had excited, I examined, with more sober thoughts, the flowery field in which I had sported, almost with the buoyancy of a schoolboy. Checking the freaks of my imagination, that boon companion

[1] The first series of lectures is reprinted in this book.

with whom I had been gamboling, I took to the plow, broke the ground, and turned myself to a more serious and useful occupation. This is, I think, clearly observable in the second series of Lectures. In the third and last series, which I now venture to lay before the public, change of tone and manner, corresponding with the authenticity and growing importance of the events which I have to record, will be still more perceptible." From that time he was measurably impressed with the duty of the historian to hold himself a credible witness of truth.

In 1854 the three series of "lectures" referred to were embodied in one book and published in two volumes with the title, "History of Louisiana : The French Domination." At the same time Gayarré said that he would continue the work and treat of the Spanish and American dominations. Hard on the heels of the promise, in 1854, he published in one volume "The History of Louisiana : The Spanish Domination," dealing with the years 1769 to 1805. It was the best part of his history ; for having discarded the tendency to romance and confined himself to sober facts, he now wrote better than before ; and having more interest in this than in the American régime, he wrote better than he was to write again. The Spanish period was filled with political intrigue and clashing personal ambition. The designs of evil men followed one another with tragic steps until at last the whole fabric of violence fell before the advent of the strong and rather

prosaic government of American democracy. This
scene of strife was a fine field for the graphic powers
of such a narrator as Gayarré, and he made the most
of it. Miss Grace King well says that his account of
it will remain "the chief standard by which emulative
writers of Louisiana history measure their failure or
success."

The "American Domination" was finished, but not
published, when the civil war broke over the country.
It was laid aside and not given to the public until 1866.
It was well done, but it lacked the movement of the
preceding volumes. The Americans brought in the
rule of democracy, and during their control, save for
the short period during which the British were before
New Orleans, public life was sober, economic, and
merely political. Gayarré was not a good historian of
the humdrum. River captains, city merchants, land
speculators, and shrewd lawyers lost some of their
charm in his handling when they were no longer iden-
tified with the fine old creole families of other days.

The latter part of Gayarré's career was as tragic as
the events he was so fond of describing. Easily among
the most prominent of the older families, he was in the
early part of his life a promising politician, being elected
senator at thirty years of age. When he returned
from France he wished to take his old place in the
procession, but it was lost irretrievably. He consoled
himself with thinking he could still live in ease and write
history. He is described as a man of dominating

temper, who brooked no opposition. For seven years he was secretary of state by the appointment of the governor. In 1853 he was seriously considered for the post of minister to Madrid, but the appointment went to another Louisianian, Pierre Soulé. In 1860, his great cycle of labor finished, he made plans for a long period of residence in Spain at his own expense. But here fate intervened. He supported the confederacy with all the fervor of his ardent nature. He defended secession with his pen, living quietly on his plantation near New Orleans. During this period he wrote a life of Philip II of Spain, but the book was based on insufficient authorities and did him no credit. The war left him in poverty, and he became that most unhappy of derelicts, an aristocratic office-seeker. In 1875 he was appointed reporter of the state supreme court, but next year the supreme court was abolished in the stern struggle to save the state from republican domination. When the court was reëstablished after the triumph of the natives, the office of reporter was allotted to another man.

In his old age — it was a long old age, for he lived to be ninety — Gayarré wrote many things that were not worthy of his fame. He tried fiction without success, he wrote newspaper articles on old Louisiana life, he gave lectures, and he rewrote in popular form some of the things he had incorporated in his larger work. Of all this group the best was "Fernando de Lemos," published in 1872, a narrative in fictitious manner, in which he really recounted scenes from his own life. He died in 1895, having outlived the old Southern régime by thirty years. As an historian he was among our best; for to the capacity of research and clear composition he added the faculty of graceful expression in a degree which few of our historians have equaled. If the original French impetus to high historical style could have been steadied in the beginning by the hand of some master who knew how to subordinate fancy to fact, he would not have been left to wander of his own will through the uncertain fields of romance to a higher ground. Self-taught in this respect, it was to his great credit that he at length reached the better style. Could he have lived in some city in which other historical writers furnished the stimulus of generous rivalry, he would probably have left a greater and more equal range of writing. As it was, he did enough to show his capacity. The South has had no other historian to whom nature was so generous of gifts.

CHAPTER II

JARED SPARKS

1. *Early Activities*

JARED SPARKS, who was destined to be for a long time the chief authority on the life of George Washington, was born in Willington, Connecticut, May 10, 1789, ten days after the first president took the oath of office. He was one of the earliest citizens born under the new government. In his boyhood the perils of the revolution and of the critical years that followed had been forgotten and our war for independence was already covered with romance. Patriotic and loyal to liberty with the peculiar intentness of the men of his day, he made it a sacred labor to preserve the story of the conflict through which liberty was established.

His early life was full of hardships. His mother was a woman of the small farmer class, married to a man of her own rank, whom her son, Jared, dutifully called father. The boy was brilliant at school and became known as a prodigy in arithmetic, doing with ease the hardest sums that could be brought him. He taught himself the principles of navigation and astronomy and at the age of eighteen was a country schoolmaster earning eight dollars a month. When

school was not in session he worked as a carpenter
and studied Latin with the village minister, Rev.
Hubbel Loomis. In this subject, progress was so
rapid that in eight weeks from the beginning he
was reading "Virgil" at the rate of one hundred lines
a day.

Such a boy was not born to build barns, nor to wield
the birch in a village school. Through the aid of
friends he was enabled to enter Phillips Academy,
at Exeter, New Hampshire, from which, after two
years of residence, he went to Harvard, in 1811, being
then twenty-two years old and very mature for his age.
He graduated in 1815. In the classics and mathematics he was so well grounded that the class exercises
were but play. President Kirkland would say:
"Sparks is not only a man, but a man and a half."
Most of his classmates were at least six years his
juniors, but he carried himself in such a way that he
won their respect as well as their admiration. Much
of his sophomore year was spent at Havre de Grace,
Maryland, where he served as tutor in the family of a
planter. His teaching was not heavy, and he so
improved his time that he returned to college and took
the examinations for the year with his class. While
a junior he taught for ten weeks in a school at Bolton,
Massachusetts. His diaries for these years show that
while a student he did a prodigious amount of reading.

After graduation he first taught a select school at
Lancaster, reading theology in the meanwhile. Next

he was a tutor at Harvard, teaching mathematics and natural history. In 1817 he was made managing editor of the *North American Review*. This periodical, then two years old, had for its chief reliance a group of men pledged to furnish articles, but the services of a managing editor were not light. His duty was to prepare the articles for the press, read the proof, and look after the distribution. He was a Unitarian in religion and had imbibed the fervor which characterized that church at this early period of its existence. To give men a form of religious faith in which reason played a larger part than in the old system seemed to him, and to many others at Harvard, the great work of an educated man. He accordingly gave himself up to the ministry, declining a professorship at Bowdoin College. In 1819 came a call to become the Unitarian pastor in Baltimore. Vast possibilities seemed to open in Baltimore. For many years it had been well known that the planter class of the South, yielding to the liberal philosophy of the day, had been very lukewarm toward the orthodox churches. Was this not the opportunity for the new faith, which rejected the mystery of the Trinity and left men free to follow their intellects? And who could carry the message of enlightenment to these people better than one who was acknowledged the most brilliant of the younger men in the movement? Sparks accepted the call, and his friends saw his departure with the greatest expectations.

For four years the fight was made in Baltimore, ably and with personal satisfaction. At the end of the time Unitarianism was a weak force in the city, and the surrounding country was no more ready to accept it than formerly. In fact, it is a form of faith that has not thriven among the Southern people. Sparks himself was highly esteemed in the city; and he won the affection of his own flock to an unusual degree. His sermons were well received by all classes. He founded a society for the distribution of books and tracts, and in 1821 he established *The Unitarian Miscellany*, a monthly periodical, which attracted the attention of many people. Controversy sprang up, in which Sparks carried himself with ability and aggression. In 1821 he was chosen chaplain of the national house of representatives in a sharp contest in which liberalism and orthodoxy were the contending sides. In Washington he gave his energy to the establishment of a Unitarian church in the capital. Hard work undermined his health, probably there was some discouragement because his church did not grow as rapidly as he had expected, and in 1823 he resigned his pastorate and returned to Boston.

It is not possible to deny that by 1823 Sparks had lost most of his ministerial interest. This is indicated by the fact that when he gave up his Baltimore pastorate he gave up the ministry as well. He burned his sermons and there is no record that he ever preached again. Secular interests, also, had been steadily

creeping into his life. During his entire stay in Baltimore, in spite of his hard labor for his professional
tasks, he had written steadily for the *North American
Review;* and his articles in that journal were written
in the most exact manner. For an ordinary review
he would make careful preliminary investigation.
Said Edward Everett, who was the editor before Sparks :
"I am obliged to depend on myself more than on any
other person, and I must write that which will run
fastest. I am ashamed of this, but cannot help it."
Sparks could write in no such manner. When he had
to prepare an article he began by gathering all available materials. It is a practice now well enough
recognized; but in 1823 few reviewers took so much
pains. Sparks was too much of a literary man to be
content with the ministry permanently.

One of his Boston friends was William H. Eliot,
who in the winter of 1820–1821 returned from the
medical schools in Paris. To Sparks he wrote as
follows :

"Every time I think of your establishment at Baltimore I am
less pleased than the last, and when I have any reason to doubt
your recollection in addition to the distance which separates us,
and the difference of pursuits which occupy us, I am half disposed
to quarrel with those who sent you to this outer post of Unitarian
warfare. What is there in your most distant prospects to repay
you for all the sacrifices you have made and are continually making?
Is it the triumph of opinion over prejudice and bigotry, or the hope
of uniting men on subjects which have divided the world ever
since anything has been known about them? For my own part,
I was never so indifferent as I have been since I returned from

Europe about speculation in theology.   I have seen learned and excellent men on opposite sides of these questions, and I do not find that moral principle is more powerful or energetic or elevated in one sect or the other of the two which divide our country.   Nor can I believe that what is very important for us to know and understand would have been left in darkness and mystery."

Consider this letter, also, which the same writer sent to Sparks over a year later :

"How many years of exile yet remain for you?   Are you determined to devote yourself to the propagation of Unitarianism in the South, and do you believe that you are serving society and religion more by leading such a life than in doing your part in forming the character of those who are to fill your place and that of other great men in society?   I may be deceived by my friendship for you, but I really believe that if you were to come to Cambridge and live there unconnected with College, you would do more good than if you made a thousand converts a day.   The passions and vices of the mass of mankind, I fear, will always remain substantially the same, whatever doctrine they profess, but the influence of the character of one man of a fair, honest and intelligent mind upon such a jarring association as that at Cambridge would be in my opinion of incalculable value.   They would be ashamed of their little squabbles and miserable attempts to injure and degrade each other in the society of such a man. Not that I should hope for the entire reformation of this *genus irritabile*.   Ambitious men can no more be just to their rivals, when the object of common pursuit is literary eminence, than any other of the great subjects of contention in this world." [1]

Breaking with the Boston circle for four years and living in a section so entirely unlike New England would naturally have a broadening influence on Sparks.

[1] Wm. H. Eliot to Sparks, March 15, 1821, and Nov. 21, 1822.   Sparks MSS, Harvard Library.

It showed him another side of life. In his two years of service as chaplain of the house of representatives he was brought into association with the most distinguished public men. His correspondence attests the cordial relations he established with many of them. He impressed himself on their world as a man of great learning and ability; and he went on his way in life with the advantage of a reputation among the great men of the land.

In Baltimore, Sparks came into close contact with slavery, and it is interesting to note that his opinion of it was not different from that of intelligent Southerners of the day. He considered it an evil to be endured. "No dream," said he in 1824, "can be more wild than that of emancipating slaves who are still to remain among us free. We unhesitatingly express it as our belief — and we speak from some experience — that the free people of color as a class in the slaveholding States are a greater nuisance to society, more comfortless, tempted to more vices, and actually less qualified to enjoy existence, than the slaves themselves. In such a state of things manumission is no blessing to the slaves, while it is an evil of the most serious kind to the whites." [1] He belonged to a New England which had not yielded to the abolition crusade. He was of the group of Prescott, Motley, Bancroft, and Everett, who followed literature in the pure devotion to it. Twenty-five years later another circle

[1] Adams, "Life and Writings of Jared Sparks," I, 247.

dominated Boston, men who made literature the hand-maid of reform.

2. *Editor of the North American Review*

In the summer of 1823 Sparks returned to Boston without definite plans for the future. He soon began negotiations to purchase and edit the *North American Review*, from conducting which Edward Everett wished to retire. This periodical was in a hopeful state. Founded by William Tudor in 1815, it was supported by a small group of proprietors, who agreed to write for it and share the possible profits, in proportion to their contributions. Sparks while a tutor at Harvard was one of the group and was acting editor. When he went to Baltimore he was succeeded by Edward T. Channing, who in 1820 gave place to Edward Everett. Two thousand copies of the April, 1821, issue were printed, a considerable number of which were kept for back files.[1]

While the arrangement was fair to the contributors, provided there were profits to be distributed, it was eminently unfair in that preliminary stage in which the financial foundations of the enterprise were being laid. There were no profits in these days, but it was evident that the *Review* was becoming a paying prop-erty, and that the few men who wrote for it were mak-ing it such. Theophilus Parsons, one of the group, expressed himself on this point as follows: "I shall

[1] Oliver Everett to Sparks, March 15, 1821. Sparks MSS.

never write again for the *N. A.* without being paid
for it, and the question of pay or not pay is now agitat-
ing in the club.   None of the owners of the book work
but Everett and you, and I do not see sufficient reason
for giving up the spirit of my labours to Messrs.
Mason, Palfrey & Co.   Others think with me; and
if I could I would spirit up every one who has written
or can write." [1]   If the *Review* was to prosper, it was
time it was placed on a sound financial basis.

The proprietors were willing to sell and August 25,
1823, Sparks became its purchaser.   To each of the five
partners he gave $1150 and to Everett $4000 in payment for back numbers, the subscription list, and other
property.   Including his own share, the *North American*
was thus valued at $10,900.   He pledged himself to
pay $2500 at the end of the first year, $3000 at the
end of the second, $3250 at the end of the third, and
$1000 at the end of the fourth.   Everett, with char-
acteristic generosity, remitted the interest on the $4000
he was to receive.   Sparks then engaged Oliver Everett
as publishing agent, paying him $1000 a year and ten
per cent. commission on all the money received for
subscriptions above 2100 names.[2]   His first number
was issued January, 1824.

The *Review* showed immediately that it was directed
by a firmer hand.   Sparks called on his friends in
many parts of the country to write on such subjects as

[1] To Sparks, Nov. 24, 1822.   Sparks MSS.
[2] Sparks's Diary, Aug. 25 and Sept. 4, 1823.   Sparks MSS.

he considered timely. He realized that it is not the function of a good editor merely to select and print the best of the articles submitted to him, but to decide upon the subjects to be treated and secure the best writers to discuss them. He especially desired to conduct an American journal, and he wished the *Review* to be national in its scope. His efforts to draw in contributors from all sections were only partially successful; and his contributors were mostly from Boston or its vicinity.

Before his day nothing had been paid for articles. Sparks adopted the rule of paying a dollar a page, a small sum, but an evidence of good faith with the contributors. The innovation surprised the *North American* writers. Some refused to take the money, among them Judge Story and Professor Andrews Norton. The latter said: "If I were once to indulge the notion of making money by anything I write, it would lead to such continual disappointment that I must put all thought of it out of my head." [1] But the majority took what was offered, choosing to accept the gratification of the present, leaving future disappointments to take care of themselves. The practice put magazine writing on a business basis and it served to add dignity to the calling of the reviewer.

Under Sparks the *North American* became the arbiter of the fate of a new book in New England. A large part of the public, and the most cultivated part,

[1] Norton to Sparks, Oct. 15, 1825. Sparks MSS.

waited to see what this critic said. If its judgment was favorable, the book was well launched. By some its standards were pronounced arbitrary, and even biased by sectional prejudices. Prescott himself seemed to have held this view; for, in congratulating Bancroft in 1833 on the appearance of the first volume of the "History of the United States," he said: "I find that Ticknor and Sparks have both conceived a favorable opinion from what they have heard. But of one thing rest assured: if you forswear your own soil and settle in Philadelphia, it will be damned to a certainty in the *North American:* that we are resolved upon, and you know there is no appeal from that tribunal." [1]

Sparks was practical and possessed good business habits. He secured an excellent publisher, who brought the accounts into order and pressed for the collection of subscriptions. The result was that the subscription list grew slowly but steadily, until in August, 1828, it contained 3200 names. In March, 1830, when Sparks sold his share in the publication, he received $15,000 for three-fourths of the entire property. The other fourth he had sold in 1826 to his publishing agent for $4000. Adding together these two sums, we see that he had obtained $9100 more than he paid for the property. Meanwhile, he had received a salary of $2200 a year. Considering the state of literature at the time, this was doing well.

[1] Prescott to George Bancroft, March 16, 1833. Bancroft MSS.

Sparks's relations with his contributors were generally pleasant. He seems to have taken the liberty, as every editor must, of cutting or altering the material sent him to suit the needs of the journal. Sometimes he clearly went too far, as we may see in a notable case in 1826. He had for review a Greek lexicon by John Pickering, son of Timothy Pickering, and custodian of the Pickering papers. Sparks was already interested in historical documents, and he naturally wished to have the lexicographer in a pleasant frame of mind. Several persons had refused to review the book when he appealed to George Bancroft, then twenty-six years old and a schoolmaster in Northampton. From his letter the following extract is quoted:

"Write six pages on the Lexicon, if you have no more time; or as many pages as you like. It affords an excellent opportunity for discussing the question of the priority of Greek or Latin in studying the languages. The fashion of beginning with Greek is coming much in vogue, and will increase as dictionaries in Greek and English multiply. It seems to me a good notion, but it is a topic to discuss in the present stage of things; as well as other things connected therewith."

Returning to the same subject ten days later, he said:

"Be learned, or popular, or both, as you please. Criticize justly but with good temper, and with due respect for so high authority as Mr. Pickering. He has great merits for his literary ardor and acquisitions, in the midst of a laborious profession, and is not to be dealt lightly with, nor should his work be examined with the same acuteness, as one coming from a professor of the language. Besides, he makes no high pretensions, and in such case it will hardly be just to be very free with censure. I imagine he has accomplished nearly all he attempted. Moreover, his coadjutors seem to have taken the greater share of the work. And after all it professes to be only a translation of Schrevelius, and all great defects must be in the original author. Mr. Pickering may have committed a mistake in translating such an author. Of this you must judge. In short, treat the matter as your judgment dictates, only take care to discriminate in your praises and censures, both as to persons and things."

Broad as were these hints, they were lost on Bancroft. If he was sensitive on anything it was on his reputation as a supporter of the new German school of Greek scholarship; and to that school Schrevelius was the embodiment of error. Of the young scholar's review the best that could be said was that he pushed Pickering aside and delivered his blows on the back of the original author. Sparks was in dismay. His own letter to Bancroft will give us an idea of what was done. In it were these words, undoubtedly to be interpreted as the best face he could put on his conduct :

"Your review is in press, but the first part a good deal altered. It was read to two of our best Greek scholars, one of whom did not know who the author was, and they both said most unequivocally, that they thought your criticisms too severe, and your general tone of remarks not altogether suited to the dignity of the subject. In these I agreed with them perfectly. By the mode of criticizing which you adopted, Stevens himself might not only be made very imperfect, but ridiculous. You may depend the article as you sent it would have given no pleasure to anybody, but offence to many. It was important to retain the Scripture proper names, because one object of the Lexicon is to aid in reading the 'O. & N. Testament,' and pupils must know how to decline these words before they can read. On the whole I thought best to omit your verbal criticisms, and I was obliged to throw in two or three short paragraphs of my own to connect matters together. As the thing is of very little importance, I presume you will have no objection to what is done; and if you should I cannot help it, as there was no time to deliberate. Your observations on Greek Lexicons generally are so valuable that I could not part with them, and as things now stand the review of the said Lexicon is a secondary affair in the article. It is headed 'Greek Lexicography.' Pickering's enterprise was certainly a praiseworthy one, vastly more laborious, than honorable, and the result of criticisms on it should not be a severe censure, but rather a commendation, whatever the minor faults may be. It is observable that you do not point out any other single work which ought to have been taken in preference."

Bancroft, of course, was highly outraged at his treatment. He had been made to appear to condone just the kind of Greek study he had spent five years in trying to overthrow. He protested to the editor, he demanded proof-sheets, and when they came he forbade the publication of the piece as it then was; but Sparks had already printed the number to the last signature and the article could not be withdrawn. It is due to Bancroft that the following extract be given from his letters, in order that the reader may see his point of view. Taking up Sparks's objections, he exclaimed :

"But the severe mode of criticism would make Stevens ridiculous! You cannot be very familiar with Stephanus to say that. The mode of criticism is one which I learnt in the schools of the best masters and leads to the result the article states about Stevens. It is the only fair criticism, careful and minute : any other is superficial and deceptive. But the article would have given no pleasure to anybody! That is a mistake. The public is always with those that tell the truth. It would give offence to many! I knew it and told you so beforehand. You encouraged me to write freely, and rightly said to my fears, Who cares? '*It was important, however, to retain the Scripture Proper names!*' Much you have examined the subject to say that. Nobody of character has advocated that opinion for more than seventy years past. Valckenaer and Buehnken, and Wyttenbach, Schneider, Riemer, and Passow are the authorities whom I followed, and think they were right, though your two Boston advisers may remain of the old opinion." [1]

This incident reveals much about Sparks's idea of the work of an editor. Industry, knowledge of what would be interesting, and the ability to keep his periodical abreast with, or even ahead of, the times, were among his excellent qualifications for the position of editor. But he was not willing to offend the mighty. It was the same trait which in later life led him to soften the language of Washington's letters and omit expressions which, as he thought, lowered the dignity of him who wrote them. It was the greatest weakness in the achievements of an otherwise great historian.

3. *Early Historical Activity*

Why Sparks turned to history is not evident. At college he was most interested in mathematics and natural history, and later on he went into theology, giving himself for the time being to each subject with

[1] For this correspondence see Sparks to Bancroft, Oct. 30, Nov. 10, Dec. 1 and 18, 1826, and Jan 2, 1827. Bancroft MSS, Mass. Histl. Soc. Also Bancroft to Sparks, Nov. 2, 10, 10 [?], and 22, Dec. 5, 6, and 13, 1826, and Jan. 18, 1827. Sparks MSS.

the greatest energy. While in Baltimore he began to write historical articles for the *North American*, dealing with such topics as "Internal Improvements in North Carolina," "Land Grants for Schools," and "Education in Maryland." For these articles he made extensive use of documentary materials. As Professor Adams remarks, he was by nature an explorer, and he found in the quest for information in unsuspected places satisfaction for an impulse which under more favorable conditions might have made him a great traveler.

About the time he was at college he became fascinated by the story of John Ledyard, a Connecticut Yankee, who had traveled much in Africa, Asia, and the Pacific Islands, and who has been called the Henry M. Stanley of his day. Sparks was for exploring Africa himself, going into the interior by way of Morocco, but money was wanting and friends remonstrated, so he gave up the hope. He determined to do the next best thing, that is, write a life of Ledyard. During the Baltimore years and for some time afterwards the plan was in his mind. It did not materialize until 1828, but it perhaps served to keep alive his interest in historical writing, and it may have turned him definitely to that kind of literature in the days when the formative period was past.[1]

The year 1823 was a critical point in Sparks's career; for it was then that he gave up the ministry.

[1] Adams, "Life and Writings of Jared Sparks," I, 93, 165, 180, 375–387.

While in Boston and before he decided to buy the
North American, he wrote this paragraph in his diary:

"Read a little, wrote a little.   Meditating on the importance of
having a new history of America.   Thought I might undertake it
some time or other.   No ordinary task to do it properly.   I would
go to the foundation, and read everything on the subject.   The
Ebeling library at Harvard University, the collection of books in
the Boston Athenæum and Historical Society, afford facilities,
which cannot be enjoyed elsewhere." [1]

A busy editor had no time to carry out such a plan,
but the diary contains evidence that writing history
continued to appeal to Sparks's imagination.   March
25, 1824, he received a letter from Charles Folsom, an
old schoolmate, proprietor of a press in Cambridge,
which brought his historical impulses to a head.   "I
wish to publish," said Folsom, "a handsome and correct edition of Washington's writings complete.   To
this end I should wish to communicate with some persons, who could and would aid me to do it in the best
manner.   Who are they at the South?" [2]   The idea
of having a complete edition of the writings of Washington was not new to Sparks, as he himself said.
Several small volumes of Washington's letters had
come out, most of them containing letters written to
one man.   At that time it was a favorite idea for a man
who published his own recollections to include in the

[1] Under date Aug. 18, 1823.   See also the *No. Am. Rev.,* Jan. 1826,
Vol. 22, p. 221.
[2] Sparks MSS.   Also in Adams, "Life of Sparks," I, 390.

book some letters of Washington; for they gave standing to any volume in which they were found.

Sparks knew that a large collection of Washington's letters was preserved at Mount Vernon, in the possession of Justice Bushrod Washington, of the supreme court, a nephew of George Washington. To the judge he wrote on behalf of Folsom, and received a refusal. He seems to have expected it, and to have determined that in spite of it he himself would publish an edition of Washington. April 23, five weeks before he knew for certain whether or not his friend's request would be granted, he wrote in his diary: "Conversed with Dr. Mease, [of Philadelphia,] on the means of collecting Washington's papers for the purpose of publishing a complete edition of his works, a project which I have for some time had in view."

We hear nothing more of Folsom in connection with the enterprise; but Sparks did not lose interest. For a year and a half he wrote to many persons inquiring about Washington letters. He learned that a great many existed but that they were widely scattered. He also learned that Washington kept copies of most of his letters and that they were probably at Mount Vernon, and he decided to make another effort to see them. Preparing a frank and intelligent statement of his plans he laid it before Judge Washington, adding that he would find his labors much shortened if he could get all the papers he needed for his work in the convenient and authentic form in which Washington left them. Again the master of Mount Vernon was unyielding. He was about to publish, he said, three volumes of Washington's letters and more might follow, a work in which he had the co-operation of the Chief Justice Marshall. Sparks was not discouraged. He appealed to his friends, particularly to Judge Story, who became his active champion. Another letter went to the chief justice, to whom Story also spoke, and it brought the encouraging assurance that "if the publication he [Judge Washington] is about to make shall defeat the more enlarged and perfect edition which you propose, it will be a circumstance which I shall regret. It is not the object of Mr. Washington to attach any notes or illustrations to the publication he proposes making, but simply to select some of the most interesting of the letters and to offer them to the public." [1]

By this time Sparks's interest was so much aroused that he was planning to extend his investigations to the general field of the revolution; and to gain a clear idea of what lay before him he made a trip through the South Atlantic states between March 22 and July 7, 1826. He examined state archives and left orders for copies to be made, and extended his circle of acquaintances. The journal of his travels is rich in information touching the state of documents. On his return he inspected the archives of the middle states, except New York, which he visited — and

[1] Adams, "Life of Sparks," I, 405.

New England also — in the autumn of the same year.[1]
He was much interested in the state of society of the
far southern states, where he was well received and
afforded every desirable facility to promote his object.
His health, never very robust, was benefited by the
journey, and his enthusiasm for American history was
greatly increased. "I have got a passion for Revolutionary history," he exclaimed, on his return, "and
the more I look into it the more I am convinced that
no complete history of the American Revolution has
been written. The materials have never been collected; they are still in the archives of the states, and
in the hands of individuals." [2]

He did not lose sight of the letters of Washington,
and it happened that twice on his journey in the South
he met Chief Justice Marshall, the man who could
most help him in his quest. The first encounter was
in Richmond, and Sparks's journal contains such an
interesting picture of the great man's home that it
is quoted entirely. It reads:

"Called on Chief Justice Marshall; entered his yard through a
broken wooden gate, fastened by a leather strap and opened with
some difficulty, rang, and an old lady came to the door. I asked
if Judge Marshall was at home. 'No,' said she, 'he is not in the
house; he may be in the office,' and pointed to a small brick building in one corner of the yard. I knocked at the door and it was
opened by a tall, venerable looking man, dressed with extreme
plainness, and having an air of affability in his manners. I intro-

[1] The journals are given in full in Adams, "Life of Sparks," I, 414–572.
[2] Ibid., 509.

duced myself as the person who had just received a letter from him concerning General Washington's letters, and he immediately entered into conversation on that subject. He appeared to think favorably of my project, but intimated that all the papers were entirely at the disposal of Judge Washington. He said that he had read with care all General Washington's letters in the copies left by him, and intimated that a selection only could with propriety be printed, as there was in many of them a repetition, not only of ideas, but of language. This was a necessary consequence of his writing to so many persons on the same subjects, and nearly at the same time. He spoke to me of the history of Virginia; said Stith's History and Beverly's were of the highest authority, and might be relied on. Of Burk he only remarked that the author was fond of indulging his imagination, 'But,' he added in a good-natured way, 'there is no harm in a little ornament, I suppose.' He neither censured nor commended the work. . . . Such and other things were the topics of conversation, till the short hour of a ceremonious visit had run out. I retired much pleased with the urbanity and kindly manners of the Chief Justice. There is consistency in all things about him,— his house, grounds, office, himself, bear marks of a primitive simplicity and plainness rarely to be seen combined." [1]

Returning, Sparks arrived in Richmond on May 10. He noted in his journal:

"Met Judge Marshall last evening at the town of Monroe, on the Roanoke River. He was on his way to hold his circuit court in Raleigh, and traveling in a sulky. He said he much preferred the stage for its expedition, but could not travel nights. Passed half an hour very agreeably with him. . . . A case of libel is to come on at Raleigh, which the Judge seems to dread exceedingly. It is a case between two clergymen, Mr. ,Whitaker and Dr. McPheeters. A good deal of excitement exists on the subject, and the decision must involve principles which present legal difficulties and perplexities." [2]

[1] *Ibid.*, 421.   [2] *Ibid.*, 451.

Back in Boston, Sparks made another appeal to Judge Washington. He was convinced he could not proceed without access to the collection at Mount Vernon,[1] but he was careful not to let the conviction appear in his letter. On the contrary, he announced that he had found so much material that he was "very confident of procuring nearly everything which can throw light on the public character of General Washington," and he only regretted that through failure to have access to the Mount Vernon collection there would be some imperfections in his work. Then he played his last card. He had learned that the judge had offered to sell the copyright of three or five volumes of Washington letters to a Philadelphia publisher for $10,000. On this hint he now offered the judge half the profits above cost of publishing and of collecting materials, on condition that the Mount Vernon papers be placed freely at his disposal, to be used as he saw fit. The recipient of the letter consulted the chief justice, who advised acceptance, and on this basis the matter was settled.

This favorable termination of his efforts greatly pleased Sparks; and in January, 1827, he found himself alone at Mount Vernon with the coveted manuscripts in his hands. They proved richer than he had anticipated. Forty thousand letters, most of them copied into letter-books, were before him. Three happy months were spent in making a superficial

[1] Adams, "Life of Sparks," I, 417.

examination, with the result that he realized that he could not select what was most valuable without giving himself to a long study of the contents. He then appealed to the owner for permission to take the papers to Boston, where he could examine them at his leisure. Permission was given, and he returned to his home with the treasure safely stowed.

By this time Sparks was one of the heroes of Boston's literary circle. "You are our standing boast and delight," Edward Everett had said [1] in 1822. To bring back the papers of the most distinguished American made him still more a marked man. Boston hailed the feat with admiration, and probably no book that Sparks wrote brought him more consideration from those who liked him best. Samuel A. Eliot wrote to congratulate him, but added shrewdly that he hoped the judge did not force Sparks to promise too large a share of the proceeds of the publication.[2] Miss Storrow, probably the truest friend Sparks then had, wrote: "I hear you are the richest, the busiest, and the happiest man in New England, perhaps in the world. Long may all this continue!" [3] William H. Eliot wrote that he longed to touch the manuscripts which Washington himself had handled.

The general expectation that Sparks would make a great deal of money out of the " Washington " was not

---

[1] To Sparks, Feb. 4, 1822. Sparks MSS.
[2] To Sparks, March 30 and May 24, 1827. Sparks MSS.
[3] Miss A. G. Storrow to Sparks, June 23, 1827. Sparks MSS.

realized. In 1837, when the last volume of the work
had been published, he had received from its sales
$30,741.00, and his expenses for travel, stereotype
plates, etc., amounted to $15,356.37. The remainder
he divided into two equal parts. One was for himself,
and the other was divided between the heirs of Washington and Marshall. From that time the work was
published on a royalty basis, but the returns were
always shared as just stated.[1] The royalties were
never large. From this arrangement it will be seen
that the chief justice was not entirely disinterested
when in 1827 he advised Judge Washington to accept
Sparks's offer.

The Washington letters were kept in a fireproof
building while in Boston, and Sparks had an index
made. When he had finished with them they were
returned to the owners without loss or damage. His
use of the collection called attention to its value, and
in 1834 it was purchased by the national government
and deposited in the library of the state department.
It now forms the most precious part of the manuscripts collection of the library of congress.

4. *Twelve Fruitful Years*

A list of the editor's own articles in the *North American Review* shows that after he embarked on his new
enterprise, in 1827, he wrote little for that journal.

---

[1] Adams, "Life of Sparks," II, 295 n.

History now absorbed all his enthusiasm. He undoubtedly expected to go forward with the work of editing and publishing the letters, a task for which three or four years would have been adequate. But, like many another explorer, he was dazzled by the opportunities opening before him; and before the "Washington" was completed in 1837 he had undertaken six other books.[1] Although he brought to completion all but one of these additional enterprises, the scattering of energy told on him in the long run. The various works demanded an extraordinary amount of labor, and its completion probably left him without impulse for other writing. From 1840 to his death in 1866 he wrote nearly nothing, completing five of the lives in the second series of the "American Biography," the "Correspondence of the Revolution," in four volumes — a work planned at Mount Vernon in 1827 — and a few brief papers and newspaper sketches.

One of the distractions was the collection of historical materials relating to the revolution, involving a trip to Europe in 1828–1829, which will be discussed in another place. Of his writings that now followed one after the other with bewildering rapidity the following list contains the important titles:

[1] Sparks tried to extend his labors further afield. He approached the family of Alexander Hamilton to edit the papers of the first secretary of the treasury, and he wished to edit the papers of Lafayette and John Jay. In 1833 he wrote to Peter Force with an idea of taking over the "American Archives." Sparks to Force, Dec. 10, 1833. Force MSS, Library of Congress. See Adams, "Life of Sparks," II, 334.

1. "Life and Travels of John Ledyard" (1828). This book had long been on his hands, and Miss Storrow, his good angel in years of struggle, many times chided him lest the demands of editorial work should defeat its production. She had faith in the author and was concerned at the prospect that he would continue to do small things, which were not worthy of his ability. Sparks took up Ledyard in earnest in 1827, after his return from Mount Vernon, as though he meant to clear the way for larger things.

2. "The Diplomatic Correspondence of the American Revolution" (12 volumes, 1829-30). This work was published under a contract by which the federal government took a large number of copies. It was undertaken under an act of congress of 1818 authorizing the president to make arrangements for the publication. Sparks found the arrangement profitable and wished to have the work continued from 1783 to 1789. Through the efforts of friends a bill to that end was passed through congress, leaving to the secretary of state the duty of making the contract, and at that time Van Buren was secretary. When Sparks was ready to make the contract, he learned that it had already been made — with Blair and Rives, publishers of the *Globe*, the Jackson organ.[1]

3. "The American Almanac and Repository of Useful Knowledge" (Vol. I, 1830). Sparks furnished the statistics and Professor Farrar, of Harvard, wrote

[1] Adams, "Life of Sparks," II, 153.

the astronomical observations. They owned the work jointly. The first edition of three thousand copies was quickly sold at a good profit, but the labor was so heavy that Sparks transferred his share to his partner, who continued the "Almanac" for many years.

4. "The Life of Gouverneur Morris" (3 volumes, 1832). Sparks undertook to write this book because it was the only way to obtain access to the papers of Morris. He wrote a biography which filled the first volume and surrendered the second and third to selections from the correspondence and other papers. The whole was done within a year; and it has not been highly esteemed by posterity.

5. "The Life and Writings of George Washington" (12 volumes, 1834–37). The first volume contained a life of Washington, and in order that it might contain the maturest results of his work on the papers in his hands, he kept it back, until the others had been sent to the press. Volume II contained Washington's letters before the revolution. Volumes III to VIII inclusive contained the official and private letters during the revolution. Volume IX contained the private letters from the end of the revolution to the beginning of the first presidency. Volumes X and XI had Washington's letters, public and private, during his presidency. Volume XII contained his speeches, proclamations, and messages to congress. In appendices were incorporated some valuable papers which had been discovered through the industry of the

editor. A discussion of the manner in which these volumes were edited is deferred to another page in this book.

6. "The Works of Benjamin Franklin; with Notes, and a Life of the Author" (10 volumes, 1836–40). In 1832 Sparks learned that Edward Everett was thinking of writing a biography of Franklin. He hastened to inform his friend that he himself had made a plan four years earlier to bring out a complete collection of Franklin's works. As if to preëmpt the field, he sent at once to the printers a small collection of letters which came out in 1833 with the title, "A Collection of the Familiar Letters and Miscellaneous Papers of Benjamin Franklin." They dealt with Franklin's personality and were slightly political.

The larger work was begun about 1834. It consisted of a life in one volume and nine volumes of letters and other papers. As the work progressed several rich collections of papers were found which previously had been overlooked. Up to that time it was the fashion to paint Franklin as a cunning man who lacked sincerity. Sparks depicted him as a man of sagacity, honorable in his dealings with his fellow-men, patient with the weaknesses of others, and sincere in his actions and opinions. Next to the "Washington" the "Life of Franklin" was Sparks's best work.

Sparks knew that he had not discovered all of Franklin's papers. William Temple Franklin had taken a large collection to London, using some of them in the three-volume edition of his father's papers published in 1817–19. The edition sold poorly and the publishers refused to continue it. The entire collection of the papers remained in the possession of the family of William Temple Franklin after his death in 1823. But Sparks was denied access to them in 1829, on the ground that they were wanted to throw light on a claim against the government. After a while they disappeared, to turn up again about 1850 in a tailor's shop in London. They came into the hands of Henry Stevens, who applied to Sparks for information about them. A correspondence ensued in which Sparks proposed to edit the papers in a new edition of his own work. Stevens agreed, but he was unable to send the papers to America because they had been pledged to George Peabody to secure a loan. They were finally purchased by the United States government and placed in the library of the state department, whence they were transferred to the library of congress.

7. "The Library of American Biography" (first series, 10 volumes, 1834–38: second series, 15 volumes, 1844–47). The plan for the work was made in 1832. Several persons were to write short lives of eminent Americans, and these were to be published in convenient volumes, each containing from one to four of the lives. Sparks at first agreed to get out only four volumes and he had not more than begun the work on them when he found himself so busily engaged with

other things that he tried to induce George Bancroft to take his place.[1]   The publishers, however, insisted that he should remain editor, and he went on with the work. The biographies proved very popular and were continued through ten volumes.   After a while the second series was projected.   The lives were generally well written, most of them being done on the basis of original research.   Although now superseded by works of better trained men, they remain for the most part a valuable collection of popular biography.

Sparks believed that the history of a country could be presented to the reader in a series of properly related biographies.   "There are three kinds of biographical writing," he said.   "First, historical biography, which admits of copious selections from letters and other original papers.   Secondly, memoirs, which method is somewhat allied to the above, but more rambling and relating more to the affairs of a private nature. Thirdly, personal narrative, in which the individual is always kept before the reader, and the incidents are made to follow each other in consecutive order. This last is the most difficult to execute, because it requires a clear and spirited style, discrimination in selecting facts, and judgment in arranging them so as to preserve just proportions."   In neither of these divisions does Sparks include that kind of biography which may be called "the lives and times" of eminent

[1] Sparks to Bancroft, Nov. 22, Dec. 1, 1832;   April 22, Sept. 24, Oct. 3, 1833.   Bancroft MSS, Mass. Histl. Soc.

men, a kind of writing in which history is made to hang around the actions of some prominent political character. To him the biographer was a portrait painter whose medium was words rather than color, and whose art consisted in the skillful manipulation of light and shades, intelligent grasp of the principles of composition and values, and the wise utilization of backgrounds.

8. "Correspondence of the American Revolution; being Letters of Eminent Men to George Washington" (4 volumes, 1853). When Sparks began to examine the Washington papers he was struck with the many excellent letters they contained from prominent revolutionary men to Washington. He formed the plan at once to issue a special work in which they should be included. His design was not carried out for many years, but in 1853, the year in which he resigned the presidency of Harvard, the work came from the press. It was not a difficult task, since his work on it consisted in merely selecting the letters to be published.

These eight works contain sixty-nine volumes, most of them octavo. They occupy a large place on the shelves of a library. Think of what an American history section was before they were published. Holmes's "Annals," Pitkins's "History," Ramsay's and Gordon's books on the revolution, and some broken attempts to give the letters of Washington and Franklin: how small they seem by the side of the works of a man who essayed to publish all that was important in the papers of men like Washington, Franklin, and Gouverneur Morris, and who gathered up in twenty-five volumes the lives of the great Americans who had founded the national life. However we may criticize them, these books changed the face of our historical literature; and the mind that could conceive the project and carry it to completion demands respectful consideration.

In 1830 to 1840 thoughtful people in the United States had just awakened to the importance of historical documents. It was the day of the publication of the "Annals of Congress," the "Debates in Congress," the "American State Papers," and the "American Archives." Members of congress eagerly received these works from a generous government and placed them in their libraries in the belief that they were going to read them. The reviewers began to talk of a documentary history as the only real way in which history was to be written, having in mind that posterity, if not themselves, would while away its hours of ease poring over collections of laws, state papers, and political correspondence. To what extremes this feeling ran is seen in the sales of Sparks's works. In 1852 over seven thousand sets of the "Writings of Washington" had been sold. When a publisher undertook to bring out a new and more complete edition in 1889, he limited it to seven hundred and fifty copies; and in 1889 our population was nearly four times as great as in 1834 when Sparks's edition began to be printed.

Sparks himself was fascinated by the idea of writing a documentary history of the revolution. Into what definite shape he would have wrought such a book it is not possible to say; for his plans were never announced. But the idea was always in his mind. It was behind all his editing and collecting of materials. In 1838 he said of the completion of the " Franklin " : "With this work I trust my editing career will end. I have planned a history of the American Revolution, on an extended scale, having studied that subject at the fountain-head for ten years. I know not when it will be executed. I intended going to Europe the present year, for the purpose of completing my collection of materials, but amidst the late wreck of human things I have lost almost my whole property, and am obliged to abandon the project for some time, and perhaps forever." [1] The universal wreck to which he alluded was the panic of 1837, which carried away the American Stationers' Company, a publishing house in which he was largely interested. His discouragement was temporary, and in 1840 he made a second visit to Europe, seeking documents. "Having finished the literary undertakings which have been so long on my hands," he said, "what could I do better than to engage in another? I am preparing to write a formidable history of the American Revolution.

[1] Adams, "Life of Sparks," II, 346.

Most of the important materials exist only in the British and French offices." [1] He appeared very earnest in his project, so much so that he was alarmed at the thought that Bancroft was going to write about the revolution, and suggested that Prescott induce him to write about Philip II.[2] The years passed and the great work made no progress. Probably that irresolution which Miss Storrow had detected in his early life now possessed him, once the great rush of labors was ended. At any rate, the "Documentary History of the Revolution" was not written. His biographer tells us it became a subject to be avoided in the Sparks household.[3]

5. *Collector of Historical Documents*

No passion is more exhilarating than that of the collector, and if ever a man had reason to delight in it, Sparks, who found a virgin field before him, was the man. But collecting has its perils for him who would be a historian : it may become the object rather than the means for reaching an object. Whether or not Sparks carried it to this excess is difficult to say. It is certain that in the condition of historical materials then existing he could not have written

[1] Adams, "Life of Sparks," II, 378.

[2] *Ibid.*, 293 n.

[3] *Ibid.*, 554. Professor Adams excuses Sparks on the ground that he could not use his right hand with comfort after 1851 and that he had many letters to write. But Sparks had ten good years before 1851, and the letters could have been declined.

books without first amassing materials. It is also
certain that his researches stimulated in a notable
way the collection and preservation of materials. He,
George Bancroft, and Peter Force, all working to the
same end, set many smaller men to work, and the
result was seen in the local collections. They made
the thirties and forties brilliant. Moreover, their
influence reached the wealthy collectors, who began
to lay the foundations for private collections, which
were eventually to become rich features of great
libraries. In this movement Sparks may claim to
have been the first in point of time among the collectors of documents in his day.

His first appearance in the rôle was in 1827, when
he made his journey in the South. He was already
planning for the great work which he never began,
the history of the revolution. Passing rapidly through
Maryland, Virginia, and North Carolina, he began
the labors of research at Charleston. The people
received him most cordially, but they had little to
show. "Inquire about papers," he wrote in his journal,
"no one knows anything on the subject, but all are
ready to mention numerous other persons who are
presumed to be fully informed of the matter."

Next he went to Milledgeville, then the capital of
Georgia. There he found a small number of papers
that were worth copying, and gave orders accordingly.
Thence he went to Columbia, where he was cordially received by the faculty of the university. He

examined the records in the public offices, and gave orders for copies to be made of a small number of papers.   Next he went to Raleigh, where, to his gratification, he found the records in an excellent condition.   A liberal selection was made and copies ordered. The spirit of resistance to British authority which early manifested itself in the colony of North Carolina impressed him forcibly.   "Perusing the journals all day," he wrote in the diary; "find much to my purpose, and am surprised to see at how early a period, and with how much resolution, the people of North Carolina manifested their disapprobation of the English government." [1]   From Raleigh he went to Richmond, where his examination yielded much fruit. Going further north he visited Annapolis, Harrisburg, Philadelphia, Dover, Trenton, and New York.   The journey was one of exploration and he brought back, besides a mass of copies, a thirst for further acquisitions.

He had, however, seen enough of the situation to understand the difficulties against which a man must contend who at that time attempted to write a history of the revolution.   "The more I look into it," he said, "the more I am convinced that no complete history of the American Revolution has been written. The materials have never been collected; they are still in the archives of the states, and in the hands of individuals.   During my tour I have examined the public offices of every state south of New York, looked

[1] Adams, "Life of Sparks," I, 443.

at all the files of revolutionary correspondence and
the journals of that period, and have procured copies
of everything most valuable." [1] Later in the year
he took a journey through New England and New
York examining the archives and making copies. At
the end of this journey he had a better knowledge of
the condition and worth of American public documents
than any other man then living.

In all these travels he had been much assisted by
the fact that he was a well-known public character.
Throughout the country he had friends, many of them
made during the years when he was the rising hope of
the Unitarians. As the editor of the leading literary
review in the United States he was also a marked man.
His lack of prejudices and his evident superiority
in intellectual matters, together with a pleasant but
dignified bearing, opened all doors to him.

Sparks's next care was to inspect the archives of
Europe so far as they might be supposed to contain
papers relating to his country. Up to that time those
Americans who had written about the revolution
had been content to rely on American documents.
If they attempted to get the British point of view, it
was in Dodsley's "Annual Register," or in some
Briton's published reminiscences. Sparks had seen
enough of the letters, reports, and orders issued on
the American side to know that just such documents
existed on the British side, probably better written

[1] *Ibid.*, I, 509.

originally and more fully preserved. No American had asked to see these papers, and it was not known that they would be shown. He went abroad, therefore, on an errand which could not but be considered uncertain. He was to ask the British government to show him the British side of a bitter controversy then only forty-five years ended.

Difficult as his task was, no other American was better qualified to perform it. He was the editor of our only American review that had standing in Great Britain. He was a man of marked culture, accustomed to the best American society, and as apt as any of his countrymen to be at ease in the literary circles of Europe. At that time, more than in the present century, the upper circle of London society was ready to show honor to an interesting stranger. To this circle came Sparks with his hands full of letters of introduction. Some were from prominent Americans, Daniel Webster, Dr. Channing, Henry Clay, and William H. Prescott; others, probably the most valuable of all for his purposes, were from Captain Basil Hall, the distinguished traveler, who was then in the United States. He wrote in Sparks's behalf to Lockhart, editor of *The Quarterly Review*, Sir James Mackintosh, and the Marquis of Lansdowne, then the home secretary. Letters to Lord Holland were also secured, and they proved most helpful. Sparks landed at Liverpool, April 16, 1828.

His diary is full of the mention of social functions

at which he took a pleasant part. He breakfasted with Brougham at Westminster Hall, had an appointment with Huskisson at the colonial office, and dined with Lord Holland and the Marquis of Lansdowne, where there were other lords and along with them Sydney Smith, with whom Sparks became well acquainted. At Brougham's he "found Mr. Mill there, the author of a work on political economy, and another on India," and he was "surprised to find both these gentlemen extremely ill-informed " in regard to the United States. He was introduced to Wordsworth, who invited him to breakfast, and who called later with Mrs. Wordsworth. Southey he also met and saw many times. All this fine society pleased Sparks immensely, and he went out as much as he could. But he did not lose sight of the object of his visit. Pleading with officials, reading where he had gained access, and giving orders to his copyists were always his chief occupations.

In his first interview with Lord Lansdowne, head of the home office, he was told that no impediment would exist to his researches. Other officials professed themselves most willing to promote his desires. But days and weeks passed in fruitless endeavors. One official sent him to another. Sir James Mackintosh, Lord Holland, Sydney Smith, and Southey all exhausted their skill to no avail. It was the very time when the British parties were in their most constant state of ferment, due to the persistent demand for popular reforms. In May the ministry was reorganized on a purely tory basis, and after a short while there followed a period of harmony. At that moment the coveted permission was obtained. It was just before the reorganization that Sparks presented his request, and the men then in power were so much engaged in their party difficulties that they did not give serious attention to Sparks. He said later that he did not think they were disposed to deny his request, but that since it was unusual they naturally showed some hesitation in deciding upon the best way of granting it.

As soon as permission had been gained in London Sparks set out for the continent, deferring the further examination of British papers until his return. After making a short detour into Germany he came to Paris, where he was accorded a warm welcome by Lafayette and the Marquis de Marbois, the latter a former minister of the French government to the United States. They both possessed influence with the government and were able to secure speedy admission to the public archives. There is an interesting contrast between the way in which the French and British archives had to be attacked. In London each department had authority over the papers that had once been within its hands, even when they were in central deposits. It was, therefore, necessary to have permission from various sources, and in some cases the officials themselves expressed doubt as to their ability to give the required permission. In France all was certain. There was a keeper of archives with authority over his office. He took the request of Sparks under consideration, referred it to his superior, the minister of foreign affairs, and the latter gave permission. There was every reason that the French should be willing that their part in the American Revolution should be known to an American historian.

Shortly after Sparks and his copyists had established themselves in Paris at their work in the archives, the minister of foreign affairs went on a vacation, leaving his office in the hands of a substitute. To this man came information that a stranger was installed in the public archives, taking copies of official papers, a favor not before allowed, even to a French citizen. He called upon the keeper of the papers, there was a period of hesitation, and the upshot was that the American was told that he could not make copies entire, but only extracts, and that he could not have a copyist. The decision involved a large amount of labor, but Sparks did not shirk it. For over three months he went daily to the archives, copying with his own hand, and missing none of the six hours a day in which the rooms were open. At last he submitted his notes to the keeper of the archives, who cut out a few passages perfunctorily, as if some excision was expected of him. Other collections, smaller than this, were examined, and January 3, 1829, he was back in London for the completion of his labors in that city.

The British officials also allowed only extracts to be taken, but he might mark what he wanted, and

clerks in the public service made the copies. When
all was done the copies were inspected by the proper
authorities. His most important work was in the
foreign office, and Lord Aberdeen, head of the office,
handed the notes to Sparks with a pleasant speech,
thus described in the journal of our traveler:

"He said the facts of history were public property, and that
the history in which I was engaged was one of great interest, not
only to America, but to England and to Europe. He hoped to see
all means used to keep up a kind feeling between England and the
United States, and he believed that a well-digested and impartial
history of past events could have no other effect at the present day,
when time enough had elapsed to calm the excitements and angry
feelings that prevailed during the transactions themselves." [1]

It is creditable to Sparks that he was never justly
criticized for misuse of the liberty given him in the
British office. He found much new material, and
some of it presented facts on the American side of
the old controversy that might have been made to do
service in opening old wounds. He did not use it in
that way. Sir George Murray, one of the Englishmen who gave him much assistance, observed to him
that there was a wide difference between the British
and French documents: the latter, said he, were the
papers of a power friendly to America in the time at
which they were written, while the former were the
papers of a nation then hostile; and he trusted that
nothing would be done or said that would tend to

[1] Adams, "Life of Sparks," II, 127.

revive angry feelings between the powers.[1] Nothing could show better the dissolving power of history on national prejudices than the perfect agreement between these two men, Yankee and Briton, as they stood by the grave of Britain's former colonial authority and pledged each other that misunderstandings should not be revived.

While in London Sparks had access to several rich private collections, one of them being the papers of the Earl of Shelburne, placed at his disposal by the Marquis of Lansdowne. Another valuable collection he did not see. It was the papers of Edmund Burke, in the possession of Lord Fitzwilliam, who was quite old. After having his hope of seeing them excited, Sparks learned that the papers were in Yorkshire, in some confusion, and that it would be impossible to examine them. To his diary he confided his disappointment, consoling himself with the observation: "I have never had any hopes of those papers since I found they were in the hands of a lord, even a liberal and good-natured one, and that his personal labor was necessary to select them." [2]

Sparks returned from Europe with even greater *éclat* than from Mount Vernon two years earlier. The newspapers of Boston and New York took notice of his success, friends and strangers sent their congratulations, and his transcripts were looked upon as an addition to the national wealth. No book was ever

[1] *Ibid.,* 123, n.   [2] *Ibid.,* 82.

better advertised than Sparks's "Washington," could it have appeared immediately after his arrival in America. Bancroft wrote: "Let me join my congratulations with those of your friends who see you visibly on the great success which report attributes to your expedition. It falls to the lot of few men to identify themselves with a leading object of public curiosity and interest." [1]

6. *Sparks in the Hands of his Critics*

It would be pleasant to record that our first really efficient collector and editor of documents had carried his work through in such a way that no shadow rested upon it. Unfortunately, we can make no such a claim. Sparks, who did so much that was truly modern, did not shake off one fatal defect of the old methods. He thought that a sacred halo surrounded the life of a great man, which profane hands should not break lest ordinary men should lose their proper reverence for authority and for the noble ideals which were embraced in the higher specimens of the race. Holding this view, and many men besides Sparks held it in 1830, he could not make up his mind to paint Washington with small faults. He altered Washington's language and became liable to a charge of perverting the truth. But for this failing Sparks could be called the father of the modern school of American history.

In 1847 W. B. Reed, of Philadelphia, published the

[1] Bancroft to Sparks, June 4, 1829. Sparks MSS.

"Life and Correspondence of Joseph Reed," his grandfather, including in the book some letters from Washington, which had also appeared in Sparks's "Washington." Four years later a writer in the New York *Evening Post*, signing himself "Friar Lubin," called attention to the fact that Sparks's text of the letters did not correspond with Reed's. He spoke with acerbity, saying that the letters had been changed by the editor "from an imperfect appreciation of his editorial functions." In the same year was published the sixth volume of Lord Mahon's "History of England," in the appendix of which the author discussed Sparks's "Life of Washington." Mahon gave due credit for the learning and industry displayed in its footnotes, and to the good judgment with which the letters had been selected, but he also, and writing without knowledge of "Friar Lubin's" attack, pointed out the divergence between Sparks's and Reed's texts of the Washington letters, drawing conclusions nearly as uncomplimentary as those expressed in the *Evening Post*. "I am bound, however, not to conceal the opinion I have formed," said he, "that Mr. Sparks has printed no part of the correspondence precisely as Washington wrote it; but has greatly altered, and, as he thinks, corrected and embellished it." [1]

[1] In 1827 Sparks, calling attention to his project, issued a prospectus in which he published as samples some letters of Washington to Joseph Reed. William B. Reed wrote him saying that he noticed that these copies differed in the wording from the originals in his possession. Sparks ignored this warning. See Reed to Sparks, Oct. 17, 1827. Sparks MSS.

To these strictures Sparks wrote a reply. He did
not deny that he had made changes in Washington's
letters. It was the duty of an editor, he said, to correct slips of the pen, inaccuracies of expression, and
errors in grammar; but he claimed that he had gone
no further than this. He asserted that his corrections
had in no case altered the meaning of a single statement of fact. In disclaiming an intention of perverting Washington's words he said:

"I do not pretend to infallibility of judgment; probably no two
persons would decide alike in all cases of this kind, some of which
involve minute distinctions of no great moment in themselves; nor
am I sure that I should now in every instance approve my first
decisions; but I feel that I have a right to claim the credit of integrity of purpose, and of having faithfully discharged the duty set
before me, in strict conformity with the principles explained at
large to the public in the introduction to the first volume that was
published." [1]

Some of Mahon's evidence, and that which was
most damaging to Sparks, included the appearance
of a two-line sentence in Sparks's copy, which did not
appear in the Reed copy. Much was made of it,
especially since it was couched in florid language,
which lent itself to ridicule. A closer examination of
the originals showed that Reed himself had made a
mistake in copying and that the two lines really ap-

[1] Sparks's reply first appeared in the New York *Evening Post* in April,
1852, and was republished in Boston in a pamphlet entitled, "A Reply to
the strictures of Lord Mahon and Others on the Mode of Editing the
Writings of Washington."

peared in the original letter. As this point was
Mahon's chief reliance for the charge that additions
had been made to the text, he was left in an embarrass-
ing position. He did the only thing possible, withdrew that particular charge in good temper, saying
he had been misled through trusting Reed's text
implicitly. But he did not withdraw the other charges,
that is, the omission of some words and the alteration
of others.

Here are some of the corrections made by Sparks
— Mahon called them "embellishments," a term
which it is hard to condemn. Washington wrote
"Old Put.," following a custom universally popular
at the time: Sparks changed it to "General Putnam."
Washington spoke of a small sum of money as "but a
flea-bite at present": Sparks made it read "totally
inadequate to our demands at this time." Where
Washington used vehement language to characterize
the conduct of the British, Sparks, probably recalling
his conversation with Lord Aberdeen and Sir George
Murray, omitted the strong words altogether. Thus
vanishes the passage in which Dunmore is called "that
arch traitor to the rights of humanity," and another
in which the Scotch are "those universal instru-
ments of tyranny." Mahon thinks that these omissions were made in order that Washington might
not seem to speak harshly about the British. Of
course, this construction may be put upon them, but
it is as fair to assume that the passages were omitted

in order that recalling them might not needlessly excite old passions. Giving Sparks the benefit of this doubt, however, does not rehabilitate him as an editor; for there are very many corrections in which it is undeniable that the sole object was to improve the language of a man who did not write polished phrases.

Speaking in defense of his labors, Sparks said in his reply to his critics that Washington himself, in his old age, revised his letters while having them copied in letter-books, and since he, Sparks, used the letter-books it was not strange that the letters should be printed in a form unlike that in which they were sent. This excuse has been made to do good service by his defenders; but it was effectively disposed of by Mahon, who pointed out that the letters to Reed were not copied into Washington's letter-books, since he had not retained copies of them; and that the very copies that Sparks used were obtained by him from W. B. Reed, and if faithfully reproduced would have been identical with the text in Reed's book.

The earlier volumes of Sparks's edition contain many more changes in the text than the later volumes. It is possible that this was due to an improvement in Washington's letter-writing art. He was largely self-taught, and having been through the highest ranks of military and political authority, he would naturally have acquired facility in expression. Possibly, also, Sparks was a little awed by the high station Washington held and did not discover as much to correct in the letters of a commander-in-chief as in those of a backwoods colonel.

Still another possibility suggests itself. Sparks was aided in his editorial work by Samuel Atkins Eliot, his warm admirer and generous friend. Eliot was a Harvard graduate of the class of 1817. He was a business man of rather daring methods, who at that time was dazzling the Boston circles by his successes. He was a good friend of learning and his interest in the Washington papers is shown by the free manner in which he advanced money to promote their publication. But he was not suited by training for the work of editing them. Yet to him Sparks intrusted the selection of the letters in the first four manuscript volumes. The following letter, written while Sparks was in Europe, shows in what light Eliot regarded his task :

"The four volumes of Washington's letters which you left with me to select from and copy are ready, with all the notes and illustrations which seem necessary ; which are very few, for the letters explain themselves very much, leaving only enough to the imagination of the reader to exercise it agreeably. I think you have rather overestimated the amount of those letters. With all the requisite notes they will hardly cover two hundred and fifty pages, or about half a volume ; and the sources of information with regard to his early life, before the commencement of his letters, are so extremely meagre that three hundred pages will be enough for everything as far as the years 1758–59, and from there to the Revolution ten lines will tell the whole story, and as I think it very important to compress the work, as far as is consistent with the purpose of giving a full and true view of Washington's character and mind, I was quite pleased to find that such was the state of the case. They are admirable letters, and considering his time of life, the character he had already established was wonderful." [1]

Eliot continued to give assistance after Sparks's return from Europe, and his letters show that he was "even more zealous than Sparks for the reputation of Washington." [2] Knowing these facts, the question arises: Was it Eliot or Sparks who made the large number of excisions in these early letters? There is no way of answering the question, since the correspondence that is preserved gives no clew that is reliable. But the fact that two men were concerned with it, at least raises a puzzling doubt in the mind of the critic; although it must not be forgotten that as Sparks intrusted the task to Eliot he was responsible for any deficiency that may have ensued.

The Sparks-Mahon controversy attracted attention widely in the United States and in England. It divided the historians into a Sparks and an anti-Sparks group, and it left a cloud on the reputation of the editor of the works of Washington that has not yet been removed. One of his best defenders was John Gorham Palfrey, a classmate at Harvard and a lifelong friend. He wrote for the *North American Review* a long criticism of Mahon's history.[3] We may imagine with what glee he discovered that the noble author had

[1] Eliot, S. A. to Sparks, Nov. 25, 1828. Sparks MSS: quoted in Adams, "Life of Sparks," II, 267.

[2] Adams, "Life of Sparks," II, 268.

[3] Volume LXXV.

written with very imperfect knowledge of affairs in
the American colonies. Taking advantage of his
opportunity Palfrey proceeded to riddle the narrative,
pronouncing it inadequate and badly balanced. He
charged Mahon with minimizing the part played by
the colonials in the Seven Years' War, with failure to
do justice to Washington, with ignoring the part New
England played in resisting the Stamp Act, and with
doing many other things equally bad from an American
point of view.

Having thus laid the foundation by putting Mahon
in the wrong on matters of history, Palfrey took up
Sparks's defense. He skillfully crushed the criticism
that additions had been made, and came blandly to
the assertion that omissions and corrections were also
made. As to omissions, of course there were omissions! Washington's letters were numerous enough
to fill forty volumes. No publisher would undertake
an edition of that size. As to the corrections, Palfrey
said much about the correction of spelling and trivial
errors of grammar. The corrections which Mahon
called "embellishments" were justified in a cloud of
general phrases, skillfully constructed to minimize
the importance of any changes whatever. Palfrey's
defense at this point was constructed in the manner
of an advocate.

The real question in connection with Sparks's editing
is this: Should letters and other papers be published
with absolute exactness, or should the editor be allowed

the liberty of changing the text in such a manner as seems to him fair to the writer. In our own day no reputable editor would oppose exact reproduction, but in Sparks's day it was otherwise. Some men, it is true, like Ebenezer Hazard and Jeremy Belknap, were for exact reproduction, but the majority were for dressing up the letters so that they should not appear indecent. Palfrey, in the article just cited, thus states the function of the editor:

The great public has a prurient curiosity to see a great man in dishabille. If, being a good thinker, he has sometimes used bad reasonings,— if, being or not being a good scholar, he has made some lapses in spelling, grammar, rhetoric, or recollection of facts, there is a sort of satisfaction to readers in having them exposed, and in having opportunity afforded to exercise their own critical gifts, and to feel, so far, their own superiority. If hasty opinions, alien from the usual habits of thought, have somehow been put on record; if some petulant expression has been used, out of harmony with the characteristic style of comment and intercourse; if something which the man kept to himself, during his life, can be got at, now that he is no longer here to protect it, there is many a reader who especially rejoices in such spoil.

"How far is that taste to be accommodated, by one who has an editor's responsibility for a great renown? If a man may reasonably dislike the thought of having his dead body exposed to a mob of students on a dissecting table, has he no privileges whatever of exemption from a vulgar exposure of his mind?"

These considerations had great weight in Sparks's day. It was generally accepted that the mind of the great should be exposed decently if exposed at all. We have in this connection the following statement from Colonel Thomas Wentworth Higginson:

"It is only very lately that there has come to be any strict sense of the value of a quotation mark. Bancroft, Hildreth, Frothingham (R.) all revised their quotations without saying so; Professor E. T. Channing in his life of William Ellery did the same thing; and his nephew, my cousin, William Henry Channing, did the same thing constantly in the Memoirs of Margaret Fuller, of which I have the MS. letters and diaries he used. It has only been outgrown since the habit came up of printing *verbatim et literatim*." [1]

Let us give Sparks all that is here claimed for him. Let us grant that he never consciously changed the sense of a letter and that if in his edition we do not get the exact sense of the writer, it is because he erred in judgment. It remains to be said that in Sparks's day, in spite of Colonel Higginson's assertion, the belief that historical materials should be printed without alterations had already secured recognition in the world. The best editors in Europe had adopted that method, and in the United States, Peter Force was employing it in his researches. The necessity for exactness in reproducing letters destined to become historical materials is as old as the impulse to discover historical truth. Employing Palfrey's figure, the mind of an historical personage, preserved in his letters, should be presented to the student of history in its nakedness, and it is for the student to treat it with respect. If he fails, the shame is the student's, not the editor's.

Perhaps Sparks did not think about the student of history. There is much to show that he expected

[1] Adams, "Life of Sparks," II, 272, n. 1.

his work to be read by the people. He thought that he was appealing to a popular audience; and for such readers it was in keeping with his design to "embellish" and correct, lest the people should lower their respect for great men.

One other charge against Sparks, the editor, must be taken up separately. Its import was that he omitted from Washington's letters expressions unfavorable to New England men. In a letter from the commander-in-chief to Richard Henry Lee, August 29, 1775, occurs the following passage:

"As we have now nearly compleated our Lines of Defence, we have nothing more, in *my opinion* to fear from the *Enemy*, provided we can keep our men to their duty and make them watchful and vigilant; but it is among the most difficult tasks I ever undertook in my life to induce these people to believe that there is, or can be, danger till the Bayonet is pushed at their Breasts; not that it proceeds from any uncommon prowess, but rather from an unaccountable kind of stupidity in the lower class of these people which, believe me, prevails but too generally among the officers of the Massachusetts *part* of the Army who are *nearly* of the same kidney with the *privates*, and adds not a little to my difficulties; as there is no such thing as getting of officers of this stamp to exert themselves in carrying orders into execution — to curry favor with the men (by whom they were chosen & on whose smiles possibly they may think they may again rely) seems to be one of the principal objects of their attention." [1]

This passage was omitted from Sparks's edition. Badly expressed as it was, a zealous editor might have cut it out through tenderness for Washington's reputation as a writer, but such a reason is hardly probable.

[1] Ford, Editor, "Writings of Washington," III, 96.

Since it gives an important view of the situation in the new army before Boston, there was every reason that it should have been left in the letter.

Another book in the editing of which the critics have found many errors was the "Diplomatic Correspondence of the Revolution." This was a subsidized publication, issued under a contract by which the federal government purchased one thousand copies of each of the twelve octavo volumes, paying $2.12½ a volume. It was a work of reference for historical students and was not written to show what Eliot called "a full and true view of Washington's character and mind." In such a series of documents nothing but an exact reproduction of the text should have been considered for a moment. Yet here, also, Sparks took many liberties with the text.

His errors were so striking that in 1888 a congressional committee on printing took up the question of providing a new edition. Its report showed that he had omitted letters bearing on the attempts in 1776–77 of French and American politicians to secure the removal of Washington as commander-in-chief and the substitution of Marshal Broglie in his place, as well as letters in which was evidence bearing on the atrocities of the British troops and the tories in the United States during the revolution. Many of his excisions were in letters that referred to the fisheries, a subject that engaged the attention of later diplomats most frequently. One of the omissions pointed

out by the committee was made in a letter from Silas
Deane, December 6, 1776, sent when De Kalb came
to America. It contained the suggestion that Broglie
be placed at the head of the army, but this part was
cut out by Sparks, and the letter when published was
only a letter of introduction. There were also, said
the committee, many small changes in the words,
made to "embellish" the language. The report of
the committee led congress to order a new edition to
be brought out under the editorship of Francis Whar-
ton, solicitor of the state department. It appeared
in 1889, immediately after the death of the editor.
The proofs were read by John Bassett Moore.

Sparks's Diplomatic Correspondence was criticized
soon after it was published, and the criticism brought
forth a reply which may be cited as his own view of his
task. "I was employed," he said, "to publish a
selection from the Diplomatic Papers in the Department
of State. I acted under specific instruction for that
object. . . . In making the selection, it is true,
my judgment was to be the guide, aided by such particular and general instructions as were given to me.
The nature of the undertaking rendered this necessary.
I explained my method in the fullest and clearest
manner in the preface to the first volume. This was
never disapproved by my employers; nor was it ever
hinted to me that I had misunderstood my instructions, or in any degree deviated from them." [1] This

[1] Adams, "Life of Sparks," II, 157, n. 1.

defense does not exculpate. An editor is judged by the standards he himself sets up, not those of a public official. Moreover, in all Sparks's extensive correspondence there is no evidence that he had specific directions on this point. It is fair to assume that his instructions left him liberty to do all he was criticized for not doing.

It would be unfair to Sparks the editor to dismiss him without emphasizing the fact that he did a great service to historical research, in spite of his faults. While we have had to re-edit what he edited, we have not lost the influence of his pioneer work. He, more than anyone else of his day, aroused the public to an appreciation of the publication of documents. Peter Force, who had better editorial habits, had not as great an influence on his age. Moreover, it seems a fair assumption that he was set to work by Sparks's example. Sparks was so nearly an excellent editor, that we are justified in giving him the benefit of that charity to which every pioneer is entitled. He lived up to a standard which the world was in the act of laying aside, and it was his misfortune that he retained the old. Those who have come after him, and are warned by the example of his failure, deserve little credit for avoiding his mistakes. Few of them are his equal in breadth of knowledge, industry, and the willingness to undertake and carry through great enterprises, qualities which are essential in a great historian.

7. *Sparks's Methods of Working*

To understand Jared Sparks we must not think of him as a bookworm.   Like most of the New England school to which he belonged, Emerson, Edward Everett, Bancroft, and Palfrey, he began life as a minister. As such he was interested in the varied affairs of life around him.   He was a member of a serious and gentle group of men and women who loved to read good books and to talk with intellectual people.   He accepted the ideals of the community in which he lived.   In his age a radical was not popular in New England.

From Professor Andrews Norton, of Harvard, a member of the group of ministers with whom Sparks's early life was thrown, we have an interesting estimate of the literary function of a minister.   He wrote from New York, January 6, 1820 :

"The literature in any place depends much upon the character of its clergymen, and upon the specimens of correct thought and sentiment and expression, which they afford in their weekly discourses; and upon the enlargement of mind produced by just views of religion.   As for the present clergy of this place, I have been led to form not a very favorable opinion of the character of the majority of their number considered in any respect.   The standard of preaching appears to be very low; and the standard of moral honesty, to judge from some anecdotes which I have heard, almost on a level with it." [1]

In Sparks's day history had not become a matter of "movements," "forces," and "problems."   The

[1] To Sparks, Sparks MSS.   Professor Norton was the father of Charles Eliot Norton.

monograph was not yet acclimated in our country. Minute research had not at that time taken the place of proportion. History was a thing of human activities to be dressed in flowing robes and with due attention to the harmonies. A historian took for his subject a general field or some series of events with the idea of making a narrative rather than an interpretation of causes and effects. Sparks did not reject the old way, although he was not the man to carry it to the best success. In fact, he was in a sense one of the first of a new school.

This is especially shown in his "Life of Washington." Here is a book written in immediate juxtaposition with the documents. Designed for volume one of the "Washington" it was the last published, being kept back in order that the author might have the benefit of his study of the letters before he wrote the book. It is sound, concise, and dull. It ushered in a new school. Sparks was not a vivacious writer, like Bancroft. It was not in him to write a sprightly book, perhaps. But in some of the biographies he wrote clear and easy narrative. In the "Life of Benedict Arnold" he is particularly interesting. He was in that book dealing with a closely connected and rather dramatic story, the very vividness of, which carried him on. In the "Life of Washington" he was swamped by facts. They crowded into his mind and mastered it, a great army of facts ranged in even ranks. He knew his facts, but he did not master them.

Sparks trusted himself entirely to history. It would have been easy to continue his connection with the *North American Review*, retaining a part of the salary that had been paid, and giving most of his time to the historical research that he loved. But he threw himself without reserve into the new field that called to him. It is true that he was very well established in life. His profits on the *Review* were $9,100, besides such savings as he had made out of his salary, and he was a bachelor. At that time an unmarried man whose income was two thousand dollars a year need not feel embarrassed in the most select circle of Boston. The following extract from his diary, July 15, 1826, has interest in this connection: "Removed to my new quarters in the house occupied by Dr. Walter Channing, Common Street corner of School Street — I have taken two rooms of Dr. Channing, for which I am to give him $250 a year. My arrangement is to breakfast in my rooms and dine abroad." [1] Dr. Channing was a young physician, a bachelor also, and shared his house with one or two friends. His marriage in 1831 made it necessary for Sparks to find other quarters.

Literature as a profession suggests garrets and crackers in most cases. To Sparks it meant no such thing. He believed he could make a living out of it, and he made more than a living. He had a good appreciation of that which the public will read. Many a young

[1] Sparks MSS.

historian to-day becomes discouraged because his book does not sell, without realizing that he has written upon a subject in which he cannot expect a large number of people to be interested. Sparks gave as careful thought to the selection of his field as to the work he did in it. He had, also, the rare opportunity to select the best field open to a historian in his day. Washington and the other revolutionary leaders were ready for some such treatment as he gave them. His friends congratulated him that he was to pass into history in honorable and intimate connection with the Father of his Country. But his success was not accidental. He did not stumble into his field. In fact, the field had lain fallow inviting exploitation for many years before he turned into it. Many other men had passed it by unnoticed, as good fields are always being passed unnoticed. It was a part of Sparks's genius as a historian that he saw the opportunity to enter a self-supporting career and accepted it.

In proportion to the labor expended on it, the "Diplomatic Correspondence" was probably the most remunerative of Sparks's undertakings. For the thousand sets of twelve volumes each which he sold to the government he received $30,300, in which was included $4,800 for editorial services at $400 a volume. Of the $25,500 paid to Sparks for the copies themselves a large part was profit. We have no estimate on which to depend at this point; but Clarke and Force's contract for the "American Archives" was based on

Sparks's contract for the "Diplomatic Correspondence," and they estimated that their own work would cost to manufacture a little less [1] than half the amount they were to receive. If this is a guide for us in the matter, we may estimate that the cost of the "Diplomatic Correspondence" was not more than $15,000, and if that is true Sparks's profits must have been as great, including his reward for editorial work. The twelve volumes were issued within eighteen months, and for the day the enterprise was very profitable.

The "Washington" was not as profitable as was expected. We have seen that in 1852 more than 7000 sets had been sold with royalty at two dollars and fifty cents a set. Half the proceeds of the eleven volumes of "Writings" were to go to the Washington heirs. Sparks received all the royalty on the "Life of Washington" and the book sold more freely than the "Writings." There was, also, an "Abridged Life," the sales of which rose to 5,500 copies by 1852. From his other works the income must have been considerable.

Sparks tried to make literature pay, and he achieved success. Although the panic of 1837 swept away a large part of his fortune, he recovered himself and lived in comfort. The task was made easy, however, by the fact that in 1839 he became a professor at Harvard and served in that capacity and as president until 1853. He also had a fair income from

[1] See below, pages 249–251.

lectures. Unfortunately we have no means of knowing the amount of his later literary income.

It is interesting to find in the life of Sparks the same problem of adjusting his time to the social demands of a pleasant city environment that many another scholar of the present day has to encounter. Anxious friends urged him to relax by taking walks before dinner and by going into society. He was a man of steady habits, and it is probable that most of such advice was lost upon him. He arose early and worked hard from breakfast until dinner. At that time the dinner hour in Boston was from three to four o'clock in the afternoon, an arrangement that lent itself to long hours of labor, with social intercourse after they were finished.

In his study was a high desk at which he wrote standing, a custom which had the advantage of giving exercise of the body in an otherwise sedentary occupation. As a correspondent he generally expressed himself seriously; certainly he lacked the sparkle that made Bancroft's letters so vivid. But in one at least of his letters he gives us a charming view of his daily life at his tall desk. "My window," he said, "overlooks Charlestown, Cambridge, and the whole country round, and I see all that is to be seen. The famous house in Chelsea,[1] with *all* the trees in the town, is in full sight, and this moment I see the ferry-boat just

[1] The reference was to the family home of his correspondent. The letter was written in 1824, which was before he moved to the house occupied by Dr. Channing. See Adams, "Life of Sparks," I, 353.

landing at the wharf. Five or six days ago I saw the
Battle of Bunker Hill fought over again, while standing as I do now at my desk, and a noisy time it was;
the wooden monument on the 'awful mount' was
shaken to its centre, and the mount itself trembled.
Do you not think I have seen wonders? And yet I
have told you nothing of the great doings of election
week, when we had three or four sermons every day,
and the ministers walked in a procession, and held
counsels and looked very grave, and did exactly what
their forefathers did a hundred and fifty years ago."

Here is a human touch of another kind, taken from
a letter from Dr. Channing, his bachelor lodging
chum, who was writing to welcome Sparks home from
Europe:

"I offer you a sincere welcome to your home and your friends.
Your old room is friendly [?], and exactly where and what it was,
and altogether at your services whenever you will come to it. My
establishment entirely remains as it was. My brother, Mr. J.
Perkins, has a small room alone, and a charming fellow, Mr. Ed.
Lowell, is in the back room on the same floor with you. There are
recent additions : the old and more important matters to true
bachelor house-keeping are all as you left them, except the fair
Clara. Mrs. Bell, her sister, a nice buxome body, has [arrived]
and well fills her place. But come again, I hope soon, and we will
talk when others sleep, smoke when others are unconscious of
breathing,— and drink *scuppernong*, or mountain dew to the good
l .alth of the morning star as in the olden time." [1]

Scuppernong wine is made in the South from the
native scuppernong grape, and Sparks had evidently

[1] May 13, 1829. Sparks MSS.

learned to like it while in that part of the country.
Hominy was another Southern dish that he learned
to like in the South.   He had it sent to him after his
return to Boston.   In his correspondence is a letter
from the Rev. F. W. P. Greenwood, his successor in
the Baltimore church, and from it the following extract
is taken, partly to show the humanity of Sparks, to
whom the letter was written, and partly to show the
humanity of Puritan ministers in the days before the
temperance movement had made headway.   Greenwood writes from Baltimore to his friend in Boston :

"I have attended to your commission.   Last week I went down
to N. F. William's store, with Mr. Nathl. W[illiams], and we saw
the wine and the whiskey packed up ready for transportation.
There are twenty bottles of the former, that is to say four gallons,
& I believe 16 bottles of the latter, half of which is from my host,
Mr. Nat., who wishes you to say which you think best, that marked
O, or that marked W.   The barrel in which they are packed is
directed to the care of French & Weld.   My debt to you on account
of the Bossuet is now, I think, discharged.   The wine, you know,
was 5 dollars a gallon." [1]

The early life of Sparks was clouded by the prevailing opinion in regard to his birth.   His mother's
husband, whose name the historian bore, was a man of
humble position, and Mrs. Sparks bore him several
children after their marriage, none of them attaining
positions higher than that of their parents.   With them
Jared Sparks could have little sympathy.   He visited

[1] January 6, 1824.   Sparks MSS.   Nathaniel Williams was one of the
trustees of the Unitarian Church in Baltimore.

them seldom; but he supported his mother in comfort as long as she lived. Hubbel Loomis, the pastor at Willington, and schoolmaster to all the Sparks children, as well as to a host of others, acted as intermediary in providing for the support of Mrs. Sparks. Many letters are preserved from Loomis to the historian, in which we have a picture of the simple home in the village. It reflects credit on the sincere mind of their recipient that he did not destroy them but preserved them in the great collection, which his historic sense must have told him would go into the hands of the future historian. From one of these letters is taken the following account of the doings of the Sparks family in 1825:

"The family are in good health and have quite as comfortable prospects as most families in town. Daniel, you probably know, is in New York. Origen has been at home since November, and is this summer putting up a house in this [village] for Daniel Glazier, Esqr. Caleb is at Sharon in Vermont, with Freeman Holt, learning the clothier's trade in the winter and farming in the summer. Soliman is at Vernon in this county, working upon a farm by the six months. Joseph works with his Father. They are all, I believe, sober, prudent, and industrious, and promise to be reputable in society." [1]

Of Mrs. Sparks the kind-hearted minister wrote in the following year as follows:

"It is, however, doubtful whether an increased expenditure will contribute materially to her comfort. She has at no time failed of receiving all the money that she intimated she wanted; and almost constantly I have had some money of yours in my hand." [2]

[1] April 20, 1825. Sparks MSS.   [2] January 4, 1826. Sparks MSS.

He added that her nervous depression made her very
melancholy, and that she was a great care to her
daughter, Roxana, whose constancy he frequently
praised. No letters from his mother are preserved
in the large number left by Sparks, and as he got his
regular information from Loomis, it is fair to assume
that she did not send any. Many of our greatest
Americans have come up from very humble origins,
and we are very indulgent to such men. To them,
as to Sparks, low birth but enhances their triumph
over adversity; for if it is well to achieve great things
when ushered into the world under favorable auspices,
it is better to achieve them when the start in life is
hampered by difficulties.

8. *College Professor and President*

Sparks had the same interest in education that a
group of young Harvard men of his day felt, who
longed to revise the methods of instruction in American colleges. Ticknor, Bancroft, Cogswell, Edward
Everett, S. A. Eliot, and many others of the younger
men of learning around Cambridge felt that the old
habit of assigning lessons on which the students were
to recite as the sole evidence of their progress was
antiquated. They wished to secure the introduction
of methods used in the German universities, lectures
by men full of their subjects, who could stimulate the
students to research and wide reading. Sparks approved this movement in a general way, but it did

not impress him very strongly until his visit to Europe in 1828 gave him full opportunity to see how much American colleges were behind European institutions. He returned with dreams of improvement, unburdening himself to George Bancroft in the following words:

"It is a great mistake, however, to call any of our institutions by the name of universities. They are neither such, nor can ever be, without a radical change. They are mere schools, and always must be schools, while the present system of mingling dogged recitations and lectures (so called) in the same course of education [continues]. I do not believe, that a university can be engrafted on any of our old colleges. Something must be done *de novo*, before any success can be hoped. There are so many shackles on Harvard, growing out of old usages, grants of money for specific purposes, and a complicated machinery of government, that you and all the world must despair of building it up into a university. The lower, or the *school-part* of this seminary is an inherent ingredient and must from the necessity of the case keep down the upper, or *university-part*. Neither money, nor talents, nor both combined, can remedy this defect. Now let us have a university without the *school-part;* let us have an establishment where we can teach young men something about the operations of their own minds, the doings of the world, and the business of life. Europe is full of such institutions: it is time for one at least in America." [1]

These observations were well taken, so far as they dealt with general educational conditions in the United States when they were made. But it was a long time before the one real university that Sparks longed for was established. His own interest in the matter was soon eclipsed by the literary and editorial work that crowded upon him.

[1] Sparks to Bancroft, June 10, 1829. Bancroft MSS.

Sparks's interest in teaching history in the colleges was akin to his general interest in education. He was called on for advice from at least two quarters in 1835, which shows that he was considered an authority on the subject. He appealed to Ticknor, who was traveling in Europe, to gather information for him on the teaching of history by lectures. Ticknor's reply was not reassuring, so far as the British universities were concerned. Professor Smyth, of Cambridge, gave him no hope of reformation from the two English universities. Ticknor himself said he would get abundant information in Germany, where the work of Heeren was probably best worth while. He added : "Nothing would be more effective in promoting the usefulness of any college among us than to have history, statistics, and geography in its philosophical as well as its practical extent, thoroughly taught by lectures, accompanied with maps, etc., as is done at every university in Germany and most of the gymnasiums. But this cannot be done with us, as long as every student is obliged to go through every study, — a point I have struggled against so long that I am, as you know, tired out, and the result of which plainly is that no new branches, however useful, can now be introduced, nor any of the old ones carried out to practical thoroughness." [1]

In 1836 Sparks was offered the Alford professorship at Harvard. The subjects included were moral philosophy, metaphysics, natural theology, political econ-

[1] Adams, "Life of Sparks," II, 363.

omy, and civil polity. Two things caused him to decline the offer : he was too busy with other things, and he did not like "the routine of a college life as practised in our universities." To President Quincy he said that a professorship of history would be more to his liking, and the president said he hoped that Sparks would yet become connected with the university. In 1838 President Quincy reopened the question, this time offering the newly established McLean professorship of history. The offer was taken under consideration, and immediately the overseers voted to elect him. It was not until he had given the matter a long and careful consideration that Sparks finally accepted the position. His doubts were due to the fear that professorial duties might interfere with historical labors ; and it was only when concessions were made by which such interference was made unnecessary that he consented. It was agreed that his duties were not to demand more than four months in each year, that his lectures should all come within that time, and that he should have the rest of the year for his own plans. The salary was two thousand dollars a year, and the position to which he was called was the first professorship of history in an American college.

Up to 1838 the history taught in Harvard, as in other similar American institutions, was a small amount of general and ancient history, taught by tutors or instructors, generally to the members of the Fresh-

man and Sophomore classes. The McLean professor
was to have work of a higher and more advanced kind,
and his students were to be upper classmen. As
Sparks himself put it, "Mr. Quincy said it was not
proposed that I should have anything to do in the way
of teaching by recitation from books. Occasional
examinations and lectures were proposed. For anything else I am not to be responsible. Let the tutors
drill the boys." [1]

Sparks assumed the duties of his professorship on
March 12, 1839, giving this term one course of lectures
on the American Revolution, from 1763 to 1783. "I
have adopted," he said, "Botta's history as a text-
book, because I can procure no other; all the other
histories of the same period being out of print. Once
a week I shall read to the class written lectures; that
is, one of the three weekly exercises will be of this sort.
My object is to communicate instruction in all the
exercises, and not merely to discipline the students in
the habits of study, which has been done sufficiently
in the early part of their college life." [2] In the following years two courses, instead of one, were given,
on several subjects. It seems that the lecturer did
not take his responsibility for the students very seriously. He was not a pioneer in any but a temporal
sense. He filled the first distinct chair of history in
the United States, without exerting a deep influence

[1] H. B. Adams, "History in American Colleges and Universities," 21.
[2] Adams, "Life of Sparks," II, 375.

on it; and it was for his successors, men of less renown as writers, to give to history teaching at Harvard that peculiar stamp of excellence which is to-day known in all the scholastic world.

Success as a historian and success as schoolmaster require such distinct qualities of mind that it is rare to find them in the possession of one person. Love of detail, patience in drill, the power of pressing laggards to action, and a tendency to consider small things equally important with large things, are essential to success in the schoolroom: the power of seeing facts in large relations, the willingness to lose touch with human nature while the libraries and garrets are ransacked for sources: — in short, many traits which make a man seem queer, inconsequential, dreamy, or abstracted in comparison with ordinary men are too often the characteristics of a successful writer of history. Certain it is, that Sparks did not make himself a terror to his students. He disliked examinations as much as they, going on the basis of many another theorist that learning should be sought for its own sake. He proved himself, says Professor Adams, "a genial, kindly, and extremely popular man, both as professor and president." The students felt that he was on their side, and he yielded to their sense of well being rather than set up standards by which they were to be moulded into ideals higher than those he found in them.

In Sparks we have an early instance of the union, so common in our own day, of the functions of historian

and history teacher in one man. This custom has
for its excuse the difficulty a man finds in making a
living out of history alone. But it is not an ideal
system. Let him teach who can best teach, and let
him write who can best write, would be the guarantee
of the best teaching and the best writing.

In June, 1840, the McLean professor, his lectures at
college over for the year, sailed for London to gather
materials. "Having finished," he wrote, "the literary undertakings which have been so long on my
hands, what could I do better than to engage in
another? I am preparing to write a formidable history of the American Revolution." The friends he
had made in 1828 received him kindly, the records
were again placed at his disposal, and he spent five
happy months going through documents and ordering
copies in London and Paris. Lord Holland asked
him if he wished to be introduced at court. "I told
him," runs the diary, "that I had no such wish; that
my objects in coming to London were of a specific
kind, which if I could accomplish, I should be satisfied,
but that going to court would not contribute to advance
them; and that my curiosity did not lead that way." [1]

In the French archives he found a letter from Franklin to Vergennes, dated December 6, 1782, six days
after the preliminary treaty of peace was signed, an-
nouncing that the writer was transmitting inclosed
a map on which were marked in a red line the bound-

[1] Adams, "Life of Sparks," II, 380.

aries fixed by the treaty just agreed upon. In 1841 the Northeastern boundary question was acute, and Sparks began to look for the inclosure. After much searching he found a map with the boundaries marked by a red line drawn in ink; but it had nothing to show that it was the identical map that Franklin sent to Vergennes, although it was the only map to be found with the boundaries drawn in red ink. Moreover, the red line was so drawn as to favor the British boundary contention. Sparks took accurate copies of map and letter, and took them with him when he returned to Boston. He submitted them to Webster, who used them to restrain the enthusiasm of the politicians of Maine, the information, meanwhile, being withheld from the public. Webster concluded the treaty to which his name is attached, gaining for the United States more than half of the disputed area.

Soon after the treaty was signed it became known that Sparks had furnished Webster with a map according to which we had made a shrewd bargain. The news was carried to London, where much indignation was felt. Sparks, so recently admitted to the public archives, now appeared as a chief witness for his government in a great boundary dispute. It was intimated that he had drawn from those archives evidence that was used against a government which had trusted him completely. This damaging charge was widely spread in England, and it was long accepted as true; but there is no reason to believe that Sparks used the information he secured in the public offices in England for any other than historical purposes.

Later developments took away some of the feeling against him by showing that the red-line map was, after all, of little significance. The discovery of a map in the king's library, on which Oswald, one of the British commissioners making the treaty of 1782, had drawn a boundary line nearly coincident with the American claim, a map on which was written in King George's own hand "boundary described by Mr. Oswald," showed conclusively that our claim had been much better than the Paris map seemed at first to indicate. The discovery reduced Sparks's red-line map to a matter of no importance. Sparks, however, would not admit that the maps had any bearing on the controversy. There was, he said, no reason for holding that Oswald's map described the boundary actually agreed upon. He dismissed the subject in saying: "These two maps, therefore, leave the matter just where it was before they were discovered." [1]

In 1849 Sparks was elected president of Harvard University, succeeding Edward Everett, president from 1846 to 1849. When first approached on the subject, he said that he could not charge himself with the "mass of small details, which properly belonged to the subordinate instructors," and he added that if he accepted some changes would have to be made in the curriculum, "particularly in what is called the

[1] Adams, "Life of Sparks," II, 411.

'Elective System'." Assured that these difficulties would be removed, he brought up another objection : "I told him that I had also literary labors in hand, which I could not consent to relinquish, and that this should be fully understood by the corporation if they should think of electing me." [1] Again he was reassured and no further objection was made. At the inauguration he was inducted with great ceremony, a thing against which he protested ineffectually. To him faculty processions seemed tiresome, wasteful, and unimpressive. In investing the candidate the governor of Massachusetts, in alluding to Sparks's historical achievements, spoke as follows :

"Having performed this service for history and for the literary world, and done justice to the memories of distinguished men, who have served their generations well and passed away, it is appropriate that you should now come up to this seat of learning and enter upon the more important work of instructing the youth of the republic." [2] Probably most men in 1849 would have agreed that to teach was a more important work than writing history.

Reference has already been made to the existence of two parties in the Harvard faculty. One, led by George Ticknor, demanded reforms in the course of instruction, and the other wished to hold in a measure to the old system. About 1838 the reformers succeeded in getting two of their important ideas adopted.

[1] Adams, "Life of Sparks," II, 438   [2] *Ibid.*, 443

One was the introduction of a number of elective courses in all but the Freshman class. The other was the adoption of an idea which Bancroft and Ticknor had contended for as early as 1822, the division of the Freshman and Sophomore classes into divisions according to proficiency.[1] Between 1838 and 1849 several restrictions had been placed on the elective system, one of them being adopted in 1848. The recovery of influence in the faculty by those who favored the old plan was coincident with the election of Sparks as president. He was opposed to the elective system, and his inaugural address left no doubt about his opinion in regard to it. But he did not go so far as to veto all electives. He recognized the terrors of mathematics, and he was not willing to force it on all students; and some other features of the elective system continued to be tolerated. As for the division of the lower classes according to proficiency, it was abolished in favor of an alphabetical arrangement. Sparks said that the previous method sacrificed the poor students for the good. His opponents may as well have said that his method sacrificed the brilliant for the poor students.

Sparks resigned the presidency of the university January 27, 1853, having held it four years and eight days. His short term had worn his spirits. He was not fitted for the many small duties of the office, and in spite of his early resolutions he was overwhelmed

[1] Bancroft to S. A. Eliot, Dec. 3, 1822. Bancroft MSS, Mass. Histl. Soc.

with such details. There were letters to write to parents and to applicants for entrance, college discipline had to be supervised, and many tedious matters were thrust upon him. Such things were very uncongenial to a man whose most devoted pursuits had been the collection and interpretation of historical documents. His reports were well written, as became one who had such a grasp of statistics and historical narrative as he. But he was not at ease in the presidential chair. Moreover, bad health added to his distress. Neuralgia attacked his right arm, and in 1851 an accident increased its lameness. Walking across Charles River bridge into Boston on a starlit evening, he was knocked down by a chaise carelessly driven at a rapid rate. His shoulder-bone was broken and his side severely bruised. Although these injuries yielded to treatment, the nerves seemed to be permanently injured, so that the neuralgia fastened itself more firmly in the right arm. One result was the impairment of his power to write. He was not able to accustom himself to dictation, and the large correspondence he carried on during his later years was the source of much pain in the actual performance.

The domestic life of Jared Sparks was uneventful. Most of his literary work was done in the days of his bachelorhood. In 1832 he was married to Frances Anne Allen, of Hyde Park, New York, whom rapid tuberculosis took away in 1835. In 1839 he married Mary Crowninshield Silsbee, of Salem, Massachusetts,

who survived him. To his own family, as to every
one else, his actions were marked by singular courtesy
and gentleness. His widow, who was his junior by
twenty years, long lived in Cambridge in the comfortable house he bought for her. She was most careful
of his fame, and in her old age gave the most efficient
encouragement to Professor Herbert B. Adams, whom
she selected to write the "Life and Writings of Jared
Sparks." [1]

After retiring from the presidency of Harvard, Sparks
lived quietly in Cambridge until his death in 1866.
He published only one work in this interval, his "Correspondence of the American Revolution," in four
volumes. Much of his time was given to answering inquiries that came from every quarter. He was
looked upon as the Nestor of American historians, and
many a man called on him for information which
could as easily have been had in an encyclopedia.
To such requests Sparks gave free and generous response.

It is seldom that an American historian has worn
the harness of his profession until the last. Too often
his last years are spent in some form of easy occupation that leaves unemployed talents and information
that are ripe for the best kind of results. Sparks,
as has already been observed, was particularly liable
to this charge. The last twenty-five years of the
seventy-seven he lived, a period during which he was

[1] Published in 1893.

the leading scholar in American history, were given over to things which a dozen other men could have done equally well.

In the United States literary ambition is sometimes a means to an end. It is to the aspirant a means of securing wealth, personal influence, or professional appointments. When these ends are attained, literature may be bowed into the attic. Such writers, historians or what not, are, intellectually speaking, nothing less than men of commerce. The real historians are those who love history for its own sake, who love it when they are old as when they were young, and whose best wish is that when death overtakes them it may find them in the harness of actual composition. To them history is a profession, a profession worthy of its hire, and in itself a sufficient reward for the hardest efforts.

In the light of these observations, it is somewhat uncertain what should be said of Sparks. If he was attracted from his best field by the flattering prospect of the first distinct professorship of history in America, and still further by the offer of the presidency of the oldest American college, he did no more than many men would do to-day with less excuse. That he had in his early years an exalted appreciation of the intellectual life is seen in the following extract from a letter written in 1825 :

"There is, as you intimate, very little harmony between riches and the love of letters. They can hardly dwell in the same house.

It must be so; it is a law of nature; one deep passion drives away
all others, and all experience testifies, that no love is more absorbing than that of riches. Yet there is nothing incompatible between
wealth and wisdom, virtue, kindness, and good feeling. I see them
every day united in an eminent degree. My absorbing passion is
for books, knowledge, and thought; and I would not exchange it
for all the wealth of the Indies." [1]

Sparks's fame would have been higher if he had remained true to the "absorbing passion" he here
avowed.[2]

[1] Sparks to George Bancroft, Dec. 26, 1825. Sparks MSS. It is interesting to note that Bancroft himself became a rich man and divided his
historical interest with politics and diplomacy.

[2] *The Sparks Manuscripts*

The Sparks Manuscripts, preserved in the library of Harvard University,
and open by his direction to all properly accredited students of history, are
classified in one hundred and ninety-three bound volumes and bundles.
They make one of the most valuable collections in the United States.
They are arranged as English, French, Spanish, and Miscellaneous. A
calendar was prepared by Justin Winsor, containing eighty-eight pages. It
was published in the "Library of Harvard University, Bibliographical Contributions," No. 22, Cambridge, 1889. See also the "Catalogue of the
Library of Jared Sparks," Cambridge, 1871, pp. 213–230, where there is a
condensed list of the papers in the Sparks collection.

CHAPTER III

GEORGE BANCROFT

1. *Student and Schoolmaster*

GEORGE BANCROFT, like Sparks, was the product of the early and enthusiastic phase of New England Unitarianism. His father, Rev. Aaron Bancroft, was minister at Worcester, Massachusetts, and author of a Life of Washington widely read in his day and still found in the older libraries. His mother was a woman of strong character and excellent mind. The Worcester parsonage was the scene of frugality and liberal thinking. Its head was never willing to admit that he was not a congregationalist, but he encouraged his children to solve their own problems in their own ways, and he himself was openly against Calvinism.

His son George, born at Worcester, October 3, 1800, early gave promise of great ability. He was sent to Phillips Academy, at Exeter, New Hampshire, and in 1813 entered Harvard, where he graduated in 1817, before he was seventeen years old. During his first and second years in residence Edward Everett, who himself had graduated with first honors at the age of seventeen, was teaching Latin and Greek. In 1815 Everett sailed for Europe, returning in 1819, two of the intervening years having been passed at Göttingen.

In Germany he remembered his able student at Harvard and advised President Kirkland to send him to Göttingen.   The result was that Harvard men raised a purse of seven hundred dollars a year for three years and to it added one thousand dollars for a year's travel in Italy and France, which, with the small amount — five hundred dollars — his father was able to add, sufficed for four years abroad.[1]   "Little Bancroft," as one of the other Americans at Göttingen called him,[2] made a good impression on his professors and took the doctor's degree with credit in 1820.   The next year was spent in Berlin where he attended lectures.   In the summer of 1822 he returned to his father's home in Worcester.

He found awaiting him a letter from Professor Andrews Norton, of Harvard, with an invitation to visit him in his home.   The invitation was accepted and two weeks in Cambridge were divided equally between two hosts, President Kirkland and Professor Norton. On this visit Bancroft was offered and accepted the position of tutor in Greek at Harvard.   He returned to Worcester full of happiness and confidence in his future.   Soon came a letter from Norton which turned his joy into mourning.   His own words written several months later contain our best intimation of what had happened.   He wrote to a friend:

[1] President Kirkland to Bancroft, May 11, 1821.   Bancroft MSS, Mass. Histl. Soc.

[2] Anna E. Ticknor, "Life of Joseph Green Cogswell," 107.

"I had hardly been at home many days before I received a letter from Mr. Norton which contained the most unprovoked attack on my feelings and character, the most unfounded censures and unkind reproofs. You will smile perhaps at my calling the censures unfounded. I repeat it, however; they were unfounded. Never did one man more totally mistake the character of another than he did mine. Now you have been told that I was offended at this letter. I was *not* offended: I was wounded: my spirit almost bent beneath it. Why? First because Mr. Norton, I had believed, loved me, and I certainly loved him most sincerely; and now in this letter he tells me he deems it '*desirable*' that I should give over visiting at his house. Secondly, it is my misery to have lived on charity, while abroad, and Mr. Norton was one of those whose bread I ate — bitter enough is the taste of it in the belly." [1]

Bancroft kept many of his letters, but the cruel lines from Professor Norton are not among them. A copy of his reply, however, is preserved, and from it is taken this vigorous utterance: "Upon your house I shall not intrude: such is your desire: I comply with it; I promise you I will never enter it except on a visit of duty or business, till you come to me and solicit it, as I expect you will do, when the future shall have shown you, that your views of my character are unjust." [2]

No information is available on Norton's side of this affair. That he said, "You have disappointed me," we know from Bancroft himself. Perhaps we may understand the matter better by remembering how formal were New Englanders a hundred years ago. Norton himself was of the straitest sect among his fellows, and

[1] Bancroft to S. A. Eliot, April 2, 1823. Bancroft MSS, Mass. Histl. Soc.

[2] Bancroft to Andrews Norton, Sept. 18, 1822. Bancroft MSS.

he had early begun to suspect his protégé of unconventional ways. "Our society is such," he observed to Bancroft in 1821, "as to require an extraordinary degree of attention to manners, in order that one may be respectable and useful. . . . There is no place, I believe, where anything implying a considerable defect in character, anything like ostentation or vanity, anything *outre* or *bizarre* (if I may use two French words at once) is observed with a keener perception of ridicule, or tends more to the disadvantage of him in whom it is discovered." Bancroft might have replied that there were many New Englanders, among them President Kirkland and George Ticknor, to whom his manners were not repulsive. That such a man was offended in Bancroft is not surprising. The younger man possessed a very warm fancy; florid phrases and figures of speech rolled from him as rapidly as duller words come from an ordinary man. In Europe he acquired many customs which in his enthusiasm he began to use among the friends of his youth. It is said that he greeted Professor Norton — of all men! — in the European fashion, with a kiss on each cheek. The effect was consternation.

This unpleasant turn of affairs did not serve as a warning to Bancroft. He was supremely confident of himself, he imitated the German professors in external matters, he carried himself with the air of a military man, he was very exacting of the students, and finally, he had decided ideas that the college was dying of antiquated ideas. Everett and Ticknor had returned from Germany with no such affectations; and their friends had remarked with delight that they were unspoiled by their travels. Bancroft was so unlike them that the opinion spread rapidly that he was intolerable. He ventured to preach, but the hearers shook their heads, and in a few months his sermons were laid away never to be taken out again.

How much Professor Norton's attitude had to do in the crystallization of this reputation does not appear. Certain it is that he did not do justice to the young man. Bancroft was a youth of great ability, he was very emotional and very desirous of success. A little more tolerance and patience, with some kind advice and the lapse of time, would have produced much improvement. Norton was unyielding. Following the promptings of a peculiar kind of Puritan conscience, he held that a thing which was unpleasant had to be trampled on. He was an influential member of the faculty. Bancroft, on the other hand, was not disposed to benefit by opposition. When punished he rose in opposition to the chastisers; and in Harvard he soon lay on a bed of thorns.

Two broad-minded men there were who understood him and left testimonials of his good qualities, two besides George Ticknor, with whom he long maintained friendly intercourse. One was President Kirkland, who was ever generous to his junior faculty, as to all kinds of people. He made a strong impression

on the heart of the young man, who, looking back in
later life to those days of distress, recalled the kindness
of his early friend by the establishment of the John
Thornton Kirkland fellowship to aid worthy students
studying in foreign countries. "To you, and to you
altogether," said Bancroft, five years after he escaped
out of his unhappiness at Harvard, "and to you alone
do I hold myself indebted for all that renders my life
useful and honourable." The other penetrating eye
that saw beneath the mannerisms the redeeming traits
of the young instructor was Ralph Waldo Emerson's.
After hearing Bancroft preach in 1823 Emerson wrote :

"I am happy to contradict the rumors about Bancroft. I heard
him preach at New South a few Sabbaths since, and was much
delighted with his eloquence. So were all. He needs a great deal
of cutting and pruning, but we think him an infant Hercules. All
who know him agree in this, that he has improved his time thoroughly at Göttingen. He has become a perfect Greek scholar, and
knows well all that he pretends to know ; as to divinity, he has
never studied, but was approbated abroad." [1]

A man who "knows well all that he pretends to know"
is a rare gift from the gods.

It is hardly to be doubted that in 1822 the methods
of instruction in American colleges were very unsatis-
factory. Hearing boys drone through their lessons,
scolding the laggards, and commending the faithful
were the chief duties of the instructors. Harvard was
no exception to the rule. Now Bancroft, and Ticknor

[1] Howe, "Life of George Bancroft," I, 165, n.

before him, had come into contact at Göttingen with men who were masters of their subjects, men full of the critical spirit and capable by eloquent lectures of inspiring their students into enthusiastic pursuit of learning. They came back to Harvard hoping to introduce methods nearly like those in use at Göttingen. A small section of the faculty and some of the younger alumni supported them; and they were able to get their reforms referred to a committee of the faculty, in whose gentle hands the matter died. We need know little of college faculties to understand how unlikely the Harvard teaching body was to change old methods in response to the demands of two young men fresh from foreign study. Ticknor had much practical wisdom and accepted the result in a sensible way. He eventually saw many of his reforms carried into operation.

Bancroft was less submissive, and probably less persistent. The failure of his efforts, added to his personal unpopularity, greatly discouraged him. "Our hopes of a reform at college," he said, May 10, 1823, "have pretty much blown over. I was quite sanguine last term that we [should] have affected reforms of a most thorough nature. But the pillars of ancient usage stand fast, and it will require another shock to overturn them." Referring to his own experience he said: "I have found College a sickening and wearisome place. Not one spring of comfort have I to draw from. My state has been nothing but trouble, trouble, trouble, and I am heartily glad that the end of the year is coming so soon." [1]

Here we see Bancroft in one of his introspective moods. He was sensitive and very emotional. To President Kirkland he wrote in the same year : "I pray you, forgive my seeming restlessness of character. If I thought it necessary or expedient I would correct the evil, which after all does not injure others and only makes me perhaps less happy than I might be. If I were not restless I should not be so desirous of improvement, or honour, or knowledge, as I wish to be. And I believe I have gentleness of temper enough and a contented disposition. Only there is no water so tranquil, that throwing stones into it will not make waves." [2] Words like these suggest that the writer of them recovered quickly from his fits of depression and carried forward constructive labors.

Indeed, in performing his individual duties he showed great capacity for doing as he chose. In this realm he was not subject to faculty consent; and he created the divisions of the Freshman Greek class according to ability, assigning the lessons in accordance with the capacity to understand them. The result was that his best section read from four to six pages of Greek a day and were so eager to go forward that he had to hold them back, while the poorest division was advancing faster than any previous section in the col-

---

[1] Bancroft to S. A. Eliot, May 10, 1823. Bancroft MSS.
[2] Bancroft to President Kirkland, [May] 21, 1823, Bancroft MSS.

lege. A boy who showed that he deserved it was promoted to a higher division, or reduced to a lower if he was falling behind. "I have the satisfaction," said Bancroft, "of knowing that I have carried my points alone, unassisted by any co-operation whatever from any one individual at Cambridge, and supported by no man in my design except Mr. Ticknor." [1]

A year of this kind of struggle was enough for Bancroft. His spirit grew sick of the discipline inflicted on it. Even President Kirkland, full of kindness, believed that the young man should change his environment. The success with the divisions in the Greek classes may have suggested the field of secondary education. At any rate, it was into that field that he now directed his steps. At Harvard in 1823 was Joseph Green Cogswell, a graduate in the year 1806, who had traveled much in Europe and was now employed in classifying the books in the library. He and Bancroft made a partnership to found and conduct a school in New England on the model of the German *gymnasium*. Bancroft described their ideas in the following words:

"I am going to turn *schoolmaster*. I long to become an independent man, namely a man who lives by his own labours. Mr. Cogswell has seen so much of the world, that he knows it and its folly: he will join in my scheme: we will together establish a school, the end of which is to be the moral and intellectual maturity of the mind of each boy we take charge of; and the means are to be first and foremost *instruction in the classics*. We intend going into the country, and we shall choose a pleasant site, where nature

[1] Bancroft to S. A. Eliot, Dec. 3, 1822, Bancroft MSS.

in her loveliness may breathe calmness and inspire purity. We will live retired from the clamours of scandal and the disputes of the irresolute. We will delight ourselves with letters, and instead of warring against the corporation and contending with scandalous reports, we will train up a few minds to virtue and honour, and hope that when we die there will be some hands to throw flowers over our tombs. . . . We call our establishment a school, and we mean to consider ourselves as schoolmasters. We might indeed assume a pompous name, speak of instituting a Gymnasium : but let the name be modest. I like the sound of the word Schoolmaster." [1]

Thus was established the Round Hill School at Northampton, Massachusetts. It took its name from the eminence on which it was situated, a hill looking over the town itself and across meadows and river to the Mount Holyoke range, as beautiful a view as the eye and heart could desire. Here, from 1823 to 1834, the school ran its career, drawing a large number of pupils from prominent families in many parts of the United States. It was a notable experiment and attracted attention far and wide. Its failure was due to bad financial management and to the fact that its plan of instruction did not connect logically with that of the colleges. In spite of Bancroft's feeling for Harvard the new school received the moral and practical support of President Kirkland and of a large number of Harvard men around Boston. Later, when money was needed to develop its work, a considerable sum was lent to it by the college itself, all of which shows that Harvard was interested in the project.

[1] *Ibid.*

Cogswell was the executive head of the school, while Bancroft, teaching the classics, bore the heavier part of the instruction.   N. M. Hentz, whom Ticknor pronounced the best French teacher Harvard had been blessed with, took the modern languages.   The aim of the instructors was to develop to the best each boy's capacity of learning.   Said Cogswell: "I do not form any classes but allow every one to get as much of any book which he is studying, as he can do, in the time assigned for that exercise, telling him that he may recite as soon as he is ready, but cautioning him at the same time, that the least failure sends him back, and obliges him to wait till the rest have been brought to trial." [1]   Flogging was not practiced and there was an abundance of vigorous exercise in which Cogswell, or another instructor, took the part of leader.

A candid critic of Bancroft who observed his course at Harvard said that he was "as a tutor only the laughing butt of all the college." [2]   It was not because he was easy on the students; for he was most exacting. At Round Hill he took the same course.   From the Rev. George E. Ellis, a Round Hill pupil, we have in 1891 this portrayal of Bancroft as a teacher: "He was absent-minded, dreamy and often in abstracted moods as well as very near-sighted.   I have seen him come into the recitation room at an exercise held before

[1] Anna E. Ticknor, "Life of Joseph Green Cogswell," 137, 143.
[2] See *Harvard Graduates Magazine* (Sept. 1897), VI, 17, n.

breakfast, with a slipper or shoe on one foot and a boot on the other. More than once he sent me across the road to his library for his spectacles. These were generally to be found shut into a book, which he had been reading before going to bed. The boys, who called him familiarly 'the Critter,' were fond of playing tricks upon him, which they could do with impunity, owing to his shortness of vision." [1]

Dr. Ellis wrote this in 1891, less than two months after Bancroft died : twenty-four years earlier he was engaged in a bitter controversy with the historian, in which the issue came at last to a question of veracity. Can it be possible that unconsciously he allowed his feelings to become mixed with his recollections? It is true, however, that the Round Hill boys disliked the teacher of Greek ; and there is preserved a lead plate whittled out by one of their jack-knives and used to print a representation of Bancroft in the margin of their school paper. It shows him as a straight little man, with the air of a Prussian corporal and the tail of the devil protruding from the coat-tails. [2] But we must not take too seriously, either the nicknames or the pictures originated by schoolboys. They may indeed show that Bancroft was not popular with the pupils, that he was eccentric and absent-minded. But he was highly esteemed by Cogswell as a teacher, and after he ceased to be a partner in the ownership of the

---

[1] See *The Educational Review* (April, 1891), I, 341.
[2] Mass. Histl. Soc. " Proceedings," Vol. 47 (1913–14), p. 222.

school he was employed as a teacher with a salary of sixteen hundred dollars a year.[1]

Bancroft retired from Round Hill School in 1831, having given nine years to teaching. When he began he was a precocious and learned youth, his mind full of the classics, his imagination teeming with the hope of conquering the intellectual world by storm. The years had brought him hard struggles against practical things, theory had been softened, and imagination had been turned away from an ancient Pegasus to more modern things. He was becoming astonishingly practical: in fact, he was about to assume the rôle of a practical politician. In George Bancroft, the champion of Jacksonian democracy and aspirant for a place in the state legislature, it is hard to recognize the absent-minded, near-sighted, dreaming "Critter" whom Dr. Ellis described. We shall not comprehend the change in the man if we do not remember that beneath all his scholastic training was a strong will and an unusual faculty of promoting his own interests.

2. *Literary Apprenticeship*

It is not unnatural that Bancroft's first publication was a book of verse. His temperament was distinctly imaginative, and his love of the classics suggested verse-making. In Europe he met Goethe and Byron, whom he admired as the great men of their day. He came back from Europe with a sheaf of manuscript poems,

[1] Anna E. Ticknor, "Life of Joseph Green Cogswell," 165.

weakly emotional efforts, no better and no worse than the effusions of bright college graduates of our own day. In 1823 these came out in a thin volume of seventy-seven pages with the modest title of "Poems." In later life the author destroyed all the volumes he could lay hands on. He had the good sense to see that he was not born to write poetry. He said that he had the love of detail that makes a man a scholar rather than the bold sweep of fancy that characterizes the poet.

That he had great facility in learning and remembering facts is undoubted, but he had also the faculty of lively and ornate expression. His letters, extracts from which are given below, sparkle with fancy. They have, especially in his early years, more than a normal touch of youth's spontaneity. By their side the letters of Jared Sparks are as sober as a scientific lecture. I have the same feelings in reading Bancroft's early letters that I have in reading those of John Richard Green. In each case there is a tone of verdant ebullition that is nearly irritating. But it seems that this superlative degree of emotion was a good gift of nature; for when softened by experience and balanced by a vast amount of solid information, it gave light and sparkle to what would otherwise have been mere didactic writing.

During his residence in Northampton Bancroft's literary efforts were expended in preparing text-books and reviews. Undertaking to teach Greek as it was taught in Germany, he found it necessary to have better text-books than were in use in the American schools. It was like his resolute and originating mind that he prepared such books himself without delay. In 1824 he published an abridgment of Buttmann's Greek Grammar and a translation of Heeren's "Reflections on the Politics of Greece." The following year he translated from the German, Jacobs's "Latin Reader," in 1826 Nepos's "De Vita Excellentium Imperatorum" with English notes, and in 1829 a translation of Zumpt's "Latin Grammar." These books were esteemed the most modern of their kind. They were largely used in the schools of Europe and became popular in the United States. The returns from them were financially important to the translator.

It will be observed that all these books were in the classical field. Here Bancroft at this stage of his career felt his greatest interest. Had he continued to teach, posterity should have to deal with him, if it took any notice at all, as a Greek or Latin scholar. He had keen appreciation of exact scholarship and he had drunk deeply of the spirit of criticism in a day when the world needed the critical attitude more than anything else. But he was not to be a teacher. By 1831 he himself had come to realize his limitations, and he was prepared to quit the schoolroom. Perhaps the remark of Mrs. Lyman, one of the best observers then in Northampton, may throw light on the condition that determined his future course. She said:

"I am very glad you are pleased with Dr. Bancroft. There is no member of his family [in the school] who is half so interesting as he is, and, notwithstanding his cracked voice and shaking head, there are few who in the vigor of youth can write as well." [1]

In spite of the fact that he had marked peculiarities of manner, which limited his teaching, he was an interesting man socially and he wrote well. In the future it was as a writer and as a man who made friends among his fellows that Bancroft distinguished himself.

The first plain allusion to history in the Bancroft letters is encountered in 1828. Writing to President Kirkland he described a project for a complete course in history. Just a week earlier he had signed the preface of a translation of Heeren's "Geschichte der Staaten des Altertums," which appeared with the title "History of the States of Antiquity." This he considered the first volume of the course, and three others were to follow. For the period extending from 1492 to 1821, he proposed to translate Heeren's "Geschichte des europäischen Staatensystem." For the Middle Ages he would write the volume or abridge an account from some valuable books; and, he added, "For my own country I should venture to write outlines." The scheme was not carried into execution. No volume for the Middle Ages appeared, but late in 1828 came in two volumes a translation of Heeren's "Staatensystem" with the title "History of the Political System

[1] Mrs. Susan I. Lesley, "Recollections of My Mother," 277.

of Europe, and its Colonies, from the Discovery of
America to the Independence of the American Continent." This title is misleading, since the book took
the story of European history down to 1821, more than
half of the second volume being given up to events later
than 1783. Since Heeren himself had no such title, it
is hard to doubt that Bancroft thus early in his career
warped the fact to make the book attractive to American readers. The last volume, relating to American
history, was not written as such; but it may well be
that the intention to write it was the beginning of the
History of the United States.

Deferring for a time a consideration of this great
work let us glance at Bancroft's relations with the
North American Review during his residence in Northampton. On this phase of his life we have much information in his letters to Sparks, and nothing could
better show us what kind of man he was than to read
liberally from them. It was in 1823 that Jared Sparks
became editor of the *Review*. While he was preparing
his first issue Bancroft offered to write for him a review
of Edward Everett's translation of Buttmann's Greek
grammar and Jacobs's Greek reader. The offer was accepted and the author was informed that he might
make it as learned as he pleased; and he was invited
to write other articles in the future. He complied
gladly, although not all that he wrote was accepted
by the editor. Sparks wrote February 1, 1824, as
follows:

"Some of the old school here have expressed to me their appre-
hensions since your last article, that the North American is becoming too partial to the Germans, at the expense of our worthy
brethren the English. One gentleman made bold to say to me,
that the English had written as good Greek grammars as anybody,
and that they ought at least to have a passing compliment. I told
him I would give you the hint. With this view I return you the
manuscript, hoping that if you can think of anything to say in
praise of English Grecian elementary books, you will give them the
passing meed of a paragraph or two." [1]

A week later Bancroft wrote : "I have been cheating
myself of my cares by making little translations from
Goethe. Perhaps I had better correct and improve
the article on classic learning, or perhaps in lieu of it
get something ready for the ladies. Then in May you
could chuse between an argument about Greek and a
lighter article." [2] An article on German poetry was
engaged for the October number, 1824.

Sparks's attitude towards his reviewers again comes
out in a letter of March 31, 1824. Speaking of a review
requested on a book by an indifferent Baltimore writer
he said :

"You will find a very ambitious, and unformed style occa-
sionally; and the general getting up of the book indicates an
unpractised hand; but there is much historical knowledge and some
good thoughts, and I should like to have the author dealt gently
with, although not extravagantly praised. I think you can let
some parts of the book speak well for themselves; you can make a
sort of analysis of things and throw in such reflections as occur." [3]

[1] Bancroft MSS, Mass. Histl. Soc.
[2] Bancroft to Sparks, Feb. 9, 1824. Sparks MSS, Harvard Library.
[3] Bancroft MSS.

These last two Sparks citations, together with the difference of opinion arising between the editor and Bancroft in regard to the review of John Pickering's lexicon, to which reference has already been made,[1] show what kind of liberties Sparks took with a contributor. They provoked sharp protest at times, though Bancroft's anger was soon appeased. He was a man without malice, and was apt to feel great pain while he protested for his rights.

In July, 1824, he sent the editor a carefully prepared article on Goethe, asking especially that no changes be made in it without consultation before publication. Nevertheless, the piece appeared with many changes by the editor. Bancroft was genuinely grieved. He wrote:

"In writing for the N. A. R. I conceived myself in the pleasantest situation, laboring in a manner to oblige and serve a friend, quite as much as myself, and at the same time doing my little part towards disseminating a love of letters. To successful exertion of one's mind a consciousness of independence is necessary. As a friend of yours, I might desire at all times to perform any literary labor, which my habits and pursuits might have fitted me for. Whenever I express my own feelings and the results of my own thoughts, there must be no mind at work but my own. . . .

"If I mistake not the character of the American public, there is no need of keeping back any truth from it. The public is willing to be shocked. Ask yourself, if a thing appears good to your own mind; and doubt not, the objections which may arise from the fear that this or the other will be offended, will prove groundless.

I have sometimes thought of relinquishing the career of letters. I could be very happy and very useful, if I would do it. I mean

[1] See above, pages 68-71.

relinquish toiling for others. The perception of excellence in others, the love of communing with high minds Providence in its mercy has conceded me — a compensation for a thousand woes, and my most valuable possession." [1]

Sparks replied with brusque complacency, disparaging Bancroft's complaint. The changes, he said, were trifling. "Allow no good was done: what was the mighty harm? It was not a thing to worry about, and more especially after a thing was done, that could not be undone;" and with that he ventured to suggest an article on physical education, enlarging on its opportunities and explaining how it might be done. Bancroft was not quite so easily appeased as Sparks thought. He replied:

"The best is, to forget unpleasant things. Only it is also best for friends to understand each other. I know not how you can call the changes you made in the unfortunate article so trifling. For me they certainly were not trifling; for while I had been expecting to derive much pleasure from the appearance of it, I have felt only chagrin. And I cannot persuade myself, my disappointment is not well founded. Do you not know, you changed one assertion from a negative to a positive one, thereby saying something, which I do not believe, & which makes the words at least unmeaning? . . . You altered, what you would not have altered, had you understood, why and in what spirit it was written. And the changes in two cases out of three, though few, materially affected both the meaning and the style of the most labored parts. I say labored parts, and I am free to add, labored with the most success, and the most *truth and nature.* The matter is of little moment, only in so far as the whole article is of little moment, and my desire to be esteemed as a writer a childish vanity." [2]

[1] Bancroft to Sparks, n. d. [about Nov. 5, 1824]. Sparks MSS.
[2] November 17, 1824, Sparks MSS.

Bancroft concluded this letter with the assurance that he would not again trouble Sparks with articles, unless they were requested beforehand. He soon thought better of it, or at least thrust aside his resentment. December 24 he wrote enthusiastically about the article on physical education, which he had begun. The following characteristic touch may explain the breaking away of the clouds: "It is Christmas Eve, and a glad occasion. The Roman is now passing from street to street, from illuminated church to church; the Basilica of Santa Maria is filled with music almost heavenly; the faithful are rejoicing. I wish you all joy suited to the occasion, and happiness always."[1]

Relations thus continued pleasant. When Sparks found some things in an article on temperaments that he did not like he marked them out and returned the article for approval, first showing it to some of Bancroft's Cambridge friends. The author rejected the emendations, and Sparks rejected the article, remarking: "You seem not to have very correct notions of this matter of 'judgment,' in regard to the *N. A. Review.* You say you 'make it a rule to rely on your own judgment.' This is an excellent rule, — precisely the rule which I adopt for myself, and which I must adhere to rigidly if I intend to have any comfort in my labors, or any consistency in my Review. Now this is not saying that my judgment is better than yours, or any other person's; but whether good

[1] Dec. 24, 1824. Sparks MSS.

or bad I must decide by this at least. It is not the *merits* of a piece alone by which I judge, but its adaptableness to the *N. A. Review.*" He went on to say that he rarely printed an article from which something was not omitted, but that he never added anything without the consent of the author, and that, in fact, he had cancelled three sheets in an article by Edward Everett in the forthcoming number. He dismissed the subject saying: "I beg whenever you send anything hereafter, that you will make up your mind to send it on the same terms that all the other writers do, and wish you to understand distinctly, that I shall always omit what I do not like, as being the invariable rule by which I am guided in all cases." [1]

This plain statement was toned down by the addition of pleasant personal sentiments, and friendly relations continued. Bancroft was genuinely attached to Sparks, who seems to have warmed to him as much as to anyone. The former with a characteristic outburst of affection wrote about this time: "You once wrote me a long letter, and never but once. I live upon that; but wish you could sometimes add at least a syllable of Christian salutation, or friendly information. You are all too laconic." [2] During the summer of 1825 Sparks visited Northampton and was charmed by its beauty and agreeable society. Returning he carried to Boston a "parcel of flowers," sent to a young lady of that city by the schoolmaster at Round Hill. The

[1] Feb. 17, 1825. Bancroft MSS. [2] Jan. 17, 1825. Sparks MSS.

editor was disposed to carp at his sentimental errand, but Bancroft said in regard to the gift: "I came very near receiving a reward, which to me would have been without price."

These were years of intense labor for Bancroft. Rebuffed as he was by most of those around him, he clung the harder to the few Harvard friends he had, Sparks and Edward Everett being among them; and meanwhile he worked hard and long. He realized deeply a poor author's need of some accumulation of capital on which to base the execution of further plans. "You must not work yourself to death," said his friend, "nor be too greedy after the treasures of this world. But you are doing great things, and the fruits of your labors are to appear not in the present time only, but in the future ages." [1]   And Bancroft in reply exclaimed:

"'Be not too greedy after the treasures of this world,' say you in yours of the 8th Feb[ruary]. And after what else pray shall a man be greedy? Truth is the object which we profess to seek and intelligence the power under whose banners we rally; but in a better world there will be no error to be overcome, no books to be read, no doubtful reasonings to follow, no reviews to be written, no midnight lamp to be left burning, but truth will shine clearly in her own simple majesty, and there will be an end of all the apparatus of the inquirer. Not be greedy after the treasures of this world! I went to a friend's wedding last week. I hope he is a happier man than he was. A good wife, with beauty enough to satisfy, warm affections enough to cheer, intelligence enough to please, cheerfulness enough to enliven the dark hours of this mortal state — that is not to be coveted, say you? Oh you are a saint,

[1] Sparks to Bancroft, Feb. 6, 1826. Bancroft MSS.

and heavenly minded; for in heaven there is no marrying nor
giving in marriage, but men are as the angels. Be not greedy for
the things of this world. Filthy lucre and the rest: be they
abhorred and spurned : to be sure a man may be as it were the only
son of aged parents, and they be poor; and he may have seen a
race of elder brothers swept away from his side by the irresistible
hand of fearful destiny, and may have all the duties of son, brother
and man pressing upon him : yet let him not think of this world but
fold his hands in contemplative indolence, and watch the courses
of the stars or the breaking of day, and muse with unseen spirits,
never striving to have his name respectfully uttered, where things
are doing, and satisfying all the ties of nature by a cold obedience
and barren affection. Fie on your morality !"[1]

In this connection I cannot refrain from quoting the
following sentiment, for it shows Bancroft in his loneliness and in a mood of stage heroics peculiar to his
nature, in spite of his many strong qualities. He wrote
to Sparks :

"I was once dining at the house of a gentleman of great wealth,
who had assembled, (I had reason to think in part or particularly
to show me a little attention) some of the pleasantest and most
distinguished persons of the opulent families in Boston. Miss M.
Lyman was there, to speak but of the ladies, Miss Otis, now Mrs.
Ritchie, and another. The conversation was various. It turned
on the lives and fortunes of men. I took little part in it : was
cold and reserved. Presently some one observed of men of letters
with something of a contemptuous sneer that they were always
poor and lived in garrets. I might have replied triumphantly, that
in that they pronounced the severest judgment on rich men, which
for the honor of human nature I trusted was 'not a just one. I
preferred not to do so : I remained nearly silent, and least of all
appeared to perceive any want of delicacy in those who made the

[1] March 10, 1826. Sparks MSS.

remark. All the persons present were my friends. One of them proved it by giving me his name for $2000 at a time when my name in business was worth little and when his only security was in my character. But observe this: there is an essential difference between the friendship of men, who are nearly on the level in their external fortunes, and the relation which grows up between the wealthy and those who have no estates but their own time." [1]

Words like these make us understand how the talented young man, conscious of his literary ability, must have formed his purpose to make authorship yield wealth as well as distinction. Text-books and reviews were produced with great rapidity, while a thrifty disposition enabled him to save a considerable portion of his income. Every man who has struggled through the initial stages of authorship will have sympathy for Bancroft's position and his feelings in regard to this matter.

Moreover, Bancroft was developing an independence in thinking that was sure to bring him into conflict with Sparks, a man little inclined to tolerate startling things. He was one of those intense men who think acutely and see nothing but the ends of their reasoning, persons who are always out of step with their fellows, and are apt to die unblessed, unless, like Bancroft, they have immense determination in bringing themselves into public recognition. Such a man was not capable of writing reviews acceptable to Sparks, and the following letter shows that Bancroft had begun to recognize it:

[1] Nov. 14, 1825. Sparks MSS.

"MY DEAR FRIEND,

"When a friend gives me an opportunity of saying yes, it is very unpleasant not to do so. You would not like my views about Judge Story's address. I do not think so highly of it, as many express themselves. The generous enthusiasm for letters is honorable to him; but there is no point, no consistent and continuous train of thoughts. Besides, just at this moment the whole care of organizing the school for the new session comes upon me, and I see no hope of a day's leisure before thanksgiving. Ready to promise and faithful to perform: this was the character you gave me of old. You must not consider me as forfeiting it by my declining now. Do you not remember too how angry Somerville was with you and me? And do you know, that while you reproached me for praising Popkin so much, Popkin was vexed at being spoken of so little?

"In great haste, very truly yours." [1]

To refuse to praise Judge Story was an alarming symptom, and Sparks might have known that he was dealing with a man whose course could not be predicted from the standpoint of prevailing Boston ideals. He should have been warned, but blindly persisted, the next offer he made being the review of a Greek lexicon by John Pickering,[2] son of Timothy Pickering, and Nestor of all that was left of the prim school of New England federalism. Pickering was a judge, and his pursuit of Greek was of an amateurish nature. Before the young gentleman who worshiped at the shrine of the latest German criticism he had the slightest chance in the world. Yet the powerful judge was thrown to the young lion, not without many soothing

[1] Bancroft to Sparks, October [24], 1826. Sparks MSS.
[2] On this incident see above, pages 68–71.

requests that the lion would be gentle for once in his
life. And he was gentle, after the manner of the gentleness of lions. He softened his roar, but he could not
make it the song of a lark. Sparks cut out all that
was properly criticism, wrote some pages to replace
the deleted ideas, and published an article that pros-
trated Bancroft with rage and chagrin. Pickering himself must have been disappointed; for his chief connection with the review was that the title of his work
stood at the head. The only respectable part in it
was a summary of the development of lexicons, by
Bancroft, but it appeared so poorly supported by the
rest of the matter that it was out of place. Bancroft's
fierce protest could secure no redress, and the incident
made a painful impression on him for the time being.
But it soon passed, and although he continued on
friendly terms with Sparks, he wrote few reviews for
him in the future.

It was about this time that Bancroft turned his attention from classical subjects and gave it to matters
concerning the life around him. His letters give us
little explanation for the change. Probably he was
influenced by Sparks's rise in popular esteem through
taking up the history of his country. He was bent on
having a literary career, and here before his eyes was
the example of a success that he could never promise
himself as a classicist. The idea was also connected
with his desire to do good. Referring to an article on
Baltimore by Sparks he said that he thought it "worth

a dozen doses of sentimental criticism, and that similar articles on various sections of the country would be of great and general value." At this time he was thinking of writing an article on the growth of the towns and cities of the Connecticut Valley, and proposed to make a journey to them gathering materials.

Bancroft's acquaintance with Sparks was a fortunate influence in his life. It gave him a medium of publication and the editor's constant call for articles stimulated the writing habit. Sparks's efforts to hold back the spirit of the young man were not entirely a failure. While they hardened the author's sense of independence, they caused him to look to his gait and to gallop with care. Bancroft had his faults, and they will be treated in their place, but in contending with Sparks he was generally right. He was developing a spirit of self-direction destined to remove him far from the group in which he had spent his earliest years; but it was the necessary mark of individuality. As Mrs. Lyman well said, "Notwithstanding his cracked voice and shaking head, there are few who in the vigor of youth can write as well." It was chiefly his faculty of writing well that made his history the glory of his countrymen in his own age.

3. *A Literary Politician*

In October, 1829, Bancroft wrote: "I should be grateful could I obtain that personal leisure, which might enable me to enter the career of letters with some reasonable expectation of doing myself justice. But at present I am doomed to bear with the petulance, restrain the frivolity, mend the tempers, and improve the minds of children." [1] Those who, like Dr. Ellis, censure Bancroft for being a poor teacher, should remember that he himself realized that he was not well fitted for the work of the pedagogue, and that he gave it up as soon as he could. Good teachers usually make poor writers. In the one case success comes from the reiterated and detailed statement of fact, in the other from clear and lively statement of ideas. Bancroft's mind was suited to the latter process, and it would have been a sin against nature to force him to give his life to the former. It was his good fortune that his thrift and an advantageous marriage enabled him to throw himself after 1831 into the field of authorship. But before we follow him into that phase of his career, let us see how it was that he became a leading democratic politician.

Our first glimpse of Bancroft's political opinion comes as early as 1823, the year after his return from abroad. Writing to President Kirkland he said: "I love to observe the bustle of the world, but I detest mixing in it. I like to watch the shouts of the multitude, but had rather not scream with them." [2] Such words would seem to indicate that at the age of twenty-three he was no democrat. A similar impression is

[1] Bancroft to Sparks, Oct. 4, 1829. Sparks MSS.
[2] Bancroft to President Kirkland, May 21, 1823. Bancroft MSS.

gathered from the following reference in the same year to the state of parties in Massachusetts: "Of the strange doings at our elections you must have heard. A democratic Governor and a democratic Senate, and now a prospect of a democratic House. Our class-mate Cushing has trimmed and wrote against Mr. Otis. So he is now in high favor with '*the Patriot*,' as the 'impartial writer in the Newburyport *Herald*.'" [1] That Bancroft, destined to be regarded in Massachusetts as a renegade equally with Caleb Cushing, should now have joined in the storm of reproaches that greeted that act of defection has in it something of the irony of fate.

The fourth of July, 1826, was celebrated generally as the fiftieth birthday of the nation, and many orations were spoken and published as a result. One of the best was made by George Bancroft at Northampton. It was a review of the progress of republican institutions in the world, particular attention being given to the proposition that most that had been accomplished was the result of our own initiation. The orator supported strongly the Jeffersonian theory of popular government, using words that must have made to wince the descendants of Caleb Strong and the relatives of Theodore Dwight, numerous in the town. What could be more unpleasant to them than words like the following:

[1] Bancroft to S. A. Eliot, May 10, 1823. Bancroft MSS. Harrison Gray Otis was defeated for governor in 1823 by the first republican governor since the beginning of the war of 1812. Caleb Cushing belonged to the Harvard class of 1817.

"Government is based upon population, not upon property. If they who possess the wealth possessed the power also, they would legislate in such a way as to preserve that wealth and power; and this would tend to an aristocracy. We hold it best, that the laws should favor the diffusion of property and its easy acquisition, not the concentration of it in the hands of a few to the impoverishment of the many. We give the power to the many, in the hope and to the end, that they may use it for their own benefit; that they may always so legislate, as to open the fairest career to industry, and promote an equality founded on the safe and equitable influence of the laws. We do not fear, we rather invite the operation of the common motives, which influence humanity." [1]

There can be little doubt that these words were sincere. They represented the creed of a man who had as yet formed no other party alignment than that to which he was born. He was a supporter of John Quincy Adams in 1828. "The election is lost," he wrote to Edward Everett in November; "but Adams is not more defeated than Calhoun. I hope New England may rise with [the] new party, that will be formed. If I can in any wise serve you this winter, don't omit to allow me." [2] From which it seems that he was beginning to drag the anchor of his party allegiance.

Jared Sparks sold the *North American Review* to Alexander H. Everett, brother of Edward, in 1830. In passing over the property to the new editor he suggested Bancroft as a reliable and useful contributor. Accordingly, Everett asked Bancroft to review the report of the Committee on Ways and Means on the

---

[1] Bancroft, "An Oration," etc., p. 20.
[2] Nov. 18, 1828.   Bancroft MSS.

condition of the Bank of the United States. Jackson's message of the preceding December had said that it was not too soon to begin to consider the recharter of the bank, and had cast doubts on the wisdom of continuing the institution beyond its charter limits, 1837. Clay and all who supported him, including Calhoun's friend McDuffie, of South Carolina, chairman of the Committee of Ways and Means, took the opposite side, investigated the condition of the bank, and issued the report of April, 1830, completely exonerating the bank from the imputations of the president. This report became a rallying cry for all who opposed the administration; and if any journal in the country could be expected to sympathize with its sentiments, it was the *North American Review,* whose editor was the brother of the distinguished representative from the Middlesex district. To Bancroft, intent upon writing what he thought, and jealous of his independence, the political leaning of the *Review* was as nothing.

Up to this time the coming historian had, probably, never taken stock of his principles. We have seen that in 1826 he was an out and out republican in theory, while he held openly with the friends of John Quincy Adams. His review of the defense of the bank led him to state what he believed about a crucial subject. He began by observing that Jackson was not mistaken in saying that it was a proper time to take up recharter. "This opulent institution," he continued, "enjoys an exclusive privilege; it possesses a capital so immense as to have an almost controlling influence on the money market of the country." But the conduct of the bank had been such as to entitle it to the fairest hearing. Its immense power had been used mildly. This was not to say that the bank gave services that no other institution could give. Other banks were as well conducted and could, if called upon, perform the services that the existing bank yielded to the public. "In sober truth," said he, "there is very little reason to doubt, that the sun would still rise and set, and the day be spent in its usual business, and merchandise be bought and sold, and bills of exchange be negotiated, even without a machine so vast and so very useful as the Bank of the United States." As for the report itself, he pronounced it an *ex-parte* statement, — assuredly the truth, — and charged that it contained much exaggeration.

What Jared Sparks would have done with an article so much out of sympathy with what he thought the *Review* should teach, it is hard to say. Everett did not omit some parts and change others, as his predecessor did with the ill-fated review of Pickering's lexicon; but he could not let the article stand for the policy of the magazine. He published the article but added to it this astonishing statement: "The expediency of renewing the charter of the present National Bank has not been brought into [this] discussion. On this question our opinion is decidedly in the affirmative; and we propose in a future paper to assign the reasons which lead us to that conclusion." In the following number there was, indeed, another article on the bank, but it was not written by Bancroft. It was a strong defense of the institution, and to it was appended a footnote stating that it was not from the author of the former article, who would probably continue his discussion in the October number. The note closed with the following assertion: "There is some divergence between the views of our two correspondents on particular points; but their general objects, those of showing the utility of the Bank, and the expediency of continuing it, are substantially the same."

While Bancroft had not declared himself openly against recharter, all his arguments ran against the bank. To say, therefore, that he thought it expedient to continue the bank was false, and he took it as a wrong. Wishing to exonerate himself he wrote a second article in which his opinions were clearly stated, but the *North American* would not publish it. He was able, however, to force the editor to sign a statement that the last sentence in the article published was not written by the author of that article.

The announcement that he was opposed to the bank was a turning point in Bancroft's career. The leading class of New Englanders were fervid supporters of the bank. They were long accustomed to view government by the lower classes as a supreme calamity; and they were good haters. That a man born in an upper rank, educated, and accustomed to think deeply about public matters should become the champion of leveling ideas was nothing less than shocking. They concluded that Bancroft had acted from selfish motives, and they applied to him the term "trimmer," which in 1823 he had applied to Caleb Cushing. The Jackson men, however, hailed Bancroft's article with delight. Here was a man of the educated class raising his voice in their behalf, and they made him a political asset. He was too astute to refuse, and he followed the lead they opened to him until at last he reached the highest places in the party. There is no reason to believe that he planned his article on the bank with a view to such a course.

In 1831, five months after his bank views were published, he was in Washington, where he seems to have had an eye to political advantages. "I found by diligent inquiry at the sources," he wrote to his wife, "that my course, as it respects the U. S. Bank, was well approved of." Later in the year he visited Cleveland on a project to establish a bank there in which his father-in-law was interested. When rumor said that his article had been connected with this project he denied it very positively. A state bank at Cleveland would derive benefit from the destruction of the bank of the United States. Late in 1831 he was in Washington trying to forward the same scheme,

continuing there well into 1832. "I almost abandon
the pursuit," he said; "yet $8000 are worth a little
patience and a sturdy effort." [1] How the affair was to
yield him so large a sum is not explained, neither is it
clear that he succeeded in his scheme. He complained
that the secretary of the treasury was ill and could
not sign the papers on which the success of the scheme
depended.

Back in Northampton, he settled down to three
years of literary labor. The excitement raised by the
bank article passed with the comment of a few of the
more radical friends of recharter. His personal friends
accepted the situation, and he had reason to believe
that he had not lost their esteem. It was, meanwhile,
an evident satisfaction to see the steady progress of
Jackson's attack on the bank.

In the autumn of 1834, Bancroft was suddenly called
into the front of the political field. Isaac C. Bates,
a whig, with an eye on the United States senate, announced that he would not be a candidate for re-election
to congress, and a card in the Northampton *Gazette*
suggested Bancroft as a candidate to succeed him.
Immediately a number of gentlemen sent him a letter
requesting a statement of his opinions on the issues of
the day. Bancroft's reply was dignified and republican in tone. It was not as extreme as the address of
1826. The editor of the *Gazette* said it would perhaps
have the opposition of extreme men in both parties;

[1] Howe, "Life of Bancroft," I. 197.

and some of the most liberal whig editors spoke approvingly of its spirit, while all expressed admiration for the style in which it was written.[1]

At that time the whig party was very powerful in Massachusetts, and its opponents, Jackson men and anti-masons, were organized as a working-men's party. It was members of this party who sought to have Bancroft nominated for congress. The nominating convention met at West Springfield and Bancroft was a promising candidate for its favor, but at the last moment he withdrew in favor of Oliver Warner, who was nominated and defeated at the polls by a whig.[2] Bancroft's friends then brought him out as one of Northampton's candidates on the working-men's ticket for the lower house of the general court, and in this contest he was defeated. His personal views on the election are interesting. He wrote thus to Edward Everett, whom he wished to see governor:

"The secret spring of the political movement in this quarter grew out of I. C. Bates' aspirations after a seat in the United States Senate. A powerful combination was entered into with the Springfield junto; the aid of the clergy was called in; sermons were preached; and the community was made to believe, that there was danger the bible would be taken out of their hands. Democracy was said to be a branch of atheism. We held our own in this town notwithstanding; but the Sunday night previous to election an immense crowd was gathered in the town hall; Mr. Bates, Lewis Strong, Forbes, a high mason, and Dewey, all assembled, and never was such an appeal to the stormy passions.

[1] Northampton *Gazette*, Sept. 24, and Oct. 8, 22, 1834.
[2] A statement by Andrew Parsons, n. d., in Bancroft MSS.

The charges against their opponents were Jacksonism, infidelity and atheism. A perfect fever was got up. The public did not perceive that this was merely a scheme to help Bates forward. I saw through it, and on Monday morning infused what courage I could into the people. It was a great triumph, that under such circumstances we could poll for an independent ticket 167 votes. The like was never known here before. Had Bates been quiet, we should have carried the town by a decisive majority. *The church*, orthodoxy was made to bear upon us. . . . It will be some years before a popular party can become powerful in this state. But it will rise, and within six years it will culminate. Webster will run for Presidency, and will get at most 24 votes. Van Buren will come in; and Massachusetts will come over to his support. Scorn your enemies: spurn them from you. Mr. Webster, retiring to private life, will leave you the leading name in the East." [1]

Before passing adverse judgment on Bancroft's course in this situation, let us ask ourselves what we should have done face to face with a powerful party which could use at will the influence of social and religious conservatism to break those who were rash enough to oppose it. For the average New Englander, born to trust the clergy and to distrust democrats, political orthodoxy was no great error. But an educated and liberal minded man today would be ashamed to yield to such influences. Bancroft was ahead of his time, and he took such a stand as many an educated man of our own day and in the same situation would consider the only thing to do. Alluding to the storm that burst over him when his letter to the men of Northampton appeared, he said:

[1] Bancroft to Edward Everett, Nov. 17, 1834. Bancroft MSS.

"With respect to my letter, it was written deliberately. I abide by it. I have no wish to retract a word of it, nor to change the time when it was published. I had no idea, how indifferent I could be to unmerited censure; it does not in the least disturb my peace: I never enjoyed greater tranquility. My letter was an attack upon all disorganizers and infidels. I am radically a republican in feeling and in principles." [1]

Perhaps George Ticknor's advice brought comfort also. Said he: "You are not made by your talents or your affectations, by your temperament or your pursuits, to be either the leader or the tool of demagogues."[2] Ticknor was an ardent whig: he looked on the defection of his old friend with great sadness. At this time the first volume of the "History" had been published and well received. Its author had become a national figure, and his political course caused much comment.

The attacks of whigs attracted the notice of the democrats. Invitations to address the faithful came in, and prominent democrats began to take notice of him. Van Buren wrote, the occasion being a reply to Bancroft's offer of a copy of his first volume: "I have, as you suppose, observed the attacks which have been made upon you by the newspapers. This has ever been and will ever be the fate of every sincere friend of liberal principles." Bancroft visited Albany, where he met many men of note, among them William L. Marcy, with whom he exchanged letters after his return. He was a Van Buren man in 1836, and in 1837

[1] Bancroft to Edward Everett, Dec. 29, 1834. Bancroft MSS.
[2] In the Bancroft MSS without date.

he received as the reward of his faithfulness the collectorship of the port of Boston, a position which he filled very acceptably until dismissed on the accession of the whigs in 1841. By this time he was fully launched as a statesman. In 1834, he said: "I must insist on my old theory: the man of letters cannot have brilliant success in politics except on the popular side." [1] These words were spoken to induce Everett to come over to democracy; but they probably stated his own theory of conduct. Let us now consider Bancroft's progress into the sure position of an accepted man of letters.

4. *Early Career as a Historian*

Six months after he gave up the schoolroom Bancroft said: "It was an unwise thing in me to have made myself a schoolmaster: that was a kind of occupation to which I was not peculiarly adapted, and in which many of inferior abilities and attainments could have succeeded as well. I have felt rejoiced at being entirely emancipated from this condition." [2] He had at last found himself.

It will be noticed that he threw his classics out of the same window that served for the exit of his schoolmaster's wand. Both were supplanted by history. "I remember well," he wrote to Everett in 1835, alluding to their early relations, "advising with you on

---

[1] Bancroft to E. Everett, July 11, 1834. Bancroft MSS.
[2] Howe, "Life and Letters of George Bancroft," I, 201.

devoting myself to the pursuit of history, and for sixteen years my main purpose in life has been un-
changed." We should ever make some allowance for
Bancroft's imagination. He may have thought in 1818
of becoming a historian, and the idea was probably
remembered; but the magazine articles written on
many subjects from 1823 to 1830 show that he was
still without a dominating theme of thought. History
begins to assume a leading position in his plans in
1828, when, as we have seen, he was thinking of publishing, in connection with Heeren's two works, a
course of general history,[1] a history of the United
States making the fourth volume in the series. Even
this plan seems to have been dropped during at least
four years. There is nothing to connect it with the
appearance in 1834 of the first volume of his great
work, except identity of subject.

Bancroft is said to have derived his historical method
from Heeren, under whom he studied at Göttingen.
The assertion seems to me very improbable. If his
teacher at Göttingen had made him love history, he
would hardly have come home filled with enthusiasm
for another subject. As to historical method, Heeren's
characteristics were balanced judgment, impartiality,
and great insight; and he gave much prominence to
the economic factors of history. Probably no critic
will claim that Bancroft had these qualities in a high
degree. He was chiefly a historian of political life.

[1] See above, page 153.

Moreover, Heeren's style was exceedingly dry, while Bancroft's was exceedingly vivid. A chapter of the German's book is a series of minute statements of fact, concise and brief : one of Bancroft's chapters is a scene from a drama, in which unity of action, enthusiasm for the subject, and descriptive power are joined in a brilliant manner. But for the fact that the young writer studied under the old writer, it is doubtful if anyone would have thought of saying that Bancroft was influenced by Heeren. It is probable that Bancroft fashioned himself according to the gift he had from nature. Certainly his appreciation for the beauties of classical literature, ancient and modern, had some appreciable influence on his literary style.

The first volume of the "History of the United States from the Discovery of the American Continent" was published in 1834. It was probably written in 1832 and 1833. The preface, dated June 16, 1834, contains this statement :

"I have formed the design of writing a 'History of the United States from the Discovery of the American Continent' to the present time. As the moment arrives for publishing a portion of the work, I am impressed more strongly than ever with a sense of the grandeur and vastness of the subject; and am ready to charge myself with presumption for venturing on so bold an enterprise. I can find for myself no excuse but in the sincerity with which I have sought to collect truth from trustworthy documents and testimony. I have desired to give to the work the interest of authenticity. I have applied, as I have proceeded, the principles of historical skepticism, and, not allowing myself to grow weary in comparing witnesses, or consulting codes of laws, I have endeavored to impart

originality to my narrative, by deriving it from writings and
sources which were the contemporaries of the events that are
described. Where different nations or different parties have been
engaged in the same scenes, I have not failed to examine their
respective reports. Such an investigation on any country would
be laborious; I need not say how much the labor is increased by
the extent of our republic, the differences, in the origin and early
government of its component parts, and the multiplicity of topics,
which require to be discussed and arranged."

Much error, he continued, had crept into American
history, as it had been written, through the habit of
one historian accepting blindly what had been said by
a predecessor. He had tried to remedy this defect by
consulting sources only. There is no reason to doubt
that he examined most carefully all the available
source material within his reach in America.

Following the preface was an "Introduction." It
opened with the statement, "The United States constitute an essential portion of a great political system,
embracing all the civilized nations of the earth. At a
period when the force of moral opinion is rapidly increasing, they have the precedence in the practice and
the defence of the equal rights of man." Then follows
a long and glowing panegyric on the American government. The idea that the history of all civilized nations
is a unity was a favorite theory of contemporary
scholars and served its purpose in breaking down the
habit of treating national history as isolated from world
history. Heeren held the view, and Bancroft probably
caught the phrase from him. But the American seems

to have used it only to vouch for his scholarship of the
German brand. Having announced that the United
States were a part of a great world system, he went on
to show that they were far ahead of all the other
nations of the world; and in taking up the story of
their past he treated it much as faithful Thomas
Hutchinson or Jeremy Belknap would have treated it.
A sensible historian needs no theorization of univer-
sality to know that he should not neglect the European
background of American history. On the other hand,
American history is essentially American.

Bancroft's first volume carried the story to the
restoration of the Stuarts, 1660. It was no sooner
published than the second was begun and brought
steadily forward to its publication in 1837. Writing
was now his only employment, and we may here see
about how fast Bancroft worked. The third volume
came out in 1840 and no more appeared until 1852,
when the fourth and fifth were issued. The sixth came
out in 1854, the seventh in 1858, the eighth in 1860,
the ninth in 1866, and the tenth in 1875. The title
of the first volume announced that the work would
bring the story down to the "present time": subsequent volumes were content with the title, "History
of the United States from the Discovery of the American Continent." The author had come to realize how
large was his task, and the tenth volume completed
the story of the revolution.

Bancroft's early volumes were marred by his enthu-

siasm for democratic institutions, leading him to fervid
outbreaks in praise of liberty.   As Professor Jameson
says, they voted for Jackson.[1]   In his mature years
Bancroft himself became aware of this defect and rewrote his early volumes with many chastening touches.
Nevertheless, the first volume made a great impression
when it appeared.   Edward Everett read it through
in less than twenty-four hours and seized his pen and
wrote: "You have written a work which will last
while the memory of America lasts; and which will
instantly take its place among the classics of our language.   It is full of learning, information, common
sense, and philosophy; full of taste and eloquence;
full of life and power.   You give us not wretched
pasteboard men; not a sort of chronological table,
with the dates written out at length, after the manner
of most historians: — but you give us real, individual,
living men and women, with their passions, interests,
and peculiarities." [2]   Judge Story, after reading some
of the proof-sheets, wrote: "I think your work will be
very interesting and useful.   You have infused into
it a very spirited, chaste, and vigorous narrative." [3]
Ralph Waldo Emerson said: "The history is richer
not only in anecdotes of great men, but of the great
heart of towns and provinces than I dared believe;
and — what surprised and charmed me — it starts

[1] Jameson, "Historical Writing in America," 107.
[2] Everett to Bancroft, Oct. 5, 1834.   Bancroft MSS.
[3] Story to Bancroft, May 15, 1834.   Bancroft MSS.

tears, and almost makes them overflow on many and many a page. . . . It is noble matter, and I am heartily glad to have it nobly treated." Theodore Parker wrote: "You are likely to make, what I long since told you I looked for from *you*, the most noble and splendid piece of historical composition, not only in English, but in any tongue." [1]

These comments were made by men who stood in the first rank in their day, and they are not lightly to be set aside. They tell us plainly that Bancroft as an historian had fulfilled the requirement of his time. The statements are supported by the large sales the book had. The first volume, published in 1834, had reached its twenty-sixth edition in 1878. To both kinds of testimony add the fact that the History gave Bancroft the undisputed rank of greatest living historian of his country. It made him famous among writers, politicians, and statesmen. No other history written in our country has had the distinction of starting tears in the eyes of an Emerson, opening the doors of high cabinet and diplomatic appointment, and filling its author's pockets with the glittering coin of the republic.

And yet posterity has its doubts. Bancroft's History is now out of date, and a changing age treats it with disdain. It has fallen into the hands of a generation that demands less color and more repose. His quick and nervous summation of facts is not suited to the careful weighing of evidence.

[1] See Howe, "Life and Letters of George Bancroft," II, 107.

The weightiest charge against Bancroft is the lack of detachment. American he was in spite of the strong impression German criticism had made on him. He assumed that the United States were founded on a plan superior to that of other nations, and that their growth verified his theory. The dispute of the colonies with England, to which a large portion of his book is devoted, had for him only one side. In Bancroft's time no historian in either the United States or Great Britain had treated the revolution with discrimination. To all it was a thing to be defended or condemned, as the feelings of the writer dictated. Bancroft was no worse than the others. Strongly partisan by nature and deeply imbued with the love of American independence, he glorified the struggle of the revolutionary fathers, and saw no good in the position taken by king and parliament. He crystallized all the hero worship of the old Fourth-of-July school into a large work written in a style acceptable to the time.

George Bancroft spent eight years of his life in Boston, four of them as collector of the port, and four as a private citizen. During these years he was a leading democrat of Massachusetts. He made speeches in the interest of the party and carried on an active correspondence with Van Buren and other party leaders. It must be remembered, also, that the keynote of the democratic campaigning was the attack on the aristocracy. Bancroft's speeches on this phase of the general discussions differ from those of other demo-

cratic speakers only in style. This fact will enable
the reader to imagine the feelings Boston entertained
for him. Of all his old friends Prescott alone, whose
gentle soul found the good in every man, remained
cordial. To a high-born Boston lady Bancroft once
said: "I did not find you at home when I called."
"No, and you never will," was the reply.

To this kind of opposition Bancroft turned a face
hardened by abuse. In the letters he wrote to Van
Buren, he gloried in his martyrdom. If he felt the
sensitiveness of the scholar, it does not show in his
correspondence, not even in his letters to his wife. A
part of the period referred to he was chairman of the
state democratic committee; he tried to distribute the
patronage; he denounced the opponents of Van Buren
and was called on by that statesman to write replies
to some of the many questions that were asked him
by friend and foe; he was nominated for the state
senate; and in 1844 he was a delegate at large to the
democratic national convention.

But his crowning party effort at this time was to
write a campaign life of Van Buren. The task was
first assigned to William L. Marcy, who refused, saying:
"I abominate man worship, and to escape from the
slightest suspicion of it, should be likely to come short
of what might be said with truth and propriety." [1]
Van Buren, who was promoting the scheme, then ap-

[1] Marcy to Van Buren, Feb. 1844. " Proceedings " of the Mass. Histl.
Soc., 1909, p. 419.

proached Bancroft, who accepted readily. He worked
hard on the task, and had it nearly complete when
Van Buren's nomination was rendered impossible by
combinations of factions in the convention of 1844.
How completely Bancroft played the rôle of party
servant is seen in his words written when sending to
Van Buren a portion of the finished manuscript. "I
look to you," he said, "that not one word escapes that
is not strictly true, and further, that is not free from
the censure of being unwise. Erase, add, explain,
comment, give me hints. I have no pride of authorship. I am a calm, tranquil friend of the cause." [1]
It is hard to have patience with a spirit so little in
harmony with the attitude of a true historian. Moreover, it is in striking contrast with Bancroft's own
position when Sparks took the liberty of making him
say what he had not intended to say. For "the
cause" the author, it is evident, doffed his garb of
historian and took the habit of party hack. The life
of Van Buren was not published in 1844, as intended.
When it finally appeared in 1889 it had the title,
"Martin Van Buren to the end of his Public Career."
It proved a colorless affair, a thing Bancroft should
not have published at all.

In his "History" Bancroft accused James Grahame,
author of a history of the United States, of inventing
a statement reflecting on John Clarke, of Rhode

[1] Bancroft to Van Buren, April 22, 1844. "Proceedings" of the Mass.
Histl. Soc., 1909, p. 425.

Island. As a champion of democracy Bancroft was disposed to take the side of the men of Rhode Island against the criticisms that the rulers of Massachusetts made against them. His accusation against Grahame brought on a controversy, in which Josiah Quincy, American editor of the author named, took a prominent part. Bancroft was deluged with scorn, and wrote a cutting reply which, however, he was persuaded to leave unpublished after it had been put into type.[1]

Another notable controversy was with Colonel George W. Greene, grandson and biographer of General Nathanael Greene. Bancroft, in his ninth volume, threw on Greene the responsibility for the loss of Fort Washington, and otherwise criticized Greene's conduct in the early part of the revolutionary war. The grandson replied in a sharp pamphlet, to which Bancroft retorted in an article in the *North American Review*, followed by a second reply from Colonel Greene, published in the same journal. The points at issue were very subordinate, and it seems that if Bancroft's language was not exactly well chosen for the subject to which it referred, it was at least not as condemnatory of Greene as the critic thought. It is certain that the Colonel wrote in a bad spirit, which could not have been wholly due to his sensitiveness in defending the fame of an ancestor.

Bancroft was unquestionably a great scholar, and

[1] Howe, "Life of Bancroft," I, 138–140.

there is no reason to doubt his industry. Nor can it be said that he had any other prejudice than his intense partiality for the American side of the revolutionary controversy. If he made mistakes in his estimates of the conduct of men, they were doubtless honest mistakes. Men who write with the hastening fingers of imagination sometimes drop into obscurity details which more literally minded persons would consider very important; or they use expressions meaning less or more than they intend them to mean. Probably Bancroft, who was always a stylist, was guilty to some extent of this form of error; and on this basis most of the criticisms made upon his "History" could be explained. Such an explanation lessens our censure, though it does not remove it entirely.

5. *Bancroft as a Statesman*

In the year 1844 Bancroft was the candidate for governor of Massachusetts on the democratic ticket. He could not have expected success; for the state was strongly whig, and Clay was running for the presidency. He was in the same year a delegate-at-large to the national nominating convention of his party, going there as a strong Van Buren man. When he realized that his favorite could not succeed, he gave his attention to defeating Cass, in whose support many of Van Buren's opponents were united. He was influential in carrying a portion of his own delegation over to Polk at the critical time, sweeping along many other

New England delegates as they went. He believed
that he thus turned the tide in favor of the "dark
horse," and five weeks after the convention adjourned
he sent Polk an explicit account of his actions. On
this side of his career Bancroft did not differ from the
average American politician.

In recognition of his position in the party, Polk made
him secretary of the navy. He himself would have
preferred a diplomatic post, but he was pleased with
the cabinet position. While he waited in Washington
to know what would be offered he wrote to his wife as
follows: "The President elect keeps his own counsels
most closely; but some of those in the street seem to
think, that the husband of a woman like yourself,
should assuredly be one of the Clerks of the President;
and as people do not know the cause of my coming
here, they draw queer inferences. Time will unfold all
things, among the rest whether you are to mope in
Winthrop-place; or reign in Washington; or freeze
your nose in some German Lapland." [1]   His fate was
a brief reign in Washington, and after that the court
of St. James. It was a sudden change that a man
who had been forced to endure many slights in his
own town was set in the highest circle of the country.
But violent as the transition was, Bancroft made it
with success. The little man whose exuberant manners brought the severe rebuke from Professor Norton
in 1822 was in 1845 recognized as a remarkable success

[1] Howe, "Life and Letters of George Bancroft," I, 259.

in all things social. His house in Washington became noted for its good company, and its master and mistress were among the most desirable guests in the best houses of the city. The esteem in which he was held is shown in the remark ascribed to President Arthur, that the President of the United States was "permitted to accept the invitations of members of his cabinet, supreme court judges, and — Mr. George Bancroft." Ample means enabled Bancroft to entertain in a handsome manner, but good taste and a careful appreciation of select company united in making his entertainments successful.

As secretary of the navy, Bancroft is chiefly remembered for the establishment of the Naval Academy at Annapolis, in keeping with an idea that many persons had previously entertained. He gave himself to the routine of his office with great earnestness. He followed the advice of his friend Van Buren as faithfully as he could : "Stand aloof from all schemes and intrigues of which you will soon see abundance. Let your course be distinguished by a singleness of devotion to the duties of your Department, and the time will come when you will find an advantage from this course beyond what is the ordinary reward of virtuous actions." Van Buren's words are illustrative of the political ideal of the time. Try hard to avoid the jobmakers and stick to your desk, summed it up. Nothing was said about the duty of a secretary of the navy to know anything about the navy. Bancroft was no better and no worse than most of the men who have been appointed to the position.

As secretary he had many difficulties. He soon brought down upon himself the opposition of a large part of the service through ignoring the rule of promotion by seniority. He adopted the more reasonable method of promotion for ability; but it is doubtful if he knew men well enough to execute this method fairly. At any rate, his decisions were roundly criticized, and at last the senate seemed to give color to the charge by refusing to confirm some of his nominations. It was the signal for shifting him to the diplomatic service. McLane, minister to London, wished to come home and Bancroft took his place, arriving in England, October 25, 1846.

Of his three years in this position this sketch can take little notice; for it was not a time in which his historical activity, except in the collection of materials, was notable. "Here in London," he wrote to Prescott, "to write is impossible; except dispatches and notes of which I have indited, on little nothings and a few matters of importance, as much as would make in bulk the Conquest of Mexico." [1] Social life was very exacting, and he and his wife gave themselves up to it. It was a sphere in which they both had much ability, and they were popular in the capital. Bancroft, it is likely, found great pleasure in the acquaintances he formed among literary men, especially among the his-

[1] Howe, "Life and Letters of Bancroft," II, 43.

torians. Hallam, Milman, Lord Mahon, and Macaulay he came to know well. His own estimate of the historians is seen in his high praise of the last named, whom he pronounced the greatest of the group, and of whom he said:

"He has the most nearly universal knowledge of any man I ever met; and his memory is as much disciplined to accuracy, as the extent of his reading is boundless. I have met him in all sorts of companies, and everywhere he is the oracle of all present. Among churchmen he shows more knowledge of ecclesiastics than all the bishops; he will go ahead of Milman and keep in advance in quoting the fathers of the church and even the later Latin authors; and when Hallam falters about a letter of Pliny, he will give its date and tenour, and perhaps begin to quote it word for word. I think him, what is so rare, greater than his books." [1]

In 1847 Bancroft made short visits to Paris to collect material bearing on the American revolution. He was well received by leading literary men, among them Guizot, Thierry, Lamartine, Cousin, Mignet, Thiers, Louis Blanc, and de Tocqueville. Seven times at least, says his biographer, he visited Paris on this business between March, 1847, and September, 1849. Add to the time necessary for these visits the time he gave to the collections in London, and we see how little of the three years he was minister was really given to the duties of the legation. His avowed purpose in accepting the position was to have the opportunity to collect materials on the revolution; and he was prepared to retire as soon as that object was secured.

[1] Howe, "Life and Letters of Bancroft," II, 16.

The triumph of the whigs in 1848 gave him fair notice
that his tenure was short. He said it made little
difference, since he had from the first intended to re-
sign as soon as he completed his researches, and had
Cass been elected he would have returned early in the
new administration. As it was, he remained until
September 1, held there by his feverish desire to finish
the work in the French archives, and by the fortunate
accident that Abbott Lawrence, his successor, was not
ready to go to London until the autumn.

Back in America, Bancroft settled in New York,
buying at the same time a pleasant home in Newport
in which he spent his summers. His city house in
Twenty-first Street was the scene of much hospitality.
Here were installed the transcripts of documents he had
examined abroad, handsomely bound with gilt tops.
Here, too, were completed the fourth, fifth, sixth,
seventh, and eighth volumes of the "History." When
the fourth appeared, in 1852, twelve years had elapsed
since its immediate predecessor had been issued. They
were twelve years mostly lost to literature. For the
eighteen years he lived in New York, 1849 to 1867, he
had a better record; but even here there must have
been much waste of time. The eighth volume appeared in 1860, making five volumes in twelve years,
which was no great thing considering that the volumes
contained on an average one hundred and forty-one
thousand words. The ninth and tenth volumes appeared together in 1874, after fourteen years of silence.

It is hard to find a great German or French historian of the period who worked so fitfully.

During most of this period Bancroft found himself out of sympathy with the democratic party. A close follower of the displaced Van Buren and little known in New York, he found himself of slight account among the politicians. He was, also, opposed to the pro-slavery influence then dominating his party, and could accept neither the position of Pierce on Kansas nor the doctrines of Taney in the Dred Scott case. The result was that he was entirely out of politics as long as the democrats ruled the country, a remarkable situation for a man who had been so much engaged in this field in 1844. "I am persuaded," he said in 1857, "the South has gained nothing by some extreme notions that have been put forth; and I see and know, that we of the Northern democracy, have been dreadfully routed in consequence, and are handed over to the most corrupt set of political opponents, that I have ever encountered." [1]

During the war Bancroft's feelings were entirely with the administration. He met Lincoln and formed a poor opinion of his ability. He regarded Seward as a disagreeable man. But he kept on friendly terms with both. In 1862 a faction of the republicans in New York wished to nominate him for congress, but he declined on the ground that his candidacy would endanger the republican cause in the district.[2] Never-

[1] Howe, "Life and Letters of Bancroft," II, 128.   [2] *Ibid.*, II, 157.

theless, he called himself a democrat, and as the war
drew to an end he began to pick up again the old
threads of his party association.

Opportunity came to put them into play when Andrew Johnson, president through the crime of Booth,
took up the plan of establishing a moderate party out
of all the liberal elements then in politics. Northern
democrats who were not tinctured with copperhead-
ism, republicans who had supported Lincoln's liberal
views, and old whigs were to be united in a great
liberal movement; and to this project Bancroft gave
his allegiance and his aid, helping in an effective, if
secret, manner. Johnson was self-educated and dis-
trusted his ability to prepare a state paper. When
his first message was laid before congress, December 4,
1865, it aroused happy surprise. Newspapers and
individuals were delighted at this evidence, as they
put it, that a plain man from the Southern mountains
could write so excellent a paper. For forty years the
country continued under this impression; but at last
Professor Dunning proved that this excellent paper
was written by George Bancroft and not by Andrew
Johnson.[1] This act marked Bancroft's return to political life. It was followed by his appointment in 1867
to the position of minister in Berlin, a post he held
until 1874.

It has been a subject of comment that Bancroft,
appointed by Johnson, could have held office so long

[1] See "Proceedings" of the Mass. Histl. Soc., 1905, p. 395.

under Grant. He himself said that he was a Grant man when appointed in 1867, and that he received a letter from Grant strongly approving the nomination. It is doubtful, however, if Johnson knew of this relation, and it cannot be doubted that if the senate had known that Bancroft wrote the message of 1867 his confirmation would have had strong opposition. Our historian was a crafty man in the affairs of this world. He was too wise to trust his fate in the new administration to the chain of friendship merely, and he did some skillful polishing of the links on his own part. Probably it was not by accident that on the morning of the fateful fourth of March, 1869, the "leading liberal newspaper in Berlin" contained flattering allusion to General Grant. On that day Bancroft gave a party for Bismarck and several of the higher officers of state, and at the proper moment the chancellor toasted in glowing words the new President of the United States. Bancroft replied with a toast to the King of Prussia. Next day he wrote Grant a letter of congratulations, but he was too shrewd to tell him about the marks of approval in Berlin : that was a thing for the dispatch to the secretary of state written March 5, 1869. To the letter to Grant he added this postscript :

"Count Bismarck, who had not dined out during the winter with one of the diplomatic corps, gladly accepted my invitation for yesterday out of his desire to prove you his regard. I assure you we had a very pleasant time; I never saw Bismarck so much at his ease, so full of mirth and frolic." [1]

[1] See " Proceedings " of the Mass. Histl. Soc., 1905, VI, 223-226.

No American minister has been more popular in the capital to which he was accredited than Bancroft in Berlin. He became an intimate friend of Bismarck in the beginning of his residence, and from that vantage point it was easy to enter any door. The king showed him marked favor; princes, dukes, the queen and her highest ladies vied with scholars and writers to show him their esteem. He lived in a handsome house on the Thiergarten, where his entertainments were well known for elegance. He was very fond of horseback riding, a practice he continued until old age, and on his daily jaunt frequently had the chancellor for his companion.

Bancroft was in Berlin during the Franco-Prussian war. His sympathies were strongly on the German side, and he showed them so plainly that the French came to understand his bias. He now became the object of contempt in Paris, a city in which he had formerly received many courtesies. Victor Hugo, with that withering scorn for which he was noted when dealing with the catastrophes for which Louis Napoleon was responsible, held up Bancroft to the world in two bitter poems. In one Bancroft is told that he insults France; and the poet exclaims: "She does not perceive in her widow's weeds or her fêtes the kind of obscure and vague shadow which you are. Try to be some one, Tiberius, Ghengis Khan, the human flea, or the human volcano, and we will examine you to see if you are worth the trouble of our contempt. Have a title to our hatred and we will see about it. If not, go away!"[1] I have not been able to discover what it was that aroused the poet's ire; but Bancroft was a man of strong impulses, and it is possible that his enthusiasm for the German cause was not restrained within the bounds of neutrality.

Berlin brought out the inherent love of social distinction that Bancroft ever had. He was just the material to make a good *Junker*, and his association with the official class of the city furnished the training and the opportunity to develop his nature. Leopold von Ranke said to him one day: "Do you know what I say of you to my classes? . . . I tell my hearers that your history is the best book ever written from the democratic point of view. You are thoroughly consistent, adhere strictly to your method, carry it out in many directions, but in all with fidelity, and are always true to it."[2] On this, Bancroft's comment, expressed in a letter to a relative, was: "If there is democracy in the history it is not subjective, but objective, as they say here." Thirty years earlier he gloried in his love of democracy, and to one who found it in his "History" he would have replied that it was his intention to make the book a tribute to democracy. An anecdote told in Washington about the time of his death illustrates how much he took on the German color in his later life. It was his habit to ride past

[1] See "Proceedings" of the Mass. Histl. Soc., 1905, II, 252.
[2] Howe, "Life of George Bancroft," II, 183.

the Soldiers' Home when taking his daily exercise.
A gentleman who met him several times without knowing him, ventured to ask of the guard at the gate of
the Home who was that old gentleman with a military
look who rode by so often. The guard replied: "That
is an old German named Bancroft."

That Bancroft could so readily take on the ideals of
his environment was characteristic of his quickly imaginative mind. He was all fire, and ever ready to run
away with any glowing prospect that opened before
him. He probably thought less about principles than
about accomplishing the things that he considered
desirable. Just returned from Germany, face to face
with New England democracy, he could exclaim to
President Kirkland in 1823: "I love to observe the
bustle of the world, but I detest mixing in it. I like
to watch the shouts of the multitude, but had rather
not scream with them." In Northampton, in face of
the frowning aristocracy of the "River Gods," and remembering the dogged opposition his reforms had met
in conservative Harvard, he could turn with enthusiasm to Jeffersonian democracy; for the Jeffersonian
democrats heard him gladly and gave tribute to his
greatness. And as long as he ran forward in the race
of political preferment, he loved and defended the
principles on which his party was founded. In comfortable retirement in New York, with the tasks of his
library before him and the joys of Newport at his
command, there was no impulse to go back into the

rough and tumble contest of politics.   In Berlin at last,
with savants and courtiers in admiring circles around
him, he adopted the ideals they held.   From step to
step he proceeded, it seems, with sincerity.   That is
to say, he believed for the time being that he followed
sincere conviction.   If posterity should judge him as a
model of individual conduct it would have to say that
he was inconsistent and shifting.   But it is as a historian that we must pass on him; and may we not say
that, in spite of his lack of continuous ideals in his personal life, he was in his literary life ever a consistent
American ?   American democracy he always defended,
even when he appeared in the garb of a Teuton.

6. *Minor Activities*

Bancroft's career has been treated in its early stages:
the first attempts in literature, his political activities,
his greatest literary achievement — the "History of
the United States," — and his triumphant service as
minister to London and to Berlin.   It still remains to
consider some minor phases, in which his actions had
enough importance to make them essential to a sketch
of his life.

First of all we must consider his shorter writings.
Fairly abundant before he published the first volume
of his "History," — as his textbooks and articles in the
reviews, — writings of this class were rarely produced
after he began his great task.   In 1855 came a volume
of "Literary and Historical Miscellanies."   Like Pres-

cott's "Biographical and Critical Miscellanies," published in 1845, it contained articles prepared for the most part for the *North American Review*. The pieces are heavy and diffuse, as are most of the articles in that periodical at that time. In 1859 he wrote a "Tribute to the Memory of Humboldt," publishing it in the series known as *The Pulpit and Rostrum*. In connection with the arbitration of the Northwestern boundary dispute he published confidentially in 1872 a "Memorial on the Canal de Haro as the boundary line of the United States of America," an official publication. In 1886 he published under the title, "A Plea for the Constitution of the United States of America Wounded in the House of its Guardians," a vigorous attack on a recent decision of the federal supreme court declaring that congress had the right to make paper money legal tender.[1] The court had held that at the time the constitution was adopted, the power to confer the legal tender quality was an element of sovereignty and that as the constitution did not withhold this power from congress it was given to it along with the general exercise of the rights of sovereignty. Bancroft traced the history of paper money in the colonies and in the states until the adoption of the constitution, showing that in 1787 the right to issue legal tender was recognized as an attribute of sovereignty. He cited early opinions of judges and statesmen to show that they did not consider that the power in question was conferred on

---

[1] Julliard *v*. Greenman, 110 U. S. Reports, 421.

congress. It was a state rights plea, a strong and well presented argument, but it attracted little attention in the days when the main trend of constitutional interpretation was in an opposite direction.

After Bancroft returned from Berlin he turned again to his "History of the United States," the title of which was pronounced misleading, since the book did not deal with the union at all, but only with the colonies and the states in revolution. He was sensible of the weight of this criticism and determined to carry the story forward to the adoption of the federal constitution. The work was taken up with the old time zeal, but it was not carried through with the old time success. The two volumes which appeared in 1882 with the title "History of the Formation of the Constitution of the United States" lack the fire of originality and have not been received as an adequate treatment of the subject.

Next he prepared a final edition of his "History." A "Centenary Edition" of the first ten volumes, which appeared with alterations in 1876, was now subjected to a more rigid revision. The text was condensed and with the volumes on the constitution the whole work appeared in six volumes as "The Author's Last Revision" (1883–1885). The edition represented a large amount of alteration in style. Naturally ardent in his early life, Bancroft was now sobered by years and experience. His "Last Revision" embodied the results of reflection and criticism. Many of the expressions which had given offense to the relatives of historical characters were toned down, and some were changed outright. That exuberance of figure that gave the early volumes a florid and sometimes a fantastic form was brought down to the sober narration that an age of self-restraint demanded of its historians. What men like Theodore Parker, Edward Everett, and Emerson, who found the first volumes so "noble," would have said of such changes we know not; but they made the work more acceptable to the new generation of writers and critics who dominated literary life in the last decades of the nineteenth century. As to the point of view, it continued what it was at first. Bancroft was in theory a democrat, and his book remains our great defense of the rise of American nationality, our most fervent great apology for the war of independence in all its untutored Americanism.

Bancroft had a high reputation in his day for elegant and polished literary orations. He always read his productions, but he read with good effect, and he was sought for service on occasions in which historical information and patriotic emotions were properly blended. Some of his best efforts of this kind were published. Among them were the oration at Northampton in celebration of the fiftieth anniversary of the Declaration of Independence; his oration at Springfield, July 4, 1836, a defense of his party principles; an oration before the young democrats of Hartford, February 18, 1840; a eulogy on Andrew Jackson, Washington, June

27, 1845; an oration on "The Necessity, the Reality, and the Promise of the Progress of the Human Race," New York, November 20, 1854; an oration at the inauguration of the Perry statue, Cleveland, September 10, 1860; and two addresses on Lincoln, one in a memorial meeting in New York, April 25, 1865, and the other in Washington, February 12, 1866. The second of the Lincoln addresses was delivered at the request of congress before the two houses in joint session, and was probably the most esteemed of all Bancroft's orations. In diction, in elevated sentiment, in its power of characterizing the dead Lincoln, it has few equals in American eloquence, and it should be read by many generations.

Bancroft lived at a time when his historical investigation was dependent upon access to materials which he himself must collect. Like Sparks, and to a certain extent Belknap, he was forced to become a collector of manuscripts and transcripts. He was, fortunately, able to have transcripts made as freely as he wished. In 1869 he said : "The expenses of various kinds in collecting materials, MSS, and books, in journeys, time employed in researches, writing, copyists, money paid for examination, etc., etc., might be put without exaggeration at fifty or even seventy-five thousand dollars." The amount mentioned here should not stagger us. Any historical scholar of to-day might with all sincerity estimate the value of his time employed in historical research, the expenses of journeys to collect information, and the money spent in purchasing books and other printed matter at a rather large figure. Bancroft undoubtedly spent more freely than the average man of his day, and the large collection of manuscripts he left, now the property of the New York Public Library, is evidence of the liberality with which he collected. Few men of his day were able to buy so freely.

His transcripts were taken from the public offices in London, Paris, and Berlin. While minister in Europe he had better facilities than any other American had been given, Sparks not excepted, to secure all that he wanted. His reputation as historian had preceded him and the keepers of public archives, as well as owners of private collections, vied with one another in giving him all possible assistance. "People here," he said on leaving London, "have heaped me full of documents. Lord North's daughter gave me all she had, and all her reminiscences to boot. The Duke of Grafton sent to my house a big box holding the most private papers of the old Duke with the key and unbounded license to use the contents at my discretion; Lord Dartmouth, the papers of his pious progenitor who, you remember, was 'The one who wears a coronet and prays.' Then I have every letter written to every dog of a cutthroat that went into the wilderness to set the Indians upon us. What need of many words? I have nearly all said or written in London or Paris or Berlin, etc., etc., and as far as eyesight, which these researches wasted horribly, and money which I have spent lavishly, would permit. And when I get my papers completed, and nicely bound with gilt edges at top and nice gilt backs, I shall snap my fingers at the whole of your Whig party." [1]

While it was to Bancroft's credit that he collected many documents from abroad, the real test of his merit in connection with them is the use he made of them. And on this point he is indicted by a recent writer in the following words :

"His researches for material both in this country and in Europe are described by his friends as the most remarkable ever made. Documents and sources of information closed to all others were, we are assured, open to him. But, strange to say, we see no result of this in his published work. Nor can any subsequent investigator profit by his labors; the wondrous and mysterious sources of information remain mysterious; and many of his opinions are difficult to support with the evidence which the investigators are able to find." [2]

In temper this criticism is over-positive, but the main accusation, that Bancroft did not make the best use of the material at his disposal, is essentially correct. How a man should have used Lord North's letters without forming some respect for the British point of view in the revolutionary controversy is difficult to see, unless we are prepared to admit that his historical sense was subverted to national prejudice.

[1] Howe, "Life and Letters of George Bancroft," Vol. II, p. 44.

[2] Fisher, Sydney G., "Myth-making Process in Histories of the American Revolution " (" Proceedings " of the American Philosophical Society, Vol. 51, p. 69).

Judging by the slow rate at which the volumes of the "History" were published, we must think that Bancroft worked intermittently. There were long periods when he could have done little, if we may judge by the results. But when occupied with one of his volumes he worked hard and steadily. He rose at an early hour, frequently at five o'clock, breakfasted at 7.30, and worked steadily until luncheon, which he took at two. In the afternoon he rode horseback, dining at seven or half past seven. The evening he gave up to his friends, unless he had an engagement abroad. He entertained with old-fashioned courtesy, and he was noted for his marked attention to ladies.

In Newport he had a famous rose garden, the cultivation of which he supervised himself. He was known to rose-growers throughout the country, and a handsome rose was called the "George Bancroft" in compliment to him. But Newport was not favorable to literary work. He came to like it in the last years of his life; but in the middle years he used to desert it for his house in New York, where he gave himself up to his books. On one of these trips of seclusion he wrote to his wife: "Certainly Newport, in contrast with my life here, has many superiorities. But in the evening the quiet of my room and the comfort of a good book were worth more to me than a game of cards which I never consent to take in hand without shame for a waste of time." [1]

[1] Howe, "Life and Letters of Bancroft," II, 104.

Students of history will be interested in Bancroft's method of writing. He had blank books, quarto in size, and gave a day of the year to each page. Then he read vastly, setting down on each page all the events that happened in the year to which it was devoted. He let no event slip, even putting in the phases of the moon; for they sometimes had bearing on the actions of men. When he wrote, these books served as skeleton outlines. His mass of transcripts do not seem to have been indexed, and he probably relied on memory to reproduce the ideas in them, using his chronological arrangement of events to correct errors He had an unusual memory, and it is to his credit that it rarely failed him. Although he was many times criticized, it was generally for bad judgment rather than for mistakes in facts.

Bancroft's excellent constitution and regular habits served him well for the achievement of an active old age. When he resigned his post as minister to Germany, 1874, he was seventy-four years old, and retired because he wished to pass his old age quietly. Yet he lived nearly seventeen years thereafter, dying at Washington, January 17, 1891, in the ninety-first year of his age. Few Americans have won more distinction while they lived, or enjoyed their popularity with less diminution until the years ran out to an unusual length. Bancroft was in the full possession of his faculties until a few days before the end, and he continued to receive the visits of literary friends and admirers until death was at hand. In his old age he was looked upon, in America and in Europe, as the greatest living American historian; and although others have excelled him in several essential qualities, it is still hard to point to a man who has written our history more acceptably to his age, or who is more likely to be remembered in the future as a historian.

Bancroft's biographer speaks of him as "unwearying in the pursuit of titanic labors." At the risk of seeming repetitious it is worth while to point out that his task, viewed as a whole, does not seem titanic. His first volume was perhaps begun in 1832, his last, the twelfth, was finished fifty years later, in 1882. The twelve volumes, including the "History of the Formation of the Constitution," contain on an average 141,000 words each, or about 1,700,000 words in all. Rhodes's well-known work contains 1,410,000 words, in seven volumes, and it was written in about sixteen years. The author, like Bancroft, was a man of leisure and in a position to employ assistance as freely as it was needed, and the task was certainly not less difficult in itself than Bancroft's. Professor McMaster's work contains about 2,208,000 words and was completed in about thirty-five years, the author being at the same time engaged in the active work of teaching. Hildreth's work, which for accuracy of statement has stood the test of time better than Bancroft's, contains about 1,162,000 words and was probably written in less than ten years. If we take out of the fifty years which passed between the beginning and the end of Bancroft's work on his "History" the ten which he gave to his diplomatic career, he still appears as a slow worker in comparison with those other American historians who have a right to be ranked in the same circle with him.[1]

[1] THE BANCROFT MANUSCRIPT COLLECTION

Bancroft's manuscripts, originals and transcripts, were purchased by James Lenox in 1893 and placed in the Lenox Library, whence they have come into the possession of the New York Public Library. Among the originals were the valuable Samuel Adams Papers, including: (a) letters to Adams from revolutionary leaders, 1300 pieces; (b) minutes of the Boston Committee of Correspondence, 1772–1774; (c) letters and papers addressed to the Committee, 1772–1775; and (d) notes and proceedings of the Massachusetts assembly, 1773–1774. Other collections were: the papers of Major Joseph Hawley, of Northampton, Massachusetts, 1653–1789; the papers of General Riedesel, 1776–1783; the "Anspach Papers," 1776–1784; and the "Hessian Papers."

The transcripts include two hundred and ten bound volumes. Among them are: "Papers from the English State Papers Office," "Papers from Landsdowne House," "Papers from the French Archives," "Austrian Papers," "Bertholff Papers," "Bernard Papers," "Brunswick Papers," "Chalmers Papers"—on the Carolinas, Georgia, and Rhode Island, "Georgia Papers," "Connecticut Papers," "Correspondence of George III.," "Ellsworth Papers," "Colden Papers," "Glover Papers," "Hartley Papers," "Hollis Papers," "Hutchinson Papers," "W. S. Johnson Papers," "Langdon-Elwyn Papers," "Livingston Papers," "Mason Papers," "Marion Papers," "Patterson Papers," "Thomas Penn Papers," "Rush Papers," "Schuyler Papers," "Warren Papers," "Wayne Papers," "Strachey Papers," "Stiles Papers," "Quebec Papers," "Letters of Governor Pownall to Dr. Cooper," "President Polk's Diary and Correspondence," "General Greene's Letter-Book," and several other collections.

For information concerning the manuscripts see: Report of the Lenox Library, 1893, pp. 10–12; Palsist, "The Manuscripts of the New York Public Library" (1915), p. 14; and Sabin, "The Library of the late Hon. George Bancroft," n. d., about 1892. In the *Bulletin* of the New York Public Library, Vol. V., (July, 1901), is a calendar of the "Manuscript Collection in the New York Public Library" in which will be found the Bancroft items alphabetized with other manuscripts.

CHAPTER IV

TWO LITERARY HISTORIANS

1. *William Hickling Prescott*

WILLIAM HICKLING PRESCOTT and John Lothrop Motley have been discussed so often as literary men that here it is not necessary to do more than assign them the places they deserve in the Middle Group of our Historians. Neither wrote our own history, neither wrote history because he felt a call to set forth the story of his country, but each selected history as the form of literary achievement in which he could find an attractive and appreciated subject for his power of narration. Each wrote because it was in him to write, following an impulse which we may call professional.

Prescott and Motley belonged to a small circle of educated Bostonians, most of them Harvard graduates, who made the first half of the nineteenth century as brilliant as another group,—in which were Longfellow, Lowell, Holmes, and Emerson, — made brilliant the second half of the same century. Of the first group, Bancroft, Sparks, and George Ticknor were also members. It was a sane group, not given to reforms, untouched by the anti-slavery enthusiasm which gave a tone of provincialism to the later group. For them literature was a profession in which each man strove to succeed for the mere love of excelling, not for the easing of a conscience big with humanitarian ideals.

Prescott was born in Salem, May 4, 1796, but his father, a lawyer of great ability, moved to Boston in 1808.   In the city, William early had the run of the Boston Athenæum, already rich in historical literature, and he graduated from Harvard in 1814 with distinction, being, like many other men of old Harvard who rose to eminence, only eighteen years old. While a junior at college one of his eyes was injured by a piece of bread thrown in a boyish frolic in the Commons Hall with the result that its sight was completely destroyed. After graduation his other eye, the right, developed inflammation, heightened by inflammatory rheumatism, and for several years he could do nothing but nurse it most carefully, lest he be left totally blind.   A visit to Europe brought no relief, and he at last settled down to a state of half invalidism, sitting for weeks in a dark room, and exercising systematically in order that a good state of general health might enable him to combat the tendency of the eye to deteriorate.   Fortunately, he had ample means to employ a reader and keep up his intellectual exercises.

Great will power was one of Prescott's characteristics, and he determined that his accident should not defeat his purpose to lead a useful life.   He turned to literature and directed his reading with an idea of laying the broadest foundation in the cultivated branches. Language was mastered as a preliminary, and with it went severe drill in the art of literary expression. For a time Italian literature fascinated him; but at length he settled upon history, which, he said, had been a favorite study from boyhood.

While gathering up his mental equipment for his task he came upon Mably's essay, "Sur l'Étude de l'Histoire," published in 1775 for the instruction of the heir to the dukedom of Parma. The author had many limitations, from the modern standpoint; but he had penetration and laid great stress upon the use of dramatic form in presenting historical events. Prescott was much impressed and read the book through ten times. He also studied carefully the construction of Voltaire's "Charles XII" and Roscoe's "Lorenzo de Medici" and "Leo X".

In the spring of 1826 he definitely settled on the reign of Ferdinand and Isabella of Spain as his subject, and began to collect books upon it. It was a theme on which he could find in Spanish and French a number of good secondary works and contemporary accounts. Such as he could buy were imported, while some were obtained by copying them in manuscript. He spared no reasonable expense in securing his object. He was fortunate in having a good literary assistant, who came to him every day at ten and remained until dinner at three. All this time was spent in reading, marking passages that were deemed important, and taking notes. For writing Prescott used a nocograph, a frame with wires stretched across like the lines on ruled paper. Beneath it was a kind of carbon paper, the black side down. Guiding his hand with the wire he wrote on the reverse of the carbon-paper with an ivory stylus, transferring the mark to a sheet of white paper underneath. The rate of progress was slow, but at last the book was finished in three volumes in 1836.

The reception of "Ferdinand and Isabella" was more favorable than could have been expected. The author had serious doubts about the wisdom of an American edition, and it was only the strong urging of his friends that induced him to permit one to be brought out. To his doubts his father said: "The man who writes a book which he is afraid to publish is a coward"; and as cowardice was a quality entirely foreign to the son's nature, the attempt was made. To the surprise of all concerned the book succeeded at once. The city of Boston took five hundred copies, before any could be spared for out-of-town orders; and the first edition of twelve hundred and fifty copies, which by the terms of the contract the publishers were to have five years to dispose of, were sold in almost as many months. This rapid success was partly due to the interest his friends felt in the work. No book was ever more fortunate in its reviewers. One of them, who had read the proofs and advised about the style,

wrote a long review for the *North American ;* Bancroft
wrote for the *Democratic Review,* and still others wrote
for other periodicals.   When the Boston coterie got
behind a book, it was most likely to succeed.

The English edition was equally well received, though
the sale abroad did not reach that in America.   The
British reviews gave it long and, on the whole, favorable
notices.   The best scholar in the field of Spanish history then living on the Continent, Count Adolphe de
Circourt, gave it a review of more than one hundred
and eighty pages in the *Bibliothèque Universelle de
Genève.*   In every quarter Prescott was hailed as a
scholar and a charming writer.

Encouraged by his success, he looked around for
another subject.   For a time he thought of writing a
life of Molière, which shows how little he had come
to look upon himself as merely a historian.   But the
general approval of his efforts in the Spanish field led
him to decide to write upon the achievements of Cortes
in Mexico.   With his usual thoroughness he sent to
Madrid for books and ordered copies of the manuscripts
in the Spanish archives, which had recently been opened
to students in other countries than Spain.   Three
hundred pounds were sent to Madrid to be used in this
quest, while liberal orders were placed in London.
While waiting for this material to arrive he used the
books he found in the Harvard library.

When he was fairly at work, his friend, Joseph
Green Cogswell, in New York, encountered Washington

Irving in a New York library collecting material for the same undertaking. When Irving learned that Prescott was embarked on this task, he generously retired from the field. To Cogswell he said that his work on the proposed subject was not well advanced; but his biographer asserted years later that Irving's efforts had gone much further than, in his courtesy, he allowed Prescott to think. It is rare that we have in our literary history so noble an example of an author's self-denial; and it is a fortunate country in the ranks of whose historians are at one time two such men so well qualified to write brilliantly about an important phase of history.

In the preface to this work Prescott places a statement, quite casually, which may well be a matter of reflection for those who would understand his art of presentation. Referring to the fact that he had carried his story beyond the capture of the City of Mexico, which properly terminated the "Conquest," he says in explanation of his course:

"I am not insensible of the hazard I incur by such a course. The mind, previously occupied with one great idea, that of the subversion of the capital, may feel the prolongation of the story beyond that point superfluous, if not tedious; and may find it difficult, after the excitement caused by witnessing a great national catastrophe, to take an interest in the adventures of a private individual. Solis [1] took the more politic course of concluding his

[1] Antonio de Solis y Rivadeneyra. His "History of the Conquest of Mexico by the Spaniards" (1684) was very popular in Spain on account of its elegant literary style. It is not reliable for facts, as Prescott admits.

narrative with the fall of Mexico, and thus leaves his readers with the full impression of that memorable event, undisturbed, on their minds. To prolong the narrative is to expose the historian to the error so much censured by the French critics in some of their most celebrated dramas, where the author by a premature *dénouement* has impaired the interest of his piece."

Two things are here apparent: first, Prescott wrote with his eye fixed on the impression his writing would have on the attention of the reader; and second, he had a full sense of the similarity of the historian's and the dramatist's tasks. Each craftsman was constructing a narrative in which there was unity of thought and purpose moving to a climax.

Prescott's delight in writing spirited and dramatic narrative was tried by the necessity, as he deemed it, of incorporating at the beginning of his book an account of the civilization of the ancient Mexicans. It was the kind of didactic composition which is familiar enough to modern students of history, who may well study his book to see how it can be done without becoming tedious to the reader. Although Prescott accepted the prevailing Spanish theory that the Mexicans were more advanced in ideas and manners than we are to-day willing to admit, and gave to his story a character that is now practically worthless, his account of early Mexican life is a model of good form and entertaining reading. He said that it cost him as much labor and nearly as much time as the rest of the book, although it filled only half of one of his three volumes.

The "Conquest of Mexico" was published in 1843, five years after he had begun to investigate the subject. For three of these years he had worked most unremittingly, a thing he was able to do through a marked improvement of his eye. It was with no doubts that he awaited the verdict of the public; for he was now of established reputation, and he knew the cunning of his own hand. But he could not have been ready for the outburst of applause that came from reviewers and friends. The sales were large. Five thousand copies were disposed of in the United States in four months, and an English edition went off in six. Edition after edition was called for as the years passed, and it was a long time before the book ceased to be a popular favorite.

Allowing himself a short period of rest, "literary loafing" he called it, Prescott now turned to the "Conquest of Peru." Here, also, he introduced the narrative with a study of social conditions in old Peru. A large collection of books on the subject, imported from Europe, furnished him with the necessary materials. At times he worked with great intenseness. In fact, he was so persistent that he strained his eye, and the latter part of the task was done chiefly with the aid of an assistant. The book was completed late in 1846 and was published in the spring of 1847. A new book by Prescott was now an event. The "Conquest of Peru" had an immediate success equal to that of its predecessors. In five months five thousand copies

were sold in the United States, and half as many
in Great Britain. It was translated into French,
German, Spanish, and Dutch.

Prescott closed his series of works on the Spanish
relations with a "History of Philip the Second," for
which he had begun to gather materials as early as
1842. He advanced to the actual performance of the
task in 1847, the year after he had completed the
"Peru." Here, as in writing the "Mexico," he
learned that he was in conflict with another man.
Motley, then looking about for a historical subject,
had hit upon the same theme. Fortunately, he
learned of Prescott's plans before beginning serious
labor. Then followed an interview between the
two men, Prescott urging Motley to go on with his
plans, saying that there was room for two books on
the same subject and offering the use of his library
and manuscripts. Motley was deeply impressed with
his kindness, but was able to give his own efforts to
only a part of what might have been considered the
career of Philip, that part which related to his dealing
with the Low Countries.

Prescott, in the meantime, went on slowly with his
work. In no part of his labors was he more hampered
by his eyesight. Many days he could use the one eye
that could yield any comfort for not more than ten
minutes, and never for more than an hour. He wrote
the book, as he himself said, under the conditions in
which a blind man must have written it. Depressed by

this phase of the matter, he found it difficult to lose himself in the task. His feelings reacted on his general health, he lost flesh, and those closest to him had serious fears for his condition. They at last persuaded him to give up the work for a time and make a journey to Europe. Most of 1850 was spent in England and in a flying trip to the Continent; and he returned home in excellent spirits. He now worked with real enthusiasm; and in 1855 he published the first two volumes. Work on the third volume proceeded slowly on account of decreasing strength. February 4, 1858, when it was nearing completion, he was stricken with apoplexy and for several days the gravest consequences were feared. His system, however, responded to treatment, and in a few weeks he was again able to resume work. But the attack had given him fair warning of what he might expect, and he hastened to finish the volume, leaving off some of the finishing touches he would otherwise have given it. Late in the summer the third volume was sent to the press. A fourth, which was within his plan, was never completed. In fact, his working life was over. After a few months of slowly weakening powers his frame gave way before a second stroke of apoplexy that came upon him just as he was beginning his work for the fourth volume. He died on January 28, 1859.

Every age has its historical ideals just as it has its political ideals. In Prescott's time the world liked the narrative form best of all. He was a part of his age.

It was no clever trick of hitting that which was popular that made him seek to tell a story well, but a conviction shared by all other historians of the day, that history was one of the literary arts. He believed intensely in the school to which he belonged. As for truth, he was not indifferent to it; and he delved patiently and conscientiously into the great mass of information before him. That he was not critical in the modern sense was due to the ideals of the time.

His manner of work was very systematic. All his forenoons were at his disposal and the first hours of the afternoons. He used them conscientiously, when he was in the working mood. But he was, like many another historian, subject to fits of listlessness, from which he sought by many devices to rally himself. His "Memoranda," a kind of diary of his literary progress kept at intervals, was made the confidant of many tricks set to induce himself to live up to his good resolutions. When once the fits were over and interest in the present task aroused, he worked with happy steadiness. He was very human and was apt to take his friends into his confidence in regard to all his fancied shortcomings. In George Ticknor, the noted professor of Spanish literature at Harvard, he had a very sympathetic and useful friend; and, as it happened, a most enlightening biographer. No historian who feels the need of impulse to keep him up to his own task can do better than read Ticknor's "Life of William H. Prescott."

Prescott's financial independence was of great advantage in his work. It enabled him to secure books, to have manuscripts copied, and to employ assistants who read for him. In our own day great libraries and large manuscript collections offer the poorer student that which wealth alone could acquire a century ago, and simple living may equalize many other evils of poverty. Not every rich man uses his wealth as Prescott. It was his glory that being able to give himself to a life of pleasure, with the excuse of poor health to reconcile himself to self-indulgence, he never compromised with such a temptation and always lived as though life had as much an obligation for him as for anybody.

It is an interesting speculation as to how much he was, under the circumstances, hindered and how much benefited by his defective eyesight. While it made it impossible for him to use his eyes in long periods, it took from him, on the other hand, a vast amount of the social frivolity which is thrust on any but the most heroic men under normal conditions. Prescott's partial blindness left him free to devote most of his available energy to his chosen field. It perhaps served, also, to develop the habit of concentration. When a man knows that he has only an hour to write in a day, he is apt to make that hour express the most exact and telling thought of the whole day. By throwing much work on the memory that faculty was strengthened. During the periods of enforced inactivity he developed his ideas and thus matured in his own mind what he meant to write down.

2. *John Lothrop Motley*

As Prescott vanished from the scene of activities John Lothrop Motley was just coming upon it. He too, was of Boston, son of a wealthy merchant and born to the best things that the city could give. He was prepared for college at the celebrated Round Hill School, in Northampton, entered Harvard in 1827, and graduated in 1831, when seventeen years old. From 1832 to 1834 he was a student at Göttingen and Berlin, and returned to Boston to read law, a study for which he had little liking. From early life he was given to literary efforts, and soon threw aside thoughts of being a lawyer to attempt to win fame writing novels. His first story, "Morton's Hope," was full of his personal feelings and traced his career in Europe with fair accuracy, but it lacked plot and as a story it was a failure.

We think of Motley, as of Prescott, as a literary historian. He was brought up in a school that loved poetry and was acquainted with the great masterpieces. He had read much and his mind teemed with quotations, but his novels failed because his plots were poor. In history he had a plot ready made, and he used his imagination in rounding out the plot, marshaling the facts in picturesque array, drawing vivid character pictures, and adjusting the scenes so

as to present a wonderful picture. Richness and
warmth of color, and strong passions, were there, and
always a deep sympathy with human life. It is to be
regretted that no adequate biography of the man has
been written. The volumes of his letters that have
been published seem to be more concerned with showing what fine company Motley kept than with revealing
the manner in which he mastered his craft. It is as an
historian, and not as a man of the world that Motley
interests us. This sketch can do no more than enu-
merate his efforts in history and give the reader an
inkling of what awaits him when the proper life of the
man is written.

In 1841, Motley was appointed secretary of legation
at Petrograd (St. Petersburg), but the life at court disgusted him and he resigned in a few months. In 1849
he was elected member of the Massachusetts House of
Representatives, but one term in that body convinced
him that he was no politician. In the same year he
published another novel, "Merry Mount," written
several years earlier, but its reception was dismal. At
this time the only things he had done with real success were some historical and biographical essays for
the *North American Review*, in which he had shown
some of the qualities which were later to make him
famous. Taking stock of his achievements, he seems
to have concluded that here was the trail worth following, and he gave himself to history for better or worse.
He was much influenced by the success of Prescott,

then at the height of his renown. Turned aside, as
we have seen, from the life of Philip the Second, he
took up the field of Dutch history. It pleased him
as the struggle of a democratic people against absolute
power. It was full of dramatic incidents, as all history
is full, when the right man comes to seek them. To
get first-hand information he went to the Low Countries in 1851, settling finally in Brussels, where he
buried himself in libraries and document offices. After
several months in the place he could say that he did
not know a soul in Brussels. But he knew well the
city's past. "The dead men of the place," he said,
"are my intimate friends. I am at home in any
cemetery. With the fellows of the sixteenth century
I am on the most familiar terms. Any ghost that ever
flits by night across the moonlight square is at once
hailed by me as a man and a brother. I call him by
his Christian name at once."

In 1856 he was ready to publish the result of his
labor, the "Rise of the Dutch Republic," in three volumes. He offered the manuscript to Murray, the
leading London publisher, who refused it. Not
daunted he brought it out with another firm at his own
expense, arranging for an American edition at the
same time. The immediate success of the book was so
great that Murray wrote, acknowledging his mistake,
and asking to be allowed to publish the author's next
work. Froude, himself a great stylist, said in review-
ing the book: "All the essentials of a great writer

Mr. Motley eminently possesses. His mind is broad, his industry unwearied. In power of dramatic description no modern historian, except perhaps Mr. Carlyle, surpasses him, and in analysis of character he is elaborate and distinct. His principles are those of honest love for all which is good and admirable in human character wherever he finds it, while he unaffectedly hates oppression, and despises selfishness with all his heart." Francis Lieber praised the book highly and said : "It will leave its distinct mark upon the American mind."

In 1858 Motley returned to Europe from a visit to the United States. A brilliant social reception overwhelmed him, but he soon fled to his historical materials on the Continent. His plans had now taken definite shape, and he announced them to his friends. He would, he said, write a history of "The Eighty Years' War for Liberty,"in three epochs. The first was the "Rise of the Dutch Republic," the second he would call "Independence Achieved," 1584-1609, and the third would be "Independence Recognized," 1609-1648. This grand scheme would cut a cross section in the history of Europe at one of its most interesting and turbulent stages. The scheme was not carried out as formed.

Two years after his return — in 1860 — the world received the first two volumes of the "History of the United Netherlands." Later in the same year, the author hired a house in London, with the intention of

going on with his work.   But the outbreak of the civil
war brought him back to his native land, where, to
his surprise, he suddenly found himself packed off to
Europe again, this time as minister to Austria. The
great struggle at home absorbed his interest, and
literary labors advanced slightly until it was evident
victory was turning to the side of the Union. In his
letters he spoke longingly of his desire to get back to
the Dutchmen of the seventeenth century.

He remained in Vienna until 1866, when he resigned
in a burst of sensitive anger called forth by an irre-
sponsible accusation. A letter arrived in Washington from one who called himself an American citizen
traveling in Europe, containing coarse charges against
several diplomatic representatives of the government in Europe. Motley was charged with being a
toady to aristocrats, and with criticizing the President,
Andrew Johnson. Secretary Seward wrote to Motley asking for a denial of the charges.   The latter took
this communication as an insult. He felt that his
government had lost confidence in him, and sent his
resignation forthwith.

Two years later, 1868, he published the third and
fourth volumes of the "History of the United Netherlands."   To his friends he announced that he would
proceed at once with the history of the Thirty Years'
War, and with this his life-work would be over. But
he was not to fulfill the promise. Returning the same
year to Boston he was appointed in the following year

minister to Great Britain and left for the post at once. Of the controversy that arose over his recall in 1870, this sketch is too short to take full notice. Suffice it to say, that it is generally held that President Grant, angered at Senator Sumner's opposition to his Santo Domingo treaty, sought to humiliate the Massachusetts senator by removing Motley, his friend, from office. The grounds alleged were some indiscreet actions of Motley's in negotiations that were past more than a year and which Motley had every reason to think were condoned and forgotten. It is hard to avoid the conclusion that he was the object of very illiberal treatment.

Deeply wounded in his feelings, Motley turned to his pen for consolation. He worked with steadiness and pleasure on his great scheme, and in 1874 gave to the public the "Life and Death of John of Barneveld, Advocate of Holland; with a view of the primary Causes and Movements of the Thirty Years' War." It was something of a digression from his main object, the Thirty Years' War, but he was interested in the career of the man, and he convinced himself that its importance justified its rather lengthy insertion in his grand series. It was a splendid picture of a man's career, vivid, unified and full of force.

Motley would now have gone on with the last part of his scheme. Work was the only solace left him after the unhappy ending of his diplomatic career. But on the last day of the year in which "Barneveld"

was published, 1874, Mrs. Motley died. He was
deeply attached to her, who had been a companion
in all he did, and his sensitive nature did not recover
from the shock. Returning the following year to
Boston on a visit, in which the influence of former
scenes did nothing to restore his spirits, he went
back to London to await the end. He died near
Dorchester, England, in 1877.

As a literary man Motley must be considered the
last prominent historian of the early school, or the
first of the newer school of scientific research. He
belonged to one or the other, as you will. He was
modern in the deep devotion he showed for research.
No document was too old or difficult to balk his patient
inspection. No one ever delved deeper in archives nor
knocked more persistently at the closed doors of record
offices, pounding generally until they were opened.
On the other hand, he had not the modern historian's
sense of detachment. He frankly took sides. He
hated the absolute government of the Spanish mon-
archy, he disliked the dogmas of the Roman church,
and he could not abide the repressive spirit of the Roman hierarchy. His histories were Protestant through
and through. He drew Philip the Second as black as
he could, but no blacker than Protestants have drawn
him through many decades. Motley was a one-sided
historian.

This is not to say that his one-sidedness was utterly
discreditable. It undoubtedly puts him out of the

ranks of the moderns. He cannot be called scientific.
But what he lost in balance he gained in intentness.
Happy the historian, from his own point of view, who
has no need to weigh evidence pro and con. For him
the steady rush of narration, the flicker of light and
shade in delicate shimmers when needed, or in rich
bands of gorgeous color when the wizard who manipu-
lates the brush thinks they are essential to his picture. For him also the applause of a broad public.
American education, universal though it be, has not
yet resulted in an average man who is capable of
balanced thought on important historical matters.
The historian of the future may have the happy fortune
of knowing that his detached history will find a just
appreciation from a detached public. At present
we are in a seemingly transitional stage. He who is
venturesome enough to write a book, dares not make
it the defense of any particular view, lest he perish at
the hands of the critics; nor does he relish displeasing
the public, since in so doing he may die of malnutri-
tion. His only refuge is to flee to the house of the
pedagogue, where food and raiment at least may
be had.

Oliver Wendell Holmes aptly compares Motley's
style to Rubens' paintings. "There is a certain
affinity," he says, "between those sumptuous and
glowing works of art and the prose pictures of the
historian who so admired them. He was himself
a colorist in language, and called up the image of a

great personage or a splendid pageant of the past
with the same affluence, the same rich vitality, that
floods and warms the vast areas of canvas over which
the full-fed genius of Rubens disported itself in the
luxury of imaginative creation." The words are well
chosen. Motley was a colorist. His compositions
were large and well lit up with line and pigment.
If it is the simple and strong feeling of Jean François
Millet that you like do not look for it here. The
Dutchman painted religious and royal scenes, the
American portrayed religious and courtly struggles.
Saints, princes, and courtiers fill the canvas of the
one; theologians, rulers, and diplomatists fill the pages
of the other.

As for me, I prefer the less magnificent portrayals
of Prescott. Here are heroes also, hidalgos and stark
warriors, but they do not march in gangs. Each
man stands out in simple outlines, and it is not difficult
to see what he is doing. Prescott, also, was more
direct in his language and more symmetrical in his
chapter constructions. I get lost at times in the mazes
of courtly intrigue that Motley reproduces, and I
cannot help feeling that somehow Prescott would
have found a way of cutting vistas through them,
so that I could see my way ahead.

It is impossible to read the books of the more popular historians of the middle group without having a
feeling of admiration for their careful mastery of the
arts of narration. No living man of the new school

has won, or is likely to win, as much success as they won in their day. We could not go back to their school — that would be retrogressing; but if we could only bring forward their best qualities into our own group of scholarly and conscientious workers, the results would be well worth the effort.

CHAPTER V

PETER FORCE, THE COMPILER

1. *His Early Career*

PETER FORCE was born of poor parents at Passaic Falls, New Jersey, November 26, 1790. Three years later the family moved to the town of New York, where the boy got such a smattering of education as was then offered in the schools of the poor. His father died soon afterwards, and Peter at about the age of twelve entered the printing office of William Davis, a man of enough local importance to become an alderman. Davis's establishment was at Bloomingdale, about five miles north of the Battery; and the small village was rich in Dutch traditions. Steady habits, industry, and the faculty of accepting responsibility made young Force a marked boy among the inmates of the shop, and at the age of sixteen he was a foreman.

A story of this early period of his life represents him as sent, while still a printer's boy, to carry to the author the proof of the revised edition of Irving's "Knickerbocker History of New York." Sitting by the roadside to read the fascinating story, he came to a place in which the author had mentioned some typical Dutch families. In the margin Peter wrote several other names, gathered from his observations in Bloomingdale, and Irving allowed them to stand. Many years later Force met Irving and told him to whom he was indebted for this bit of literary collaboration. So runs the story, which Lossing says he had from Force himself. It is somewhat spoiled by the fact that "Knickerbocker" was first published in December, 1809, and the second edition, published in New York, appeared in 1812. At that time Peter Force was twenty-two years old, and had been nearly six years head of the printing shop. He was hardly likely to be sent back and forth with proof at that age.[1]

The year 1812 brought him an honor still more significant in his election to the presidency of the Typographical Society of New York. Such an elevation to high rank of a man of twenty-two indicates that he had the power of leadership. He was equally earnest in the militia of New York and during the war served two tours of duty of three months each. Here also, he inspired confidence, and in 1815, after having served as a sergeant and sergeant-major, he was commissioned ensign, and in the following year was lieutenant of militia.

[1] March 29, 1812, Irving wrote Brevoort that he had made a bargain with Inskeep, to bring out the revised edition and said he was "about publishing." He was then living with Mrs. Ryckman,' on Broadway, near Bowling Green, where Brevoort had also lived until a few months previously he had left for Europe. During the summer, however, Irving resided near Hellgate for a few weeks. See Pierre M. Irving, "Life and Letters of Washington Irving," I, 281, 283.

In the latter year his scene of activity shifted. His employer, Davis, had political influence, and being awarded a contract for a part of the printing of the federal government found it advisable to open a shop in Washington City. He sent Force to take charge of the enterprise, and immediately, or soon afterwards, the new office was conducted under the firm name of Davis and Force.

By nature Peter Force was not suited to play the part of government printer. He was a man of downright principles, outspoken, and unwilling to bend to the winds of party favor. He was such a man as would take a dominant position in whatever group he made a part, and he would not follow orders.

All through his residence in Washington he was active in local affairs. He became as prominent in the militia of the District of Columbia as he had been in New York. Promotions came in due time. He was a captain of artillery in 1824, a lieutenant-colonel in 1830, a colonel of artillery in 1840, and a major-general of militia in 1860. Throughout his later career he was generally known as "Colonel Force." At the same time that he rose in the militia he rose in local politics. He was elected to the city council in 1832, and soon afterwards became its president. Next he became an alderman and president of the board of aldermen; and in 1836 he became mayor, holding the position for four years. These successes were based on his popularity with the masses

of his fellow citizens. He was a self-made man of
fine natural parts, and the people felt that he was one
of them. One who had received better educational
advantages, or who was born to higher rank, would
probably have been little interested in the honors
which Washington politics and militia service could have
bestowed. In a city like the national capital he would
probably have aspired to fill some high federal office.

Force's love of books was another phase of his
character, and with advancing years it came to rule
all other desires. When still a boy he is said to have
written "The Unwritten History of the War in New
Jersey," a collection of revolutionary stories he had
heard at the fireside of his father, who was a revolutionary soldier. The manuscript was lost before the
boy was old enough to put it into type, but writing
it shows the bent of his mind from his earliest years.

His next literary project, it seems, was a literary
journal, the prospectus for which was dated December
6, 1817. It was to be known as *The American Quarterly Review*, and the first number, announced for
April, 1818, was to contain articles on General Wil-
kinson's "Memoirs" and Wirt's "Life of Patrick
Henry," besides a history of the proceedings and debates of the first session of the fifteenth congress.
The enterprise was rashly planned and it seems that
the first number did not appear, although the prospectus was inserted in the *National Intelligencer*,
January 3, 1818.

In 1820–1828 Force compiled and published the "Biennial Register," a book brought out by order of congress with the names of public officials and much information about the machinery of the government. Force changed the name to the "Blue Book." [1] In the same year he began to publish, on his own account, the "National Calendar and Annals of the United States." It contained matter so much like that of the "Blue Book" as to suggest that he merely enlarged the government document by the addition of other matter and published it with a change of title. The "Calendar" was issued annually, until 1838,[2] with the exception of the years 1825, 1826, and 1827. It contained statistics of both federal and state affairs.

In 1823 Force established the *National Journal*, for several years an influential newspaper in the capital. A prospectus, dated August, 1823, announced that the paper would be issued twice a week, with a weekly "Extra," containing congressional debates, reports, and laws. The prospectus was unsigned, but it directed that communications relating to the enterprise be sent to Davis and Force, printers and stationers. In August, 1824, the paper became a daily. From the first it was an Adams organ, although its editor had furnished all the money for its establishment. It was, in fact, a most independent party

[1] See an article from the *Round Table*, reprinted in the *Historical Magazine*, IX, pp. 335-338 (1865).

[2] So says Sabin, but I have found no set that goes further than 1836. — AUTHOR.

paper, and the Adams leaders were disappointed at its lack of fervor. Several of them held a meeting to determine what was to be done. They finally sent one of their number to suggest that the editor should allow a committee of his friends to assist him in his editorial labors. When the cautious emissary dropped the first hint of his plan, Force said with decision: "But I do not suppose any gentleman would make such a proposition to me!" The messenger retreated as gracefully as he could, and nothing further was said about the plan to put the editorship in commission. In 1830 Force retired from the conduct of the paper, which suspended publication soon afterwards. At that time the Adams party was a thing of the past. Clay's more energetic and less conservative leadership demanded a more partisan organ than Force was capable of conducting.

Force is sometimes said to have published the "Directory of Congress," but he seems to have had no other connection with it than to print it. This enterprise goes back as early as 1809, when there began a series of annuals, under one name or another, in which were given the names and residences of members of congress and other prominent officials. For a long time it was published by Jonathan Elliot, Jr. Blair and Rives sometimes brought it out, and sometimes we find two editions for the same year, apparently identical except as to title-page. It was a private enterprise and was probably intended chiefly for the use of those whom business or curiosity impelled to seek the federal officials. Force's name appears on an edition of 1820. The edition of 1839 contained diagrams showing the seating of the senate and the house. It was a feature likely to find favor with those who occupied the galleries in the capitol. In 1841 and 1842 an edition appeared with Peter Force's imprint. It was identical with an edition in the same years with the imprint of Robert Farnham. In 1843–1844 came an edition by W. Q. Force, son of Colonel Force, and with that ends the connection of the family with the "Directory of Congress." The remainder of this story deals with the historical activities of Colonel Force, which constitute my sole reason for laying his career before the reader.

2. *The American Archives; Origin of the Enterprise*

It is not easy to find the origin of a movement which between the years 1827 and 1837 resulted in the publication of Sparks's "Diplomatic Correspondence of the American Revolution" and the beginning of his great work on Washington, the publication of Blair and Rives's collection of "State Papers," and the fair launching of Colonel Peter Force's great series the "American Archives." We find the idea that inspired all these works in the "Documentary History of the Revolution," planned by Ebenezer Hazard just after the revolution, but never carried to completion. It reappears in Jedediah Morse's

"Annals of the American Revolution," 1824, an inadequate compilation which made only a slight impression on either contemporaries or posterity. But
while we are guessing we cannot ignore the influence
of Chalmers's "Political Annals of the Colonies,"
1780,[1] a well-written work based upon original materials
in the British public offices. Frequent mention of
Chalmers's book is made in the letters of the men of
the period under consideration, and it was a constant
reminder to them of the need of collecting and using
the scattered materials in the various parts of our
own country.

Probably the earliest compendious scheme for a
historical work at the epoch just mentioned was that
projected as early as 1819 by Judge Archibald D.
Murphey, of North Carolina. An able lawyer with
an active practice, he had no special training for
history writing; but his strong mind and deep
interest in every phase of the life of the people
led him to plan an all-embracing treatment of the
state's history. If carried out as announced it
would have required five volumes to treat of the
early charters, the military and civil affairs, the physical condition, the progress of society, and the economic
development of North Carolina. No state has, up
to this day, written its history so extensively.
Judge Murphey collected materials, mostly, it seems,

[1] His "Introduction to the History of the Revolt" was not published
until 1845.

the reminiscences of men living in his day. After a time he came to realize that he needed documents in the keeping of the British government, in London; and in 1825 he called upon the assembly for aid in publishing the work. He was given authority to establish a lottery to raise money in order to send an agent to London to collect materials and to defray the expenses of publication. The project was well received by the newspapers, and Fourth-of-July toasts were drunk to its success, but the tickets sold slowly. In 1827 the assembly took steps by which the lottery could be enlarged so that he could raise $25,000 instead of the $15,000 first authorized.[1] Nothing came of these efforts, and in 1832 Murphey died, overwhelmed with debt and disappointment. His proposed history got no further than the collection of some of the materials he needed. He wrote a polished sentence and had a proper sense of the valuable things of history. Had he lived longer, and had he found himself master of enough time and concentration to carry through his scheme as planned, we should have possessed, in all likelihood, in his five or six volumes, a noble state history.

About this time several states made feeble efforts to get copies of historical papers from the public offices in England. Perhaps the first to act was North

[1] Hoyt, editor, "The Papers of Archibald D. Murphey," 2 vols., *Pubs. N. C. Histl. Commission*, I, 146, 187–206, 208–216, 220–238, 323–324, 326, 332, 338–341, 347 *n*, 350–353, 357, 361, 364, 395, 399; II, 361–363, 414, and *passim*.

Carolina, which in 1825, as we have seen, gave Murphey permission to establish a lottery, part of the proceeds of which were to be used in making copies in London. February 9, 1827, the assembly directed the governor to apply through the American minister in England for permission to copy historical documents relating to the colony of North Carolina. Cordial replies were received, granting the liberty to make copies of the papers in the custody of the board of trade and those indicated in a list which was forwarded. In 1825 a similar favor had been granted in reference to the records of the colony of Georgia, the request in this case coming from a private individual, Mr. Tattnall. November 15, 1826, Governor Troup recommended to the assembly that the state historiographer be sent to London to obtain the desired copies. December 7, 1827, the senate of South Carolina resolved that similar copies relating to the history of that state should be made; and in 1830 Henry N. Cruger, a citizen of the state, returned from England with a report on the whereabouts of the several kinds of papers on South Carolina history in the British public offices. All these efforts were without favorable results. They seem to have been due to the activities of a few individuals, who soon ceased to press them.[1]

[1] Clarke and Force, "Report to Secretary Forsythe on the Documentary History of the United States, pp. 14–22. See also Hoyt, editor, loc. cit., II., 362.

In the same year, 1827, a similar series of efforts was made in New England. The general assembly of Rhode Island voted that the state's senators and representatives be requested to endeavor to get the federal government to obtain copies of papers in the British offices "relating to the early history of this country." January 24, in the same year, the American Antiquarian Society voted to ask the Massachusetts delegation to use their efforts to the same end; and about the same time the Massachusetts Historical Society passed similar resolutions, signed by John Davis, James Savage, and James Bowdoin.[1] It seems hardly probable that the year 1827 should have seen so many and such widely separated efforts of a similar nature without some common course. Who stimulated this action it is impossible to tell. It could hardly have been Sparks; for although he made his first journey into the South to collect materials in 1826, his ample biography and his diary as well give no intimation that he had aught to do with the state efforts. It could not have been Bancroft; for he was still engrossed with the duties of schoolmaster at Northampton, and what literary opportunity he had was directed to schoolbooks and magazine articles. Nor could it have been Judge Murphey; for his influence was strictly local. Probably the movement was in the air, and Murphey, Sparks, state officials, and learned societies acted from a general impulse.

[1] Clarke and Force, "Report to Secretary Forsythe," pp. 22–26.

It was in the midst of this revival of interest in history that Peter Force came into the field as a collector of historical documents and as a compiler and publisher. When and how he formed his great project does not appear. He had a partner in the enterprise, but since he was the sustaining factor of the plan on its intellectual side, it is fair to assume that it originated with him, and there is no good reason to doubt his statement that he began to gather historical materials as early as 1822. His design was to publish in one collection all the historical evidence bearing on the revolution. We shall see how the scheme was amplified as he became better acquainted with the conditions under which it was to be carried through. From the first it was his intention that his publication should be a complete embodiment of all the material he could find on the subject proposed.

Force's partner was Matthew St. Clair Clarke, a native of Pennsylvania, who was clerk of the house of Representatives from 1822 to 1833, when he was defeated by Walter S. Franklin, also of Pennsylvania. He was again elected to the same position in 1841, and served for two years,[1] after which he appears as sixth auditor of the treasury department. That he was a man of wealth is shown by the fact that in the latter part of his career he lived in what was popularly said to be the finest house in Washington, on what was then called President's Square. He fur-

[1] House Journals, *passim*.

nished the money for expenses, while Force collected
materials, and it is evident that the partners relied on
his political influence to get the congressional appropriation on which depended the success of the undertaking.

In a statement which they laid before the secretary
of state, 1834, explaining their plans, we find this assertion: "About twelve years ago the plan of our
work was originally fixed upon. It began by the purchase and critical examination of books, pamphlets,
newspapers, and early periodical publications, containing or referring to documents, correspondence,
speeches, parliamentary and legislative proceedings,
etc., etc. Of these a large and very valuable collection
has been made, containing many papers not elsewhere to be found. During great part of the time
our progress was necessarily slow. For the last five
years, Mr. Force, excepting a short time in each year,
expended on his Annual Register, has been devoted to
this work, to the exclusion of every other pursuit." [1]

Since Force gave up the editorship of the *Journal*
early in 1830, we may fix upon the end of 1829 as the
time at which he gave himself up entirely to his
project. In 1829 appeared the first volume of Sparks's
"Diplomatic Correspondence" and eighteen months
later the work was completed in twelve volumes.
The editor's net profits must have been very satisfactory at a time when a salary of two thousand dollars

---

[1] Forsyth's Report, 1834.

a year was considered good.   In 1832 Blair and Rives, snatching it out of the very hands of Sparks, got a contract to continue this publication for the years 1783–1789.   Gales and Seaton got a contract in 1831 to publish the " American State Papers " at remunerative prices.[1]   Seeing these fine opportunities going into the hands of other men, probably spurred Force on to action.   In 1832 he had formed his partnership with Clarke and the two men were standing cap in hand before the door of the government.   It would be pleasant to speak of these various enterprises as disinterested labors of men devoted to scholarship; but such language would be only half the truth.   They were planned by persons who saw in government contracts opportunities to make money.   The rapidity with which one application followed another shows how quickly the men concerned saw the advantage that lay in the business.   It is fair to say that Force was, probably, least selfish of all the group. He was filled with a genuine devotion to an idea, but he was saturated with the spirit of Washington City, and he held steadfastly to the idea that he could get congress to publish his work and purchase the great collection of materials he was gathering.

3. *Relations with the Government*

It was in 1831, the year in which Blair and Rives, and Gales and Seaton, secured their contracts, that

[1] See above, p. 82.

Clarke and Force also began to seek recognition. July 18, they sent a memorial to Edward Livingston, secretary of state, proposing to publish "A Documentary History of the American Revolution, from the Commencement of the Restrictive Measures of Great Britain to the adoption of the Constitution of the United States in 1789." The work was to be in six divisions, as follows: 1. The origins of the several colonies, their charters and public papers up to 1763; 2. Materials on the years 1763 to 1765; 3. Materials on the years 1765 to 1774; 4. Materials on the period from the meeting of the first continental congress to the adoption of the Declaration of Independence; 5. Materials on the years from the adoption of the Declaration to the treaty of peace, 1776 to 1783; and 6. Materials on the period from the treaty of peace to the adoption of the constitution, 1783 to 1789. The memorialists said nothing at this time about compensation, but asked permission to copy and publish the papers in the public offices. The secretary replied, July 20, giving the desired permission.

Early in 1832 the matter was before Congress.[1] Clarke now saw Edward Everett, ever a patron of enterprises that had a literary flavor. February 1 he wrote saying that he would agree to print and deliver to the government 1500 copies of his proposed work at ten

[1] G. C. Verplanck to Jared Sparks, Jan 17, 1832. Sparks MSS. Harvard University Library.

dollars a volume, the form to be like that of the "American State Papers," which Gales and Seaton were then getting out.[1] He and Force would procure the copies of the papers to be published, with the exception of those that came from abroad, which he wished the government to furnish. In making his appeal Clarke referred to the vote of congress in 1781, in aid of Hazard's proposed "Documentary History of the Revolution," using it as a precedent for his and Force's request. In June, 1832, a bill was before congress subscribing to the proposed work at the rate of eight dollars a volume of eight hundred pages. It was voted down because the price was considered excessive.[2] In the following winter another bill appeared. It authorized the secretary of state to contract with Clarke and Force for the publication of "The Documentary History of the Revolution," provided the cost a volume should not be higher than that of Sparks's "Diplomatic Correspondence." The bill became a law on March 2, 1833, being carried through at the close of a strenuous session, in which nullification and the "Force bill" were the overwhelming topics of debate.[3]

Livingston now completed the contract in due form. Sparks's work had appeared in octavo form and the government had paid for it at the rate of $2.57⅓

[1] As clerk of the house of representatives, Clarke, with Lowrie, secretary of the senate, supervised the publication of the "State Papers," nine volumes of which appeared in 1832.

[2] Debates in Congress, 1835–1836, 3303 (Vol. XII, Part III).

[3] Peters, "U. S. Statutes at Large," IV, 654.

a page, taking 1000 copies averaging 537½ pages each. As the new work was to be folio in size and the number of copies were to be distributed liberally among the congressmen and the persons and institutions to which congress would wish to give them, 1500 copies were to be ordered. A practical printer was called on for an estimate transmuting the cost a volume of Sparks's book into that of the proposed work. The result was that it was agreed that the government would take fifteen hundred copies of the work in folio at the rate of one and seven-eighths cents a page a copy. Clarke and Force were to do all the work of collecting, editing, and printing at their own expense. In the rate hit upon, a small sum was allowed for indices, which were not in the "Diplomatic Correspondence." As each volume would have about eight hundred pages, the publishers would receive about fifteen dollars for it; that is, about twenty-two thousand five hundred dollars for each edition delivered.

Among the Force manuscripts are some memoranda which Force submitted to Clarke, who was not a printer, February 1, 1832, showing what the two men then thought of the enterprise as a business venture. Force said that five volumes would be required to carry out his plans, and for all of them in the size and style of the "State Papers," which he thought the preferable form, he gave the following estimate of the cost: "Paper, $9,375; composition, $6,912; presswork,

$4,320; binding, $7,500; total, $28,107." He proposed that the volumes be delivered for ten dollars each if a thousand were taken, or for eight dollars each if fifteen hundred were taken. The figures quoted are on the basis of five volumes with fifteen hundred copies of each. Force's memorandum also places the receipts from the sale at $75,000, showing that he was thinking of ten dollars a volume, instead of eight. On this basis he made the profit of the enterprise $46,893. But from it he has subtracted $15,000 without indicating the purpose. It is a fair guess that he meant that amount, $3000 a volume, to be deducted as the editor's pay for his services.

The estimate just given was modest in comparison with what came later. It showed Force's idea of the project in 1832, when he could hardly have had a correct view of the nature of the work upon which he wished to enter. Clarke, long accustomed, as clerk of the house, to the ways by which the government may be made to yield its favors, had a better realization of the opportunity before him. Among the manuscripts is the following for 1833, representing what the partners had in mind when the contract with the secretary of state was actually made: "Expense per volume according to the accompanying estimates, all of which are of the *highest rates*. The calculation is for a volume of 850 pages. 1. Printing, $3,612.50; 2. Binding, $2,250.00; 3. Paper, $2,232.00; 4. Index and other expenses, $2,580.00. Total, $10,674.50.

Leaves, over and above estimated expenses per volume, $11,000. The contract price for a volume of 850 pages, $21,675.00." Along with this memorandum is an estimate from a printer, R. S. Coxe; and in it is the following: "P. F. Shall, if he chooses, print and bind the work, in the manner and form required by the contract with the secretary of state on the following terms: 1. For Printing (including composition and press work), four dollars and twenty-five cents per page; 2. For Binding, one dollar and fifty cents per copy." It seems that Force and Clarke were thus paid at a higher rate than Gales and Seaton, although they claimed that their compensation was at a slightly lower rate than that of Sparks. Force himself, just quoted, said that the former were paid at the rate of eight dollars a volume for fifteen hundred copies and ten dollars a volume for one thousand volumes. But his own volumes, which contained only eighty-three per cent. as many words on the page as Gales and Seaton's, were sold to the government at fifteen dollars a volume for fifteen hundred copies.[1] This point should be borne in mind in connection with the great popular dissatisfaction when the terms of the agreement become known.

The contract signed, the two partners turned with zeal to the work of collecting materials. Force, it is true, had been collecting pamphlets and books for many years, but he had probably done little in gather-

[1] Force MSS. Library of Congress.

ing the actual manuscript materials. In the autumn of 1833 he was in New England, visiting state capitals, selecting documents and leaving orders for copies. Clarke was paying the bills, and at one time had so much difficulty to get money that his partner, at Concord, New Hampshire, was seriously inconvenienced. Clarke himself was in Boston and looked over the manuscripts in the possession of the Massachusetts Historical Society. When he saw how many there were he was horrified.[1]

He soon had other cause for anxiety. Both he and Force were supporters of Clay, and as such they were likely in 1834, when Clay was making his bitterest attacks on Jackson, to be the objects of the resentment of the supporters of Jackson. The attorney-general, Butler, of New York, was called on for his opinion on the legality of the contract. He could not deny that the agreement was legally made, but he declared that it was a bad bargain for the government, since it was unlimited as to the number of volumes and the final cost might be very great. To meet these objections Clarke, April 17, appealed to Polk, chairman of the ways and means committee. It was the nature of a work like this, he said, that it was impossible to tell how large it would become, since the materials were still unearthed. He and Force had suggested in the beginning that congress should

[1] Force to Clarke, Sept. 14, 1833; Clarke to Force, Sept. 12, 1833. Force MSS.

create a tribunal to determine what should go into the series, but the suggestion was ignored. They did not think the American people would object to paying thirty or forty thousand dollars a year to preserve their history in a form more reliable and complete than any other nation could hope to have of the history of its early years. Clarke closed by asking for an advance to pay for the expenses of preparing the first volume for the press. He said he hoped to bring out in 1835 all the documents on the years from May, 1774, to the end of 1776.[1] To Senator Chambers, of Maryland, who had said that the number of volumes might reach one hundred, Clarke replied it had been agreed that this was a matter which should be left to the judgment of the compilers, but that he was willing, if it was thought wise, to limit the work to twenty volumes.[2]

Livingston ceased to be secretary of state May 29, 1833. He was followed by Louis McLane, who seems to have had little interest in the "Documentary History." After him came John Forsyth, whose commission was dated June 27, 1834, but who actually entered office on July 1, not to leave it until March 3, 1841, when the Whigs came into power. Forsyth was a senator from Georgia in 1833 and had at that time opposed the bill granting the request of Clarke and Force. Two days after his commission was dated, and two days before he entered office, congress instructed the

---

[1] Force MSS.
[2] Clarke to Chambers, June 20, 1834, Force MSS.

secretary of state to examine the contract with the two partners and to report on the nature of the materials to be included in the work, the number of volumes, and the estimated cost of the whole. There are evidences that the partners were in a panicky state of mind, and in Force's manuscripts is a copy in his own hand of an "additional covenant" dated June 7, when the blow was foreseen, offering to limit the edition to twenty volumes and to submit all the material before printing to the approval of the secretary of state. This proposal was not then accepted.

December 22, 1834, Forsyth sent in the report required of him. Neither the contract nor the law, he said, indicated what kind of materials would be used in the proposed work. The compilers referred to it as a "Documentary History of the American Revolution from the Commencement of the Restrictive Measures of Great Britain to the Adoption of the Present Constitution of the United States"; but from the plan announced it seemed that the materials would begin with the origins of the colonies. The compilers reported, he continued, that they had examined the archives of ten of the original thirteen states and that they had made copies or were about to make them for the other three. In all they had copied, or were about to copy, 60,000 manuscript pages distributed as follows: in the state department and referring to the continental congress, 30,000; state records in Georgia, New Hampshire and elsewhere, 20,000; from old

periodicals etc., 5000; and on New England, 1774–
1776, 5000. Material was on hand for several volumes, though there were some gaps which the compilers were trying hard to fill up. They added that
they would soon begin to print the first volume of
Series IV and hoped to deliver it early in the next
session of congress, that is, in December, 1835.
They had not, however, been able to get permission to
take copies freely from the public offices in England.
Thus spoke Clarke and Force to the secretary of
state.

Forsyth said that the contract was "uncertain and
defective," but he was unwilling to say how far congress
could remedy the deficiency. At present the only
control over the compilers was to withhold payment
if the work was not done as agreed. He reported that
Clarke and Force were willing to limit themselves
to twenty volumes, saying that if at the end of that
number the work seemed incomplete they would
ask congress to continue it. On this basis the total
cost would be limited to $20,400 a volume, or $408,000
for the twenty volumes. These concessions were not
satisfactory to the secretary, who recommended in
closing that congress take steps to regulate the size
and number of volumes, and fix the time at which the
work should be completed. He also thought that there
should be a proper supervision of the selection of the
matter published, that much might well be omitted,
and that in general papers already in print and very

trivial papers of any kind ought not to be included.[1] Nothing was done at the time to carry out the recommendations of the secretary.

However much we have at heart the cause of historical publication, we must agree that Forsyth had much truth on his side. Livingston had made a loose arrangement under which a designing man could have saddled the government with a large and indefinite expense. Force's character was such that we cannot charge him with entirely selfish motives; but Clarke was a politician, and there is no reason to believe that he was better than the average of his kind in his day. Certainly, Forsyth and many others looked upon the two men as persons who had secured a fat job at the expense of a careless congress and secretary of state, and the impression thus formed embarrassed the partners as long as their enterprise continued.

They suffered also through the impatience of the congressmen to get the free copies which had been voted them. As the months ran into years and no copies of the "Documentary History" were sent out, members began to inquire what progress was being made. To one such inquirer Force wrote February 3, 1837, quieting his anxiety and saying that one volume was in press, that materials collected were sufficient to make ten volumes, and that he would be pleased

[1] 23d cong., 2d sess., House of Reps., State Dept., Doc. No. 36. Appended to the report were petitions and statements by Clarke and Force, from which fact the document is frequently catalogued under their names.

to have congressmen inspect what had been done.¹
The view of the public at large was expressed by a
correspondent of the Boston *Courier*, April 21, 1836,
who said that the scheme began with Hazard in 1789,
who issued two volumes and made money out of them.²
"From the year 1789 to 1833, a period of forty-four
years," he said, "the work was forgotten, but in the
latter year Matthew St. Clair Clarke, losing his office
of clerk, memorialized congress," which agreed without
stopping to inquire how many volumes could be printed.
It now appeared that if the compilers went on as they
intended, the work would cost the public $500,000.

This notice in the *Courier* was probably called forth
by a warm debate in the house of representatives in
April, 1836.   Clarke and Force at this time had been
collecting materials for some time and they had accumulated debts to the amount of $35,000 on account
of the enterprise.³   They were anxious to have an
appropriation authorized, so that it would be immediately available on the completion of the first volume.
When the general appropriation bill reached the committee of the whole in the spring of 1836 it contained an
item of $20,000 for the "Documentary History."   This
item provoked the discussion to which the *Courier*
undoubtedly referred in the extract cited.   The com-

¹ Force to Edmund Deberry, February 3, 1837, Force MSS.
² The statement was entirely erroneous. Hazard's two volumes were
not issued under a grant from congress, and he made no money out of them.
See Belknap Papers, Mass. Histl. Soc., " Col.," Ser. V, Vol. III, p. 361.
³ Clarke to Cambreling, January 25, 1836, Force MSS.

pilers sent to the chief objectors a long statement in their own justification, but it did no good. The committee of the whole voted to strike out the item making the appropriation. On reporting to the house there was another debate in which John Quincy Adams, Edward Everett, Vanderpoel, and others came to the aid of the proposed work, while Cave Johnson and Huntsman, both of Tennessee, were the leading critics of it.

Adams's argument for the appropriation is not preserved, but a part of Cave Johnson's speech is in the "Debates in Congress," and it shows the basis of opposition to the work. He attacked Livingston for failure to guard the interest of the government in making the contract. The bill authorizing it, said he, was most modestly named. No member who voted for it had an idea that he was voting for the publication of a book larger than "a volume or two of moderate size." And who could have expected a work so large that it might cost the government a million dollars or more? It is true the publishers were willing to limit the number of volumes to twenty, costing a little more than $400,000, but this was excessive and would never have been granted had congress realized what it was doing. The most he would agree to was that a fair estimate be made of the expense Clarke and Force had incurred in their work and the sum expended be repaid to them, together with a liberal payment for their time and efforts.

Johnson attacked very properly the practice of publishing and distributing books at the expense of the government. Since 1826, he said, congress had paid for such purposes the sum of $397,994, and it was now proposed to add to that sum an even larger amount in only one item. This vast expenditure was sufficient to procure for congress the best library in the world. He was willing to vote for the liberal purchase of books for the library, but he thought that congress should cease to be a publisher. He thought the sad error into which the national legislature had fallen in the contract with Clarke and Force was sufficient proof of this opinion.

In attacking the contract Johnson made this statement: A bill authorizing the publication of the "Documentary History" was before congress in June, 1832, and it said specifically that the price should be eight dollars for a volume of eight hundred pages. At the time the publishers thought that a fair price; but congress thought otherwise and the bill failed. When re-introduced in the next congress the price was not named specifically, the only allusion to the subject being the statement that the work would not cost more a volume than Sparks's "Diplomatic History," a book in small volumes, octavo size, of about 544 pages, for which the government paid two dollars and twenty cents a volume. No one suspected that under this general description of the cost a contract would be made by which an indefinite number of folio volumes could be printed at fifteen dollars for each volume of eight hundred pages, especially since in 1832 the publishers were willing to take eight dollars for the same size volume.[1]   By such an argument Johnson sought to show that the contract was made through fraud.

Huntsman was a less able man than Johnson, and his speech was colored by deep popular prejudice. But at one point it illuminates the subject by showing the unavowed opinion many congressmen had of the part Clarke took in the transaction.   John Quincy Adams had said that one of the men to whom the contract was given "was long a clerk in this House, was a clerk at the time, and that he is advantageously known as a gentleman."   In reply Huntsman said: "Sometimes these clerks become very popular among the members; they pass to and fro amongst them, and render many little services.   Sometimes, in a convenient anteroom, there may be some cool, wholesome water to drink; and the members are invited in.   The conclusion is, that this clerk is a very clever fellow; and by these and other little attentions the clerk gets the contract, the members the books, and Uncle Sam is taxed with the costs." [2]

The upshot of the discussion was that the house voted, yeas 85, nays 93, against the motion to strike out the appropriation.   The publishers had won,

[1] Debates in Congress, 1835–1836, 3300–3307.
[2] Ibid., 3306 (Vol. XII, part III).

but their majority was narrow. From that time they proceeded for many years with little restraint, although there was much to annoy them. Of Forsyth the following opinion was written by Force in this controversy: "No matter how widely he may have differed from us in opinion [1] [he] has acted with candour and fairness in the whole matter."

4. *The Work Published*

In December, 1837, was published the long expected first volume. It bore the title, "American Archives: consisting of a collection of Authentick Records, State Papers, Debates, and Letters and Other Notices of Publick Affairs, the Whole Forming A Documentary History of the Origin and Progress of the North American Colonies; of the Causes and Accomplishment of the American Revolution; and of the Constitution of Government for the United States, to the Final Ratification thereof." There were to be six series as follows: 1. From the discovery of the continent to 1688; 2. From 1688 to 1763; 3. From 1763 to the king's message to parliament, March 7, 1774; 4. From March 7, 1774, to the Declaration of Independence, 1776; 5. From the Declaration of Independence to the treaty with Great Britain, 1783; and 6. From 1783 to the adoption of the constitution, 1789. From this statement it is evident that

---

[1] Force to Clarke, January 7, 1836, Force MSS.

the compilers had yielded nothing to the reiterated demand for a short series.

The volume which appeared in 1837 was the first of the fourth series. In a dignified preface were explained the purpose and plan of the compilers. "We now submit to the people of the United States," it began, "the first fruits of our long and arduous labours. We offer the present volume as a specimen of the manner in which our work will be accomplished. The undertaking in which we have embarked is, emphatically, a National one: National in its scope and object, its end and aim." Other nations had been making collections of their original documents at great expense and with vast amounts of labor, notably the collections made in England under the supervision of the Record Commission, and in France under the supervision of the minister of public instruction in accordance with the suggestions of M. Guizot. If such collections were made abroad, was there not more reason that they should be made in the United States while it was possible to gather up a very large part of the necessarily transient material ere it was destroyed?

The volume began with the king's message to parliament, March 7, 1774, in reference to the "disturbances in America," and contained the proceedings thereupon with other proceedings in relation to the state of affairs in the colonies, extending to May, 1775, in all over three hundred folio pages, reprinted from British official sources. The rest of the book was filled with proceedings of the assemblies and councils of individual colonies, the journals of congress, copies of the proceedings of committees of correspondence, and many important letters by individuals. The time covered was about fourteen months. The same rate of progress was not to be maintained in the succeeding volumes.

The second volume of the fourth series came next, October, 1839. It was followed by others in the following order: the third volume, December, 1840; the fourth in April, 1843; the fifth in April, 1844; and the sixth, completing the series, in March, 1846. The five volumes following the first dealt with a period of a little more than a year. The first volume of the fifth series appeared in April, 1848; the second in May, 1851; and the third in January, 1853. At this point publication was suspended.

Actual publication did not remove the friction with congress. The process of getting money out of the treasury to pay for work already done proved very hard for Clarke and Force. In November, 1839, when the material for the second volume was about to be printed, Clarke, anxiously observing the trend of events, discovered that the item relating to it had not been put into the printed general appropriation bill, then being prepared for the use of the committee. This seemed ominous. Inquiry elicited the fact that it had not been sent to the ways and means committee, which was still more alarming. Clarke wrote to

Force: "I don't like this: I wish you would look about it. My patience has been so much tried that I cannot trust myself to talk with them for fear of insulting them. You can command your temper better. See Stubbs and Forsyth and Woodbury to-day, if you get this in time." [1] The following letter, dated February 20, 1839, and addressed to Hon. James J. McKay, of North Carolina, is an illustration of another kind of annoyance:

"Sir: — I received to-day at two o'clock, a paper without address, name, or verification, but which is, I presume, a copy of a Resolution adopted by the Committee on the Public Printing, of which you are the Chairman, directing an examination of the Printing and Printer's accounts, for the House of Representatives for the 23d and 24th congresses. It was left at my office in my absence, this forenoon, by Mr. Kincaid, foreman of the *Globe* office, with a verbal request that I would attend at the Treasury, at three o'clock to enter upon the examinations.

"It would give me great pleasure to comply with the request of the committee, were it possible to do so: but the great number of documents and accounts to be examined, and the numerous calculations that must necessarily be made by myself, before I could assent to any Report, would, in my opinion, occupy, of the time I could devote to such a purpose, at least a month, instead of three days to which the time is limited. As I could make no statement under the Resolution, but one founded on my own careful and deliberate examination, and as the time is inadequate to such an examination, I feel myself obliged to decline attempting it. I have the honor to be very respectfully, etc."

In this letter Force shows his nature most characteristically. Rigid and bold, he was the last man to

[1] Clarke to Force, November 28, 1839, Force MSS.

leap when the whip of authority cracked. He knew his rights under his contract, and no threat of a presuming chairman of committee could frighten him.

He was not yet done with McKay. In June, 1840, two pointed questions came from the gentleman. The first referred to the charge that Force's work was not valuable, that he merely printed material from the department of state, convenient at hand, and from newspapers, books, and other printed sources. This charge implied that good faith was not kept with the government. McKay asked what portion of the "Documentary History" was from printed sources and what part was taken from documents in the state department.

Force replied at length, urging the wisdom of not confining himself to manuscript materials. Much of the printed matter was so rare that it was inaccessible, and he asserted that this kind of material was the most difficult to collect. He thought about three-fourths of the papers in the first volume and one-half the matter in the second volume were such as had previously been printed; and that not more than fifty pages of the first and one-fourth of the second were from manuscripts in the state department. The residue of each volume was from manuscripts obtained elsewhere.

McKay asked a second question, "What is the expense for Printing, Paper, and Binding of each of the volumes now published?" Force said: "To this I answer, that for fifteen hundred copies of each volume it amounts to about $11,000; or $7,33⅓ per copy." Force's reply to the chairman of the committee was dated June 26, 1840.[1]

In 1843 the affairs of Clarke and Force came to a turning-point. Clarke this year gave up connection with the enterprise, and John C. Rives, partner of F. P. Blair in the publication of the *Globe*, took his place.[2] His withdrawal was probably an advantage to the enterprise. Friction had appeared between the two men, and that may have been the reason of the dissolution. In March 1843, we find Force protesting to an assistant in the office of the clerk of the House of Representatives because Clarke had secured an order for the payment of more than $5000 for a number of volumes congress had bought for the members. It seems that Clarke, then clerk of the House, had issued an order to himself and pocketed the entire sum. Force gave notice that Clarke did not speak for the other partner and that he, Force, would not deliver the books in fulfillment of the transaction.[3]

At the same time Force was able to clear up his relations with congress. In the general appropriation bill of March 3, 1843, was introduced a clause to pay Clarke and Force $6,826 due for more than two years on volume two, and $27,650, the whole cost of

[1] Force MSS.

[2] Force to John C. Rives, March 28, 1843; Rives to Force, March 29, 1843. Force MSS.

[3] Force to Robert Johnson, March 16, 1843. Force MSS.

volume three, published in the preceding December. This money was to be paid only on condition that the owners should in ten days agree that the whole work was not to contain more than twenty volumes at an average cost of $20,400 each, and that the secretary of state must pass on all the matter that went into the series.[1] More than once during the past ten years of wrangling the compilers had expressed themselves as willing to accept these terms. Failure to accept them seems to have been due to congress, which was unwilling to give the publishers the benefit of a twenty volume contract, hoping to deny to them proper compensation for their efforts, and otherwise to tease them into a more disastrous surrender.

Probably the adjustment of 1843 was in some measure due to the fact that both branches of congress were whig. Seizing the opportunity Force quickly issued volumes four and five and carried six so far forward that it was nearly off the press when the democratic administration of Polk came into existence.[2] Buchanan, new head of the state department, now controlled the fate of the "American Archives." Force sent to him, May 31, 1847, a statement of the materials to be included in volume one of the fifth series. They were in four chief divisions as follows: 1. The proceedings, papers, and correspondence of

[1] Peters, "U. S. Statutes at Large," V, 641.

[2] Although the title page has the date 1846, there appears at the end of the volume the date May 20, 1845, indicating that the printer finished his work at that time.

the continental congress; 2. The same documents of the assemblies, conventions, and councils of safety of the several states; 3. The same documents of the British government and of the officers acting for it in our revolution; and 4. "Letters and Papers, not included in the preceding enumeration, which relate to, and are necessary to illustrate the events of the period of the Revolution." [1] All these classes of papers were to be such as related to the events between the adoption of the Declaration of Independence and the battle of Long Island, August 27, 1776. Buchanan rejected the fourth division.

Soon followed another Whig administration. To John M. Clayton, secretary of state, Force sent, April 18, 1849, a statement of materials for two volumes, second and third of series five. No objection was made, and they appeared in 1851 and 1853 respectively. The division of matter was the same in the statement to Clayton as in that made to Buchanan.

It would have been better for Force if he had sent another volume before the Whigs gave up office. In 1853 a democratic administration came into power, and William L. Marcy became secretary of state. February 12, 1855, Force sent him a statement of the character of the contents of volumes four and five of the fifth series — using the fourfold divisions he had used in previous similar statements. Two months later he wrote to the secretary as follows:

[1] Force to Buchanan, May 31, 1847, Force MSS.

"I have the honour to submit, herewith, for your examination, a quantity of the Papers collected for the Fourth and Fifth volumes of the Fifth Series of the American Archives, having been informed that you consider such an examination indispensable." [1]

The note was short and to the point, as were all of Force's communications; but it brought no answer. Finally, on November 1, after six months of silence, came a note from the secretary which ran as follows:

"P. Force, Esq.; I should be pleased to see you in regard to the documents which you left with me for examination. Yours truly, W. L. Marcy."

Peter Force has left no written account of what happened in the interview that followed; and the account left by a friend to whom he talked is so much at variance with the preserved documents that it is impossible to rely upon it. The essence of the story is that Marcy said: "I don't believe in your work, sir! It is of no use to anybody. I never read a page of it, and never expect to." [2] No other answer was ever given to the persistent compiler by the strong tempered Marcy. Force was compelled to realize that it was the end of his enterprise. His hope revived in 1857, when Lewis Cass, a man of literary pretensions, became secretary of state. To him was sent a statement in the usual form, with the request that the materials be approved for the fourth and fifth volumes of the fifth series, carrying the story of the

---

[1] Force to Marcy, Feb. 12 (2); April 18, 1855, Force MSS.

[2] G. W. Greene, "Col. Peter Force — the American Annalist" (*Mag. of Amer. Hist.*, Vol. II, p. 229).

revolution to the surrender of Burgoyne. But Cass gave no encouragement. The publication of "The American Archives" was thus suspended.

Before condemning Marcy we should consider his point of view. He had before him a work that had been authorized in a careless moment by congress twenty-two years earlier. It was vastly expensive. At that time it had cost $228,710, which was 56.1 per cent.[1] of the $408,000 authorized in the adjustment of 1843. It would have been as much as could be expected if the work reached the end of 1778, had it gone on uninterrupted. If it had proceeded at the ordinary rate until it contained the material up to 1789 it would have cost at least $1,250,000 to complete the fifth and sixth series, and it is hard to see how the first, second, and third could have been published for less than $1,000,000. Such a liberal expenditure the government at that time could not be expected to make. It should be said, also, that the assertion that Force overcharged for the volumes is supported by the fact that when in 1879 a proposition to continue the series was under consideration, the public printer estimated that an edition of one thousand copies, in style identical with Force's volumes, could be issued at $4.00 a volume.[2]

[1] The estimate is based on the agreed price, $1\frac{7}{8}$ cents a page.

[2] Sen. Miscel. Doc. No. 34, 46th cong., 1st ses. The public printer's estimates are apt to be too low, but still there was room for ample correction without discounting the argument.

Force was a man of rigid purpose. Having determined that the country should have a work in which every valuable kind of historical material relating to the revolution should be included, he never relaxed his purpose to carry through the work on that basis. A more practical man would have recognized the weight of the objection to reprinting a large amount of material from Hansard's debates of the British Parliament, and from the published laws and journals of the states and the continental congress. Popular criticism, however, erred in trying to analyze Force's motives. It assumed that he used these materials merely to pad a work which yielded him a good profit. On the other hand, he had a dream of a vast and complete repository of revolutionary history, whose very completeness made it necessary to include the papers that had been printed, as well as those which were still in manuscript.

A source of trouble for Force was the habit that grew up of distributing back volumes to members of congress who took their seats after the regular distributions. As there were from one hundred to one hundred and fifty new members in each congress and as a member once on the list for the distribution received all the volumes at the expense of the public as long as the work was being published, the cost on this account grew every second year by several thousand dollars.[1]

---

[1] Force to B. B. French, March 20, 1845; to Robert Johnson, March 16, 1843; Force to . . . . February 22, 1847 (draft), Force MSS.

It was an insidious form of jobbery; for what congress would refuse to make itself the beneficiary of the habit, in order to put an end to a bad practice? Marcy may well have felt that this was another reason why he himself should assume the responsibility of putting an end to the series.

Force is not to be described as an editor. The material he printed was rarely illuminated with notes. His task was to collect and reproduce. He had a faculty for detail and was accurately acquainted with the outside of books and documents relating to his subject. He seldom ventured into the field of authorship, and then in such small attempts that he cannot be called a historian. To historical scholarship his chief service was his indefatigable energy in collecting, rather than in any constructive use of materials. His "American Archives" is nearly forgotten: it is not even a model for the many collections that have been published since its day. Its arrangement is poor, being entirely mechanical. The fourth series has not even a good index, a deficiency which, however, was remedied in the fifth series.

Force's work is defective because he did not secure and incorporate in it manuscript materials in the British public offices. His excuse that he could not get permission to make copies is not sufficient. Sparks in 1828–1829 got such permission, both in London and in Paris. Force made applications through agents and when refused allowed the matter to lie. By going to London himself, he could probably have secured his object.[1]

Force was minutely accurate in making reproductions of documents, and in this respect he was ahead of most men of his time. To Sparks, for example, it seemed sufficient to give the text of a letter as he thought the writer of it might desire it given. Force had the more correct method of exact reproduction, leaving the reader to determine in what light imperfections of style should be viewed. The following letter to Joseph Gales, Jr., March 12, 1838, will show Force's attitude on this point, and give an idea of his knowledge of the materials that passed through his hands. He wrote:

"Dear Sir: It gives me great pleasure to furnish the information you request, in your note, received this morning.

"The Journal of the Congress of 1774, was first printed under an order of the 22d of October of that year. It has been reprinted several times since. The best of the old editions is that printed by Robert Aitken, at Philadelphia, in 1777, under a Resolution of Congress of the 26th of September, 1776. Folwell's was printed from that, and Way & Gideon's from one or the other of these. It may be difficult to procure Aitken's; but I suppose Folwell's may be obtained in Philadelphia — if not Way & Gideon's can certainly be purchased either there or here for a reasonable price — four dollars a volume or thereabouts.

"I think I may venture to say, however, that the best copy of the Journal of that Congress will be found in the volume of the Documentary History just published. In the preparation of this volume I examined the MSS. Journal carefully, and *as far as*

[1] See Force to Obadiah Rich, Sept. 23, 1834 (2 letters, drafts), and Rich to Force, Feb. 20 and May 21, 1835, and Nov. 8, 1838. Force MSS.

that goes, I followed it closely. Several papers omitted there were inserted in the first printed copy; which, besides containing these papers, departed from it in some other respects. I have noticed and corrected all these variations, and have also supplied some other matter which is neither in the MSS. nor in the printed copies.[1]

"You may, therefore, if you can confide in my judgment, refer Mr. Reed to the volume I have named, folio 893 to 939. One has, I presume, been sent to the Atheneum, at Philadelphia, by the Secretary of State.   Yours etc.   P.F."

Force's reprint of the journals of the continental congress compares favorably with the edition of the Library of Congress, under the editorship of Mr. Worthington C. Ford and, later, Mr. Gailliard Hunt. In fact, Mr. Ford, in the preface of volume II pays this excellent tribute to our compiler: "The larger number of the surviving papers [of the continental congress] are printed in Peter Force's 'American Archives,' and it is safe to assume that if he did not include a letter or a report in that monumental compilation, it was not to be found in the Papers of the Continental Congress in his day." [2]

5. *Peter Force as a Collector*

In collecting the vast mass of copies of documents Force came into contact with the men most active in the field of historical collecting and writing. His

[1] Force MSS. The text gives no intimation of what papers are "supplied." Two foot-notes are given, without indication of the sources, though one is evidently from a Philadelphia newspaper of contemporary date. — J. S. B.

[2] Journals of the Continental Congress, Vol. II, p. 5.

correspondence affords us an interesting view of the state of research in his time; and to know that cannot fail to be of real service to American historical students of this or any future time. There was hardly a man in the country then engaged in research who did not write to Peter Force. Not only the great collectors and the minor historians, but such important major writers as Jared Sparks and George Bancroft are thus revealed in their intimate labors. Most pertinent of all in this place is the view we have of Force's own efforts as collector.

"I first proposed the American Archives, and drew up the plan of the work, in 1822. Since January, 1830, my time has been almost wholly occupied in collecting materials for it, and preparing them for the press. The work is the result of my own labour, and the copyright belongs to myself alone." [1] Thus wrote Colonel Force in 1848. Collecting materials meant buying books, newspapers, and pamphlets as well as copying manuscripts. Of the first class he had a considerable collection when he formed the partnership with Clarke. He soon became known to the dealers in second-hand books as a good customer, and with some of the large dealers in the chief cities he was on the basis of a preferential customer, buying largely when he was financially able. The invoices preserved with his papers show that his purchases were not exclusively American, as the following

---

[1] Force to Thomas J. Campbell, August 19, 1848, Force MSS.

items, taken at random, but successively, will show: "Appianus, $4.50; Le Blanc, $3.75; Proposals for a Q. Settlement in Penn., $5.25; Holyoke, $4.50; Tryal of Pyrates, $5.00; Agreement between Penn and Baltimore, $3.12; Franciscans, $5.25; Ptolemy, $18.37; Life of Whitefield, $1.62; 3 Tracts at 75 cts., $2.25; Zeno, $3.62." A man who wedged in Ptolemy between the Franciscans and the Life of the great preacher of Methodism was certainly a man of broad interests.

The following letter reveals his relations with the book dealers, and, incidentally, shows his interest in books on the art of printing:

"Dear Sir: — I am gratified to learn from yours of the 8th instant you can furnish all the books ordered in mine of the sixth. Annexed is an additional order. I thank you for suggesting Dibdin, but Arres [?] must serve me for the present. I have several works on the history of Printing, and a few early printed Books. I wish to add to them and would order Pliny (no. 2170) but I think the price too high. I have not added Hakluyt to the list solely from an apprehension that I may find the Bill without it inconveniently large. Has your Discovery of America by the Welch been published? Respectfully etc." [1]

Again Force wrote:

"I have received your two letters. I will attend to the nomination of the gentlemen you named for Corresponding Members of the Institute. There has been no meeting since, and probably there will be none before November. Mr. Broadhead called upon,

---

[1] Force to John R. Bartlett, of New York, July 9, 1776 [sic]. Bartlett was a member of the firm of Bartlett and Welford, booksellers. He was the author of "Bibliotheca Americana" and other bibliographical works.

and spent an hour or so with me. You know what has been done about the appointment of secretary. What will be done hereafter it is impossible to conjecture. Mr. Marsh should have been one of the Regents.

"I was much mortified with my seeming want of courtesy to Mr. Ludewig. I could not intentionally omit to thank him for his kindness to myself, or for his extremely well executed Book, for which he is entitled to the thanks of all who desire to read or to study the History of this country. Enclosed are your two Lists. The twenty-eight books I have marked you will please send me. I have, just now, occasion for Herrera, Barcia, Pigafetta, Cardenas, Navarete, De Laet, and Hollingshed. Will you return the lists with the Books?" [1]

Force was an omnivorous reader, and it is probable that he desired these books for his personal use. He was not at that time engaged in any investigation that would have required works of such varying character as Holinshed and Navarete.

To Hermann E. Ludewig, mentioned in the letter above, he wrote in 1857 as follows:

"You are mistaken, my dear sir, in supposing that nobody takes an interest in your American bibliographical researches. All who take an interest in American history must acknowledge the value of your Book, and thank you for the industry, perseverance, and especially the ability, you have shown in the preparation of it. It was unfair to throw the expense of publication on one who had

[1] Force to John R. Bartlett, September 11, 1846, Force MSS. The "Broadhead" mentioned here was probably J. R. Brodhead, of New York; and the position mentioned seems to have been the secretaryship of the Smithsonian Institution. Herman E. Ludewig was a Saxon bibliographer who arrived in America in 1844. He published his "Literature of American Local History" in 1846 at his own expense. The edition was given away by the author, who received acknowledgments from only thirty of the recipients.

voluntarily incurred the expense of preparing it for the press.   **For** a second edition, with your additions, it must be arranged otherwise.   I am sure you could make some additions here, where I should be glad to see you at any time, while I hope for the pleasure of meeting you in New York the coming summer.   I wish I lived nearer our friend Gowans, or rather, I wish he lived nearer me, (for I cannot change my location).   I never visit his collection without meeting with something desirable." [1]

Among other correspondents were Lyman C. Draper, Charles Deane, Henry Onderdonck, J. B. Moore, Samuel G. Drake, George Livermore, William B. Reed, and Buckingham Smith, all men of note in some special field of history.   To most of these men Force was an object of high consideration, and a source from which came help of many kinds.   Lyman C. Draper wrote in 1847 — then in his thirty-third year — "Upwards of a year since I took the liberty of sending you a printed *circular* explaining my aims and my historical collections.   Limited and unimportant as they are, compared with your great researches and achievements, I yet hope, in my humble way, to effect something for the biographical literature of our country." [2]

John H. Wheeler, author of an indifferent history of North Carolina, wrote as follows in acknowledgment of the aid he had received: "You will receive by this mail, the *first form* of my History of North Carolina.   Your god-child, for whom at the baptismal

---

[1] From an undated draft in reply to Ludewig's letter of Oct. 6, 1857. Force MSS.   [2] September 20, 1847.   Force MSS.

font you are made to stand, is before you. I fear almost that you will disown the ungainly bantling. But 'it must be so, Plato'; and perhaps after all it may do, as it is 'only for *Buncombe*' that the work is written. Let me hear from you by return mail, and your opinion as to the typography; and your suggestions will be respectfully heeded." In another letter Wheeler speaks of Force, Bancroft, and Governor Swain as "having stood at the fount as sponsors for my bantling." [1]

From Edward D. Ingraham, of Philadelphia, came a letter which must have startled the collector. It was nothing more nor less than a request for the loan of a rare copy of Archibald Loudon's "Indian Narrative," [2] which a "client of mine" wished to publish in a "superior edition." The writer gave assurance that the book would be returned if the new edition was not published. Force said in reply: "I will lend *you* Loudon with great pleasure to be returned to me safe and sound, in the same condition it now is; but there is an awful squinting in your 'unless,' etc. that alarms me. A copy of a new edition, no matter how superior, would not replace this old one on my shelves. Will not a MS copy serve to print from? I would rather make one than have my Book destroyed; and I would much rather copy it twice than disoblige you,

[1] July 3 and September 13, 1851.   Force MSS.
[2] Loudon, Archibald, "Interesting Narratives of Outrages Committed by the Indians in their Wars on White People," 2 vols., Carlisle [Pa.], 1808–1811.

to whom I am indebted for so many favours." [1] Ingraham was a man of education, a lawyer of ability, and a bibliophile. It is, therefore, amazing that he should have thought a rare book, mutilated in the hands of the printers, could be replaced by a copy from a new edition.

Of all the collectors with whom Force came into contact the most notable was Henry Stevens, second of the name, probably the prince of Americans who were accustomed to collect and dispose of old American books, pamphlets, and manuscripts. Stevens's father, likewise called Henry, was himself a collector. He lived in Barnet, Vermont, and made a thorough search of Vermont garrets for material on the history of the state. His researches brought together the greatest treasury of Vermont history that has been seen in one place. Left in the state house in Montpelier, it suffered severely in a fire which destroyed the building in 1857. Force bought duplicates from him and a friendship existed between the two men. On a certain Christmas day Stevens wrote: "I have been thinking about going to Washington this winter, but how to manage to get there, as yet I have not determined. If I could sell you a few hundred dollars worth of old manuscripts, from four to six hundred volumes of newspapers, a few hundred pamphlets for a reasonable reward over and above expenses I might be induced to make you one more visit. Come,

---

[1] Force to E. D. Ingraham, December 13, 1850. Force MSS.

give me what may be termed solid comfort. I will pack up and clear out for Washington. Write me soon after you receive this, so that I can look about and consider what is for the best." [1] Stevens, senior, was possessed of average Vermont shrewdness, sharpened by years of ferreting in garrets, and he could not restrain its working, in spite of his genuine admiration for Force.

His son, Henry Stevens, Junior, was to be a greater man than the collector of Barnet; and it was Force who first gave him an opportunity to develop his talents. In 1843 the young man was a senior at Yale, facing financial difficulties which threatened to interrupt his stay at the college. By some means, possibly through his father, he became acquainted with Force and made arrangements to copy manuscripts for him. The young collegian had his father's faculty of nosing out rare materials, and Force trusted to him to select what was valuable. Students were employed to do the actual copying, and through the spring many valuable parcels were sent to Washington. In the autumn of 1843 Stevens entered the Harvard law school. He was in debt to a New Haven bank, and Professor Kingsley had become his security. There was, therefore, more reason than ever that he should earn money by copying. To his earnest plea that he should go on, Force at first refused on the ground that he was himself in need of money. But later he

[1] December 25, 1851. Force MSS.

relented and authorized Stevens to furnish copied manuscripts to the amount of $350, the sum for which the young man was in debt.[1]

The money was not applied to the debt, and Professor Kingsley wrote in deep concern to Force, saying that Stevens gave as the excuse for failure to pay that Force owed him money for copying, and asking that Force would accept a draft for four hundred and fifteen dollars. To this request, so badly based, Force gave a polite refusal. To Stevens he sent the amount then due, $253.76, saying that he had informed Kingsley of the fact, and directing Stevens to cease copying.[2] Force was the soul of honesty, and loose methods of business were very distasteful to him. But the two men were mutually necessary to one another, and the estrangement did not last long. A year later Stevens was collecting manuscripts and sending books. The following letter written to him will cast interesting light on the methods of collecting in general, as well as illustrate the personal habits of the writer of it:

"Dear Sir: I have just received by the express yours of the 13th with the catalogue. It came in excellent time. I was about leaving for Boston to-morrow (at great inconvenience to my business) to attend the sale. If you will attend and buy for me you will do me a great favour. I want the books I have marked. Get them as cheap as you can, but buy all that do not sell at extravagant prices.

[1] Force to H. Stevens, Jr., Dec. 27, 1843. Force MSS.
[2] Force to H. Stevens, Jr., Feb. 8, 1844, to J. L. Kingsley, Feb. 8, 1844, Kingsley to Force, Jan. 29, 1844. Force MSS.

Of course I except such as you want for yourself. The auctioneers do not know me; but I suppose they will be satisfied if I remit immediately on receiving a Bill, and before *any* Books are sent, the balance for whatever amount you buy for me, above the two hundred dollars I now enclose. Instead of returning the catalogue, I annex the numbers I desire of the first day's sale. To-morrow I will send you the 2nd and 3rd Days. Your draft will be attended to: it has not yet been presented. I very much wish to procure full sets of the old copies of all the Colony Laws, and will take any you can gather for me. If you can get me a copy of Ingersoll's Letters I beg you to send it. Respectfully, etc." [1]

Stevens had previously called Force's attention to certain manuscripts to be included in the sale, and he seems to have suggested that George Bancroft, then in Boston, be asked to look over them and advise him, Stevens, as to their value. In reply Force said:

"With regard to the MSS, I am unable to give directions. A mere transcript, no matter how neatly written, without evidence of its authenticity, is of no value to me. I am unwilling to trouble Mr. Bancroft, but may, perhaps, write him about them. It is proper to say, I consider this a matter of business and that I expect to pay you a commission for your trouble." [2]

One can see something of the spirit of treasure-hunting that lent a glamour to the life of a collector in the suggestion conveyed by Stevens in the following words, the allusion being to the sale above mentioned: "I think there will be no long pursed competitors in the field. The Harvard Library has already many of the works. Sparks has gone to Halifax, and all the anti-

[1] Force to Stevens, July 19, 1844. Force MSS.
[2] Force to H. Stevens, July 20, 1844. Force MSS.

quarians of the Law School and college are off. Bartlett and Welford's agent will probably be the only high bidder." The sale went off favorably, Force securing $485.57 worth of the books. Stevens gives us a glimpse of still another side of book collecting in the following : "I shall have a tale to tell you of the wonderful conduct of our George B—— to whom you wrote, and who, I believe, did his best to manœuvre me out of some of the best of the books, particularly no. 240." [1]

By this time Stevens had drifted far into the current of the collector's life. Law, which he still called his dearest pursuit, was fast receding into the distance. From Boston he made many journeys into the interior, buying books freely and selling them where he could find purchasers. When he accumulated a quantity that he could not sell privately he placed them with an auctioneer. He was an ardent buyer and was apt to purchase rashly. The result was that he often lost money. In the spring of 1845, while embarrassed, he got Force to accept a draft on an auction house in Boston, claiming that the house owed him several hundred dollars. The draft was drawn in favor of a Washington man, indorsed by Force, and sent to Boston for collection, where it was promptly protested. Force waited two weeks in daily expectation of a letter from the agent. When none came he wrote him as follows : "I paid Mr. Morrison, with the ex-

---

[1] Stevens to Force, July 15 and 27, 1844. Force MSS. "George B—" was Bancroft.

penses on the draft, $63.75, and expected you would immediately replace the money, without being reminded of the necessity of your doing so. Your silence compels me to request you will send me the amount, forthwith. At the same time I take the liberty to advise you, never hereafter, under any circumstances, to resort again to such an expedient to raise money. You cannot succeed in it without the loss of friends and of character." [1]

This reproof brought a prompt explanation. The draft was issued, said Stevens, in the faith that he had funds enough to meet it at the auctioneers'. It was protested during his absence from Boston. When he returned he learned of the occurrence, went to the auctioneers, and was told that his balance was eighty-one cents. In despair he ran to the bank, only to learn that the protested draft had gone back to Washington. To his expressions of grief the bank clerk gave him the consoling assurance that he would soon have ample opportunity to pay. Stevens wrote very contritely, accused himself of lack of business knowledge, and made a strong appeal to the benevolence of his patron. "I cannot bear the idea," he said, "that you, to whom I am so much indebted for my past successes, and for the facilities afforded me in my favorite study, should have occasion to withhold the confidence once reposed in me; for I am free to confess that to you, more than to all others, except my kind

[1] Force to Stevens, April 8, 1845. Force MSS.

father, do I owe my education,   I have often boasted of you as a friend, and hope by my actions hereafter to merit the same appellation."

The hard-hearted patron was not appeased. He began to examine his invoices of books more carefully than formerly, and the conclusions he reached prompted him to write in the following strain :

"When I proposed to you last summer to collect books for me, I agreed to pay you a fair price (without regard to their cost to you) for what you might gather of such as could not be procured in the regular way of purchasing, and were without an ascertained value; but it was expressly understood that this arrangement did not include such as were found in bookstores or on sale Catalogues with fixed prices : on such I was to pay you a commission merely. I advanced you money and took the Books you offered me, without scrutiny, at your own prices. On the present occasion I have looked into it.

"Of the whole sent me on the 18th instant, there is not more than one for which I will give what you ask. The prices throughout are extravagant. The two lots, of 144 for 75 cents each, and 82 for one dollar each, I would not take in the lump, as you say you expect me to do, at the average price of 25 cents each. Of those sent on the 5th I have found some on the catalogues from which I have no doubt you ordered. For instance, I find the price of Lettres Edifiante [*sic*], for which you charge [$]27.00 is 26 shillings; Norrici [?], $3.75, is four shillings; Mirror of Cruelty, $4.50, is ten shillings; Fernandez Relation, $10.00, is ten shillings and sixpence; Gage, $5.75, is four shillings and sixpence; and so of others. The catalogue price of the five I have named is *fifty-five shillings*, and you have charged me for them *fifty-six dollars!* The Bookseller's commission for importing the same books would not exceed ten per cent. I find others in the same bill, on Towne's Catalogue, which you probably purchased of Mr. Morrison, in this city, charged at more than four times his price. I now write to inquire if you adhere to the prices you have fixed in your Bills; if you do, write me, at once, and I will return you the Books immediately. Respectfully &c."

To this protest Stevens replied that he had charged the same prices that Harvard College, Messrs. Dowse, C. Dean, Lawrence, Livermore, Chapin, Crowninshield, Norton, and Bowditch paid him. But he added: "I am convinced I have charged you, *in the aggregate* extravagant prices"; and he proposed that Force should deduct twenty per cent. on one and twenty-five per cent. on another of the bills complained of, and send back all the books he did not wish at these reductions.[1]

At this time the course of Henry Stevens, Jr., in America was nearly run. He had, as he said in the letter just cited, established a trade with the wealthy Boston collectors; and he had sold to them at liberal profits. He was about to be translated to a wider sphere of activity. Some of his rich patrons, among them Messrs. John Carter Brown, of Providence, Governor Slade, of Vermont, and J. R. Brodhead, of New York, sent him to London to search the market for rare Americana. Before this time Obadiah Rich, of London, had sold many of the books ordered by Americans; and now and then some New York or Boston dealer would go to England and run through the stalls to see what he could find. It was in the latter

---

[1] For this correspondence see Stevens to Force, April 12, 1845, Force to Stevens, April 27, 1845, and Stevens' reply, May 4, 1845. Force MSS.

capacity that Stevens reached London. He examined the London shops thoroughly, visited the out-of-town booksellers, and finally met Panizzi, the head of the British Museum, who was so impressed with him that he gave him an order to purchase books on America for that great library.[1] It was an unlimited order, and carried with it admission to every part of the Museum. Rich was completely overshadowed by the young American, and the other booksellers were in despair. Bartlett, of New York, wrote to Force in these words: "Soon after my return from Washington our Mr. Welford went to London. He writes me that our friend Hy. Stevens is the great monopolist of American books in London. He not only buys everything of value, but prevents all the respectable dealers from selling to others. . . . The fact is, he has some rich customers in Boston and Providence, and I understand that he makes them pay high prices. He is also employed at the British Museum, and has free access to every part of the institution. Mr. Welford has been in London more than three months and has not been able to send me a single book on America of variety or value."[2]

The prosperity of the young American did not wipe out immediately the resentment Force had felt in 1845.

[1] It was in this year, 1845, that Panizzi made his most celebrated report on the reorganization of the library of the British Museum. He pointed out the deficiencies in the collection of printed books, and parliament was led to vote £10,000 annually to keep up the collection.

[2] Bartlett to Force, July 8, 1846. Force MSS.

The short business letters Stevens wrote seem to have remained unanswered. It was not until 1848 that correspondence was resumed between the two men. In 1851 the last trace of harshness was gone, as we may learn from the letter that follows.   Force wrote:

"I wrote you last week by Mr. Cunningham, who is on his way to England, to see the Elephant. I hope you will give him the benefit of some of your London experience : it will be of great value to him. I have had much to do with old England for some months past, in the way of 'Contributions' to the great Industrial Exhibition, and I have been urged to present myself to the Royal Commissioners in London, as one of the 'natural products' of America. I had a strong desire, too, to go; not altogether to visit the Crystal Palace, (though I have no doubt that will be worth looking at) but to learn something certain about the quantity and accessibility of the papers relating to America, preserved in the State Paper office, and other depositories about the Metropolis. I supposed that in three or four months a general examination might be made; but I learn from an article in the March number of the Gentleman's Magazine, they are guarded by such a fearful array of bars, and fees, and favours of office, that they must be totally inaccessible to one who desires to obtain a general knowledge of what there is there that he wants. There is at least one black spot of the Dark Ages of Albion not yet rubbed out. So, I shall not visit Mr. John Bull this year. . . .

"Brunet[1] gives four early editions of Froissart's Chronicles. The 1st without date; 2d, 1505; 3d, 1518; and 4th, 1530. All these editions, if they exist, should be in the British Museum.[2] You will much oblige me by making an examination and a comparison of the first volume of each edition, and when you write let me know in what respect they severally differ. It would tax your time

[1] Jacques-Charles Brunet, a celebrated French bibliographer.
[2] The publication of the British Museum catalogue began in 1841, when the letter A was published. It was not carried further until 1881.

too much, or I would ask you for a similar examination and report on each of the volumes. I don't believe in Brunet's four editions." [1]

These extracts from Force's letters give us a view of his activity as a collector. Although he read constantly and knew a great deal about miscellaneous things, he can hardly be called a great scholar in history. In fact, he lacked early educational advantages, and the effect is seen in all he did. As his friends said to him in 1851, he was a natural product of America. But nature gave him a genius for historical collecting, a gift which would undoubtedly have been expanded into larger proportions, if he had been so fortunate in his early life as to have enjoyed the opportunities of a sound and liberal education.

6. *Other Activities of Peter Force*

One of the outcomes of his collecting of rare Americana was the four volumes of " Tracts and other Papers relating to the Origin, Settlement, and Progress of the Colonies in North America." The first appeared in 1836, the second in 1838, the third in 1844, and the fourth in 1846. In an "Advertisement" the compiler explained that he had experienced much difficulty in collecting the early pamphlets and tracts on the colonies. Of the vast number that were issued only a few had survived the waste of time, and these few were in libraries connected with public institutions. It was proposed, therefore, to reprint such tracts as were of

[1] Force to Stevens, April 5, 1851. Force MSS.

most value and to make them accessible to a larger number of readers than could otherwise see them. Of the thirteen numbers in the first volume two had not been printed before that and two others were now for the first time published in connected form.

Force's "Tracts" have long been considered an indispensable work among the collections of early Americana, although they are somewhat superseded in recent times by the inclusions of most of the tracts in various local or modern collections. The preparation was to Force a labor of love. He was not a rich man and was frequently in straitened circumstances. It was, therefore, not an easy thing to get out the volumes. He said in this connection : "Whenever I found a little more money in my purse than I absolutely needed, I printed a volume of Tracts." [1] They were brought out without notes or other editorial amplification.

In his old age Force became interested in Arctic exploration and the invention of printing ; and he was one of the many men of his day who tried to solve the fascinating puzzle of the authorship of Junius' letters. In 1852 he published a pamphlet in defense of the claims of the American expedition that went out in search for Sir John Franklin and his party. The title was "Grinnell Land, Remarks on the English Maps of Arctic Discoveries in 1850 and 1851." Controversy

---

[1] Spofford, A. R., "Life and Labors of Peter Force," in *Records of the Columbia Historical Society*, Vol. II, p. 4.

followed, and the next year he published a second pamphlet called a "Supplement to Grinnell Land." In a controversy Force was likely to speak with biting words, but he was always patriotic. In 1856 he published in the *Smithsonian Contributions to Knowledge* a treatise called " Record of Auroral Phenomena observed in the higher Northern Latitudes." His fervent desire to defend his country's history led him in 1855 to publish a pamphlet in reply to some of Lord Mahon's strictures on the outbreak of our revolution. It was called "The Declaration of Independence, or Notes on Lord Mahon's History of the American Declaration of Independence."

Force is also remembered for other services to historical literature. He discovered the proclamation of Governor Josiah Martin of North Carolina, in which mention was made of certain treasonable resolutions passed in Mecklenburg County. This proclamation had been taken as supporting evidence by those who believed in the twentieth-of-May "declaration." But searching in the contemporary newspapers Force discovered in the *Massachusetts Spy*, July 12, 1775, an abbreviated copy of the resolutions passed in Mecklenburg County, May 31, 1775. He published them in the *National Intelligencer*, December 18, 1838, pointing out that they answered fully the resolutions to which Governor Martin alluded in his proclamation. Later on, these resolutions were discovered in other newspapers, and more diligent research has established that it was to them that the governor referred, and, in fact, that the so-called "twentieth-of-May resolutions" never existed in fact, but were only a figment of the imagination.[1] Force's discoveries in connection with the controversy were but incidental to his long and minute examination of the sources of revolutionary history, but they attest the care with which he pursued his tasks.[2]

7. The Last Years of Activity

After the secretary of state, William L. Marcy, refused to accept for publication the material for the tenth volume of the "American Archives," Force's life passed into a period of disappointment and sorrow. It was the failure of the great scheme on which his best

[1] For a full discussion of this subject see Hoyt, "The Mecklenburg Declaration of Independence." Force's share is mentioned on pages 16–17.

[2] Force seems to have believed the resolutions of May 31, 1775, were really a declaration of independence. In his statement to McKay's committee, June 26, 1840, he said, while arguing that it was proper to include in the "Archives" matter which had once been in print: "The controversy about the Mecklenburgh Resolutions, begun more than ten years since, is well known. During all that time, notwithstanding the earnestness of research and investigation of the parties engaged in that controversy, no written or printed contemporaneous evidence was discovered, either to affirm or disprove the claim of North Carolina to the first declaration of a separation from Great Britain. Yet such evidence exists, and it is contained in a Paper affirming the fact. This is a printed paper. Who will say, that because it was printed sixty-five years ago, it is not now entitled to a place in the Archives of the Country; but that after having been buried in oblivion for more than half a century, it should be left there to perish forever?" McKay was from North Carolina, and the allusion to the Mecklenburg resolutions was probably a piece of guile, but it can hardly be believed that Force would have affected a belief in the resolutions which he did not feel. The statement from which the quotation is taken is in the Force MSS.

hopes were staked. Never a man of strong social qualities, he retired into his home life and surrendered himself to the impulses of a book-loving recluse. George Bancroft in his later years lived in Washington, the center of a prominent group of prominent men. To a society that was amply endowed with official distinction he added the much desired finish of literary reputation. Senators, cabinet members, ministers from European courts, and the president himself were pleased to entertain him and be entertained by him. To support this high state he had ample means, as well as the fondness for high social dignity. But Force had neither the money nor the taste for such a life. His home was in a roomy old house at the corner of D and Twelfth streets, Northwest, looking over Pennsylvania Avenue. The adjoining house was the shelter for his library and behind the two was a large garden in which he exhausted his ingenuity to provide areas for flowers, lawn, and trees. One particular corner contained shrubs and trees intermingled and was known as his "wilderness." Love of flowers is often a characteristic of the scholar who retires from the observation of the world, and it has been peculiarly present in our American historians. Bancroft, Parkman, and Prescott were devoted to gardening; the first had a rose named for him and the second originated several new varieties of plants, the most noted being the *Lilium Parkmanni*, to which his name was given. An ugly brick building now stands where Force's garden used to be.

In his library, Force was ever the serious student and devotee of learning. To curious persons who sought to see one of the reputed wise men of the city he was never at home. But to students seeking his aid, and to book-lovers like himself he was the soul of hospitality. By eight o'clock in the morning he was at his table "collating and writing amid heaps of historical lore." Severe simplicity marked his environment, partly because such was his fancy, and partly because he was not able to afford rich surroundings. "More than once," he said, "did I hesitate between a barrel of flour and a rare book, but the book always got the upper hand." Dr. Spofford, the librarian of congress, often visited him and together the two men went through the treasures of the library. The following picture of the seven ample rooms in which the collection was crowded is given to us by Dr. Spofford:

"No luxurious library appointments, no glazed bookcases of walnut or mahogany, no easy chairs inviting to soft repose or slumber were there; but only plain, rough pine shelves and pine tables, heaped and piled with books, pamphlets, and journals, which overflowed seven spacious rooms and littered the floors. Among them moved familiarly two or more cats and a favorite old dog, for the lonely scholar was fond of pets, as he also was of children. He had near bits of bread or broken meat or a saucer of milk to feed his favorites in the intervals of his work. Clad in a loose woolen wrapper or dressing-gown, the sage looked up from his books with a placid smile of greeting, for (like that of many men of leonine and somber aspect) his smile was of singular sweetness." [1]

[1] Spofford, A. R., "Life and Labors of Peter Force," *Records of the Columbia Historical Society*, Vol. II, p. 8.

In physical appearance Force was tall and erect. Curling hair covered his large head even to his old age. His carriage was firm and dignified, as became the military man. He wore well the rank to which he was advanced in the militia of the District of Columbia. This marked presence was probably one of the things that commended him to the voters and resulted in his election to the mayoralty of Washington. Having resided in the city from its early years, he was well known on the streets, where the citizens courteously saluted as he took his daily walks, and where visitors turned to remark his striking figure. Those who saw were apt to remember him long.

To his friends his conduct was gentle and helpful. "His manners," said Dr. Spofford, "were gravely courteous and simple, his conversation deliberate rather than fluent, his tones modulated and low. His talk was often enlivened by an undercurrent of genial humor. Without egotism or pretension, he was ever ready to impart to inquirers from his full stores of wisdom and experience, while cherishing a wholesome horror of pretenders and of bores." [1] This warm nature beneath a stern exterior was not apparent to the men who dealt with him in a business way. A more expansive manner to strangers would have enabled him to avoid some of the disappointments that overtook his hopes. He who would succeed in a world of politicians

[1] Spofford, A. R., "Life and Labors of Peter Force," *Records of the Columbia Historical Society*, Vol. II, p. 9.

must have address and open sympathy for casual as well as for real friends.

Colonel Force lived in happy family relations. Seven children of his household came to maturity, two dying young. One of them, Manning Ferguson Force, a graduate of Harvard in 1845, and of the law school in 1848, became a historian of note in his day. He wrote several books on the Civil War, among them "From Fort Henry to Corinth," in Scribners' "Campaigns of the Civil War." He lived in Ohio, and was elected a corresponding member of the Massachusetts Historical Society. He served in the Civil War as an officer of volunteers and reached the rank of brigadier-general.

As Peter Force approached an advanced age, he became concerned about the fate of his collection. He had long thought that it might be bought by the government and kept together as a great national collection of historical lore; but the suspension of the publication of the "Archives" and his consequent strained relations with the officials left little encouragement for his hopes. During the civil war he could not expect that a government straining every nerve to raise funds for the expenses of that struggle would devote a portion of its resources to book buying.

In 1865 efforts were made to secure the collection for the New York Historical Society. Force, as an old New Yorker, was willing to sell to the society, and the terms agreed upon were: 1. The collection to be kept together and known as the "Force Library"; 2. The price paid to be $100,000; and 3. Force himself to subscribe $10,000 toward the sum. George H. Moore, librarian of the society, set about the task of raising the remainder, $90,000. At the end of more than six months he had to report that he could not raise the money, and the negotiations came to an end.[1]

Then the matter was again taken up by persons who wished to keep the library in Washington. A bill was now carried through congress, March 2, 1867, appropriating $100,000 for the collection, and the library with its manuscripts was transferred to the library of congress.[2] The transaction was largely due to the efforts of Dr. Ainsworth R. Spofford, librarian of congress. He made a report on the character of the contents of the collection, dividing the materials into the following seven classes:

1. Printed books of several categories, including early voyages, statutes, documents, and other materials relating to America; and books in Spanish, French, and German languages bearing on the general or special fields. It was, said Dr. Spofford, the largest private collection ever made in its field. In all there were 22,529 printed volumes.

2. Extensive files of early American newspapers, dating from 1735 to 1800, and relating especially

[1] Force to Moore, May 29, 1865; Moore to Force, May 20, October 5, and December 11, 1865. Force MSS.
[2] U. S. Statutes at Large, Vol. XIV, p. 464.

to Massachusetts, Virginia, Pennsylvania, and New York.

3. Pamphlets in the same field, in all about 40,000. How valuable these pamphlets were may be seen from the fact that the library of congress then had only 6000.

4. Maps and atlases referring to American history, many of them describing events of the revolutionary times.

5. Incunabula, collections of early specimens of the art of printing, many of them examples from the work of the most notable printers.

6. Autographs and miscellaneous manuscripts, relating chiefly to the revolutionary period, among them many letters from American generals.

7. Transcripts, materials collected and prepared for publication in the Archives. Some of them represented documents that had been destroyed after these copies were made. These transcripts remain a promising un-worked field of research to this day.

It was in the spring of 1867 that the collection was moved to the capitol, which then held the library of congress. Force, left alone with the empty shelves, was overcome by loneliness and sought refuge in daily journeys to the library. But to see his favorite books in a new and strange setting was no relief. His physical powers began to fail, and he died January 23, 1868.

In 1879 efforts were made, probably through the initiation of the librarian of congress, to continue the publication of Force's papers. The matter was introduced into the senate by Senator Voorhees, and the committee on the library was directed to report on the papers from 1776 to 1783. This called forth a report from the librarian, Dr. Spofford. He was not specific, estimating merely that there was enough material in the collection to make thirty folio volumes of 800 pages each, which if printed like the original volumes could be published for $4 each, according to the estimate of the public printer. No further action was taken.[1]

The Force collection of manuscripts formed the nucleus of the treasures of the manuscripts division of the library of congress. Dr. Spofford's description of the collection already cited does not enable us to discover how many of the manuscripts were original and how many were copies. Inquiries at the division show that the originals were received in about forty bound volumes, and that they have been cut up and the sheets distributed with other papers,[2] so that it is difficult to make a list of those that were obtained through the Force collection.

The transcripts have been kept together and the most valuable have been bound. They consist of papers relating to the following states: Massachusetts,

[1] Cong. Record, 46th cong., Vol. IX, prt. 1, p. 77, and prt. 2, p. 1350 (March 27 and May 15), Sen. Miscel. Doc. No. 34, 46th cong., 1st sess.—1879.

[2] In this investigation I have received much assistance from Mr. John C. Fitzpatrick, of the MSS. Division, Library of Congress, always an efficient friend of investigators.

45 volumes; New Hampshire, 17 volumes; Vermont, 7 volumes; Connecticut, 3 volumes; New York, 40 volumes; Pennsylvania, 4 volumes; Maryland, 5 volumes; South Carolina, 2 volumes; and Georgia, 6 volumes. The rest of the thirteen original states are not represented in this collection, although it is known that Force had papers relating to some of them.

The character of these collections may be seen by examining the volumes for one of the states, and for this purpose Massachusetts will serve. On it were more volumes than on any other state. Resolutions of the towns filled six; letters relating to the revolution, five; petitions, four; papers of the board of war, six; provincial congress journals, four; provincial congress resolves, one; council papers, four; council letters and messages, three; committee of safety journal, one; papers relating to military affairs, three; house of representatives journals, three; general court resolves, four; and committee reports, etc., one.

Thirty-one of the total number do not extend beyond the year 1777, and of the rest only a small part of the contents go beyond that year. Nor is there evidence that Force had collected many documents for the period earlier than 1773. His habit seems to have been to make copies as he needed them of the well-known collections in various states. But if he came across an interesting thing that covered an earlier or later period, he took that also, on the ground that he would need it some time. My examination of the transcripts does not support the theory that he had intact a vast collection ready to be sent to the printer and complete for the revolutionary period. It would seem that he lived from hand to mouth, as it were. Of course, it is impossible to say how many originals he had in his collection. If these were very numerous, however, they would bulk large in the general collection in the library, where they were distributed. On this point a more careful research than I have had opportunity to make would throw light on the interesting question of the value of Force's collection.

CHAPTER VI

THE HISTORIANS AND THEIR PUBLISHERS

In the preceding sketches little has been said about the arrangements of the early historians with their publishers, a subject of such interest to the historians of the present day that it cannot well be omitted.   We do not see the writing of history on a sound and respectable basis in any country until it is, like other professions, on a self-supporting footing.   The laborer is worthy of his hire; and it is significant that those historians have had greatest national influence who have reaped the best rewards from their efforts.   Any consideration, therefore, of the growth of historical literature in a given period should include a consideration of the economic aspects of the subject.

At the time with which I have been dealing a book that may be described as popular did fairly well in both Great Britain and the United States, as is shown by the fact that Washington Irving was paid three thousand pounds for the copyright of a British edition of his "Life of Columbus."   The demand for such works was certain.   It was a time when people wished to have good books in their homes; and while the book-buying class was not large, it had a real desire for something to read.   History, also, was still considered among the branches of "polite and entertaining literature." It had not at that time taken on the character of philosophy, economic statistics, and political science which makes it a thing to be dreaded by the mass of present-day readers. These conditions made the task of the popular historian a century ago somewhat better than today, although he had still many difficulties to encounter.

Belknap and Hazard were not to be classed as popular. It was theirs to write scholarly books, and their chief reliance for the favor of the public was the desire to perpetuate the deeds of a heroic past. No publisher waited to assume the risk of publication, guaranteeing the author a profit in the form of royalties or bonuses. To get their books published they must assume the risks, and their first step was to secure subscriptions in advance of publications. Blanks were prepared, with spaces left for the names of subscribers below the descriptions of the proposed works, and sent out to persons who would circulate them through friendship or for commissions. After the lists had passed from hand to hand they were sent back to the author, who then knew whether or not he might proceed with the enterprise. Some of Belknap's lists were left in the hands of booksellers who displayed them where customers could see them. He himself sent out those that were intended for New England, while his friend, Hazard, looked after those sent out in Philadelphia and New York. Hazard insisted that an advance pay-

ment of half the price should be paid by the subscribers, which was not the custom in New England.
Belknap thought that this demand lessened the number of subscriptions.

The next step concerned the actual manufacture of
the book. Belknap made his arrangements with
Robert Aitken, of Philadelphia, a Scotchman whom
Hazard recommended as a better printer than could
be found in Boston. The estimate of cost furnished
by Aitken, which proved to be a little too small, was
as follows: For printing, including the type-setting,
5 pounds 10 shillings for each of the twenty-five sheets,
the edition to be 1000 copies. For stitching 50 pounds.
For 58 reams of paper at one pound each, 58 pounds.
The whole edition would thus cost 245 pounds and 10
shillings, equal to about 5 shillings for each book furnished. The estimate was in Pennsylvania currency,
worth 60% of sterling money. By "stitching" was
meant not only the sewing of the books but binding
them in boards, the customary form for books of the
day. In this connection an amusing situation arose
in connection with the New Hampshire subscribers.
When the natives read that the book was to be sold at
10 shillings "in boards," referring to the binding, they
assumed that it meant that the payment was to be
in clapboards, an article in which they were accustomed
to pay their bills. Belknap discovered the error in
time to save himself from being overwhelmed by this
kind of boards.

When the book was at last ready for distribution prospects seemed good for large sales at 10 shillings each. But so many subscribers failed to take their copies that the author found himself under a debt to Aitken which he had not the means to discharge. In despair he lowered the price, but to no good end; and it was ten years before he finally paid the obligation. The publication of the second volume in 1791 and the third in 1792 gave impetus to the sale of the first. In 1791 the legislature of New Hampshire allowed him 50 pounds in token of the esteem in which his labors were held. Moreover, he was at this time in receipt of a respectable salary as minister, and the "American Biography" and the "Foresters" were yielding him something. All in all, Belknap was beginning to prosper in a worldly way when death cut short his career in 1798. Had he lived longer he would doubtless have found that literature was slightly profitable. That it was not notably so is shown in the following statement from Hazard in 1795:

"I am sorry that so many [of the Histories] remain unsold here. It must be charged to want of taste in the age, I believe. I more than *sympathize* with you, for I have not sold enough of my Collections yet to pay for printing the 1st volume! and I believe you have. Our friend Morse seems to be the only successful author in the triumvirate. What a pity it is that *we* had not been geographers instead of historians."

"Friend Morse" was Jedediah Morse, whose geographies and gazetteers were then in great demand.

When Belknap began to write, congress had passed
no copyright law. Under the old congress that was the
function of the states. But in 1790 the new congress
passed such an act, thus protecting authors against
pirating. When a newspaper editor in New Hampshire
announced that he would bring out the " History " in
installments, Belknap invoked the law in the following
sarcastic words : "As I am particularly interested in
the success of that literary adventure, I beg you would
set me down for a subscriber for the *Cheshire Adver-
tiser* for one year, to commence from the first portion
of the said History which you may reprint, and send
the papers regularly to me by the post. If you are
desirous of reprinting the certificate from the Clerk
of the Federal Court which secures the copyright of
the said History to me and my heirs, agreeably to the
laws of the United States, be so good as to let me know
it, and I will send you an authenticated copy." The
"literary adventure" was carried no further.

When Jared Sparks took up the work of a historian,
the condition of the literary market in the United
States was more promising than in the time of Belknap
and Hazard. The era of manufactures had brought
solid prosperity to New England, planting cotton
had made the South wealthy, and trade and advancing
land values had proved a boon to the people of the
country generally. Better still, the establishment of
the *North American Review* had raised the standard
of taste in regard to serious books. Sparks was a man

of unusual ability in discovering what kind of books the people would buy. He divined that the existing generation was deeply interested in the revolution, and in the men who laid the foundation of the new nation. Here lay the field into which he decided to carry his efforts.

He possessed much business shrewdness, and his bargains with the publishers were usually advantageously made. Mention has already been made of the financial considerations of his "Diplomatic Correspondence," which must have yielded him a net return of several thousand dollars.[1] When he first made plans for the "Writings of Washington" he expected to appoint agents who would conduct an active canvass for subscriptions in advance. Several such agents, in fact, were appointed. But before publication he changed his method for a plan then coming into general use and destined to be followed for many years by the historians in the United States. He had the type set at his own expense and ordered stereotyped plates, for which he paid. He then agreed with a Boston firm to allow them to publish and sell 4000 sets of the work, paying him a royalty of about sixty cents a volume. This firm, however, failed before the work was issued, and he made a new contract, by which he was to be paid fifty cents for each volume of the "Writings" and eighty-five cents for each volume of the "Life." On the "Writings" he had to share the pro-

[1] See above, page 117.

ceeds with Marshall and Washington, but all the returns from the "Life" belonged to him.   In 1852 he said the 7000 sets of the "Writings" and 8500 copies of the "Life" had been sold, together with 5500 copies of an abridged "Life."   The last, in two volumes, yielded a royalty of twelve and a half cents a volume. Sparks changed his publishers several times, and it is not certain that the same royalty was paid by each. But it could not have varied much from the original rate, and on that basis he would have received $8,600 on the two editions of the "Life," from which should be deducted probably $1,600 for making plates.   From the "Writings" he would have received $38,500, on which the expenses to be deducted were by his own statement [1] $15,356.37.   Subtracting this amount from the total receipts we have $23,143.63, half of which was paid to the heirs of Washington and Marshall. From these sources the work would yield $18,571.81 in fifteen years after the completion of publication. But these are not all the sources.   In 1846 Sparks made a contract with Harper & Brothers for a cheap edition at a royalty of twenty-five cents a volume. There were, also, editions in abridged form in the French and German languages, from which something was received.   Besides, it must be remembered the "Washington" had a moderate sale after 1852, when the figures were made for the estimate here introduced. These very figures, in fact, were submitted to pub-

[1] Adams, "Life of Jared Sparks," II, 295.   Also see above, page 118.

lishers in making arrangements for a new edition. All in all, it seems safe to assume that Sparks received as much as $25,000 for his labors on this work. Nor were these labors necessarily great. The "Life" was a task of considerable burden, but it was in one volume octavo. Editing the "Writings" was not as laborious as the size of the volumes may suggest. A better edition has been made within recent years in less time than it took Sparks to prepare his, and for a small fraction of the money he was able, through his financial ability, to extract from the process.

Sparks sold the copyright of his "Works of Franklin" for $2,000, retaining his right in the "Life" that accompanied it. The "Life of Gouverneur Morris" was undertaken with the agreement that Sparks should have half the profits. His returns from it were inconsiderable, as the sale was small, and in 1839 he relinquished to Mrs. Morris his claim to further proceeds. For the "Correspondence of the American Revolution," the "Familiar Letters of Franklin," and the "Life of John Ledyard" he probably received little. The "American Almanac," in which he sold his half interest after a year's ownership, proved to be very profitable; but it was impossible for him to carry it on while engaged in his other work.

In the "Library of American Biography" Sparks probably possessed his most profitable literary property. The enterprise began in coöperation with the publishers, who paid one dollar for each 16mo page.

Sparks allowed each contributor seventy cents a page, reserving thirty for himself as editor. In return for the advance by the publishers, he agreed that they might print and sell 2,000 copies. But he himself owned the copyright, and as the contributors were no longer to be dealt with he received all the royalties on the later editions. As the work was published in twenty-five volumes, and ran through a large number of editions, the receipts of the editor were exceedingly large.

Of course, his profits were taken at the expense of the contributors, who were in the larger sense the real authors of the "Library of American Biography." By accepting a cash sum for their labors they threw away future possibilities. It is an unwise author who will sell his labor for that sum which a publisher feels he can afford to offer under such conditions, since no publisher could afford to offer more than he thinks is absolutely sure to come back to him. In entering into such a contract the author surrenders all the contingency in his work, accepting only that which it can hardly fail to pay. Report says that for a series of small volumes in American history that appeared in recent years the authors were paid five hundred dollars each; yet these books have sold to the extent of more than a hundred thousand copies.

Sparks's plan of retaining the copyright and manufacturing the plates, while he contracted with publishers to sell limited editions at specified royalties, was followed also by Bancroft, Prescott, and Motley. In fact it became the accepted way of bringing out a book at a time when the publisher was not so important on the business side of literature as to-day.   The tendency was for the author to retain control of his enterprise, and to take a strong position with reference to the publisher. To-day the publisher occupies the stronger position. He is the *entrepreneur*, and the author looks to him for the initiative, or waits anxiously to see whether or not his ideas, once formed, will prove agreeable to the source from which comes the only opportunity to put them into force.

It is impossible to say what returns Bancroft received from his "History of the United States." The earliest volumes were in the twenty-fifth edition in 1878, and the demand for the book was still active.   In his old age the author was in very comfortable circumstances. Although he had married a woman of wealth it was generally supposed that a considerable part of his fortune was derived from the receipts from his books, which his sagacity had enabled him to invest advantageously.

Prescott's method of publishing was like that of Sparks. He had stereotyped plates made and then contracted with publishers for editions of a limited size for specified sums or royalties. For the first edition of the "Ferdinand and Isabella" the publishers were to sell 1,250 copies within five years and to pay him $1,000 in advance. The edition was sold in five months and other editions followed in rapid succession. For the "Conquest of Mexico" Harper & Brothers paid $7,500 for the privilege of issuing 5,000 copies. Here, also, a new edition was soon called for, and it was issued with a new contract. For an English edition he was paid 650 pounds, and it too was followed by a second edition soon afterwards. For the "Conquest of Peru" he was paid $7,500 on the day of publication for an edition of 7,500 copies, the edition to be sold within one year, and later editions to be issued at the same rate unless the author wished to make other arrangements. Throughout all the years of publication the demand for the earlier works was considerable; so that his total receipts must have been very large. For the copyright of an English edition of the "Peru" he was paid 800 pounds. These were unusually good terms for the day. To obtain $11,500 for a book on a history topic the day it is published would be considered a remarkable achievement in these days, although the population of the country is now several times what it was in 1847.

The historical books of Washington Irving afforded him a handsome revenue. Before 1835 his receipts from the "Columbus," the "Voyages of Columbus," "Astoria," "Bonneville," "Grenada," and "Alhambra" amounted to $66,375; and of this sum $41,875 came from the American editions. On these works from 1835 to 1842 his receipts were $8,050. For a few years his works were out of print; but from 1848 to

his death, 1859, the return from all his works was
$88,143. Assuming that in this period the same pro-
portion of the total came from the historical books as
in the former period, he received from this source in
this latter period the comfortable sum of about $44,000.
We may thus conclude that at his death Washington
Irving's historical works had paid him at least $118,000,
and were still selling well.[1]

We have little information of Motley's financial
arrangements with his publishers. We only know that
his books sold in large numbers. A year after publication the "Rise of the Dutch Republic" had been purchased to the extent of 15,000 copies, and the "United
Netherlands" and "John of Barneveld" went off quite
as well. They long remained in active demand: in
fact, they are still sold in considerable numbers.

Thus we see that the middle of the nineteenth century was a happy time for the abler historians then in
the United States. A great change had come over the
historical situation since Hazard and Belknap, after
they had made their gallant attempts in authorship,
had found themselves with hands full of unsold books.
Genuine interest in history had spread throughout the
country, and a prosperous people were willing to purchase well-written books which dealt with it. History,
a plant of slow growth, had come to maturity in the
United States. It was nourished by men of great
literary skill, who gave their energy of mind as much

[1] Pierre Irving, "Life and Letters of Washington Irving," IV, 410.

to the task of expression as to that of collecting information.

The old school came to its end with the advent of the critical spirit, whose greatest impulse was to test old statements, to bring to the surface new views, and to set forth phases of life that were formerly ignored. Criticism has made history a new creature. It is a thing for the readers who like originality. In spite of the great emphasis that is now being given to history in the public schools the circle that reads history is perhaps not as large in proportion to population as in the days of Prescott and Motley. Why this is true and how it may be remedied are not parts of my subject. They are problems for historians to solve, problems that require as much mental ability and as much originality of judgment as any of the phases of criticism that have to be met and determined.

INDEX

Aberdeen, Lord, and Sparks, 98, 103.
Adams, Charles Francis, influence as a critic, 47.
Adams, Herbert B., 135.
Adams, John Quincy, supports Clarke and Force, 258, 260.
Aitken, Robert, 40, 305.
American Antiquarian Society, plan to obtain British documents, 243.
"American Archives," 88; the origin of the idea, 239, 275; approved by Congress, 247–248; contract with Livingston, 248; detailed plan, 254, 261; criticized by Forsyth, 255; in Congress, 257–261; published, 261–263; purpose explained in preface, 262; contents of volumes, 265, 267, 271, 272; suspended, 266–270; agreement of 1843, 267; the series discussed, 270–274; plans to revive, 299.
"American State Papers," 88.
"Annals of Congress," 88.
"Annual Register," a source of revolutionary history, 12.
Arthur, President, on George Bancroft, 190.

Bancroft, Rev. Aaron, 138.
Bancroft, George, 46, 215; reviews Pickering's lexicon, 68–71; and Sparks, 100; method of editing, 109; and methods of education, 123; his birth, 138; education, 138; relations with Andrews Norton, 139–141; instructor at Harvard, 139–146; attempts reforms,

141–146; his part in the Round Hill School, 146–148; as a teacher, 148–150; his early literary efforts, 150–153; his "Poems," 151; editing textbooks, 151; Mrs. Lyman on, 152; turns to history, 153, 177; translates Heeren, 153; relations with the *North American Review*, 154–160, 162–165; early connection with Sparks, 154; article on Buttman and Jacob, 154; on German poetry, 155; on Goethe, 155, 156–158; on Pickering's lexicon, 156, 163; on the necessity for thrift, 160; on popular contempt for authors, 163; thinking of an article on the Connecticut Valley, 165; influence of Sparks on him, 165; longs for literary career, 165; his dislike for teaching, 166, 177; early political views, 166; on Caleb Cushing, 167; his Fourth of July oration, 1826, 167; supports John Quincy Adams, 168; his article on the bank, 168–172; effects on his career, 171; visit to Cleveland, 172; visit to Washington, 172; drawn into politics, 173; on Bates, 174; indifferent to his critics, 176; relations with Van Buren, 176; with W. L. Marcy, 176; influence of Heeren on, 179; "History of the United States," first volume published, 179; his historical ideals, 179, 181; order of publication of volumes in the

317

"History," 181, 193; the book commended, 182; criticism of, 183; ostracized in Boston, 184; collector of port at Boston, 184; political career, 185; supports Van Buren, 185, 188; writes life of Van Buren, 185; controversy with Josiah Quincy, 186; with G. W. Greene, 187; criticism of, 187; supports Polk, 188; appointed secretary of the navy, 189–191; distinguished in society, 189; establishes the naval academy, 190; minister to Great Britain, 191–193; on Macaulay, 192; collecting documents in London, 192; his period of residence in New York, 193; out of sympathy with the democrats, 194; relations with Andrew Johnson, 195; minister to Germany, 195–200; flatters Grant, 196; relations with Bismarck, 196; attacked by Victor Hugo, 197; his pro-German qualities, 197–199; von Ranke on, 198; his democracy weakening, 199; his "Literary and Historical Miscellanies," 200; his "Tribute to Humboldt," 201; "On the Canal de Haro," 201; "The Constitution Wounded in the House of its Guardians," 201; "History of the Formation of the Constitution," 202; revises his "History," 202; his orations, 203; address on Lincoln, 204; as a collector of documents and transcripts, 204–206; his manuscripts in the New York Public Library, 204–206; criticized by Sydney G. Fisher, 206; his literary habits, 207; interest in horticulture, 207; lagging interest in history, 209; relations with Force, 275; H.

Stevens, Jr., on, 283, 284; social life in Washington, 294; love of flowers, 294; his literary profits, 312.

Bancroft Manuscripts, contents of, 210.

Bank of the United States, the second, Bancroft's article on, 168–172.

Bartlett, John R., 276 n. 1, 277 n. 1, 288.

Bates, Isaac C., 173; Bancroft on, 174.

Belknap, Jeremy, 181; his "History of New Hampshire," 15, 30–32, 40; as a historian, 24; relation with Hazard, 24, 31, 35, 39–43, 304; his early life, 25; as a minister, 25–27; controversy at Dover, N. H., 25; settles in Boston, 27; early leaning to history, 27; and Governor Wentworth, 28; to Captain Waldron, 29; a Whig, 29; "The Foresters," 31–35; "American Biography," 35; and the Massachusetts Historical Society, 35–37; on the task of the historian, 41; "The Pleasures of a Country Life," 41 n.; as a historian, 43; conditions under which he published his histories, 304–306.

Beverley, Robert, his "History of Virginia," 4.

Bismarck, Otto von, relations with Bancroft, 196.

Blair, F. P., 266. See also Blair and Rives.

Blair and Rives, 82; diplomatic correspondence, 246.

Bozman, J. L., 48.

Bradford, William, 2; his "History of Plymouth Plantation," 5.

Brodhead, J. R., 48, 287.

Brown, John Carter, 287.